'This insightful volume opens up new interpretations of Hughes's texts and will prove valuable to any reader interested in his poetry.' – **Rosario Arias**, *University of Málaga, Spain*

...ng critical
...popular and
influential British poets of the twentieth century. In twelve new essays, international authorities on Hughes examine and debate his work, shedding new light on familiar texts.

Split into two parts, the first half of this book examines Hughes's work through cultural contexts, such as postmodernism and the carnivalesque, while the second part uses literary theories including postcolonialism, ecocriticism and trauma theory to interpret his poetry. Providing fresh inspiration and insights into the various diverse ways in which Hughes's writing can be interpreted, this volume is an ideal introduction to both literary theory and the work of Ted Hughes for literature students and scholars alike.

Terry Gifford is Visiting Scholar at the Centre for Writing and Environment, Bath Spa University, UK, and Senior Research Fellow and Professor Honorífico at the University of Alicante, Spain.

New Casebooks
Collections of all new critical essays

CHILDREN'S LITERATURE

MELVIN BURGESS
Edited by Alison Waller

ROBERT CORMIER
Edited by Adrienne E. Gavin

ROALD DAHL
Edited by Ann Alston & Catherine Butler

C. S. LEWIS: *THE CHRONICLES OF NARNIA*
Edited by Michelle Ann Abate & Lance Weldy

PHILIP PULLMAN: *HIS DARK MATERIALS*
Edited by Catherine Butler & Tommy Halsdorf

J. K. ROWLING: *HARRY POTTER*
Edited by Cynthia J. Hallett & Peggy J. Huey

J. R. R. TOLKIEN: *THE HOBBIT & THE LORD OF THE RINGS*
Edited by Peter Hunt

DAVID ALMOND
Edited by Rosemary Ross Johnston

NOVELS AND PROSE

JOHN FOWLES
Edited by James Acheson

POETRY

TED HUGHES
Edited by Terry Gifford

Further titles are in preparation

For a full list of published titles in the past format of the New Casebooks series, visit the series page at www.palgrave.com

---

New Casebooks Series

Series Standing Order ISBN 978–0–333–71702–8 hardcover
Series Standing Order ISBN 978–0–333–69345–2 paperback
(*outside North America only*)

You can receive future titles in this series as they are published by placing a standing order. Please contact your bookseller or, in the case of difficulty, write to us at the address below with your name and address, the title of the series and the ISBN quoted above.

Customer Services Department, Macmillan Distribution Ltd, Houndmills, Basingstoke, Hampshire, RG21 6XS, UK

New Casebooks

Ted Hughes

Edited by

TERRY GIFFORD

 macmillan education   palgrave

First published 2015 by
PALGRAVE

Palgrave in the UK is an imprint of Macmillan Publishers Limited, registered in England, company number 785998, of 4 Crinan Street, London N1 9XW.

Palgrave Macmillan in the US is a division of St Martin's Press LLC, 175 Fifth Avenue, New York, NY 10010.

Palgrave is a global imprint of the above companies and is represented throughout the world.

Palgrave® and Macmillan® are registered trademarks in the United States, the United Kingdom, Europe and other countries.

ISBN: 978–1–137–30112–3 hardback

ISBN: 978–1–137–30111–6 paperback

This book is printed on paper suitable for recycling and made from fully managed and sustained forest sources. Logging, pulping and manufacturing processes are expected to conform to the environmental regulations of the country of origin.

A catalogue record for this book is available from the British Library.

A catalog record for this book is available from the Library of Congress.

Typeset by MPS Ltd, Chennai, India

Printed in China

In memory of Keith Sagar,
pioneering Hughes critic and generous scholar

Contents

Contents

Series Editor's Preface

Welcome to the latest series of New Casebooks.

Each volume now presents brand new essays specially written for university and other students. Like the original series, the new-look New Casebooks embrace a range of recent critical approaches to the debates and issues that characterize the current discussion of literature.

Each editor has been asked to commission a sequence of original essays which will introduce the reader to the innovative critical approaches to the text or texts being discussed in the collection. The intention is to illuminate the rich interchange between critical theory and critical practice that today underpins so much writing about literature.

Editors have also been asked to supply an introduction to each volume that sets the scene for the essays that follow, together with a list of further reading which will enable readers to follow up issues raised by the essays in the collection.

The purpose of this new-look series, then, is to provide students with fresh thinking about key texts and writers while encouraging them to extend their own ideas and responses to the texts they are studying.

Martin Coyle

Notes on Contributors

Laurence Coupe is Visiting Professor of English at Manchester Metropolitan University. He is the author of *From Myth to Ecology: Kenneth Burke* (2013), *Myth* (2009) and the editor of *The Green Studies Reader: From Romanticism to Ecocriticism* (2000). Other books include *Marina Warner* (2006) and *Beat Sound, Beat Vision: The Beat Spirit and Popular Song* (2007).

Alex Davis is Professor of English at University College Cork. He is the author of *A Broken Line: Denis Devlin and Irish Poetic Modernism* (2000) and (with Patricia Coughlan) co-editor of *Modernism and Ireland: The Poetry of the 1930s* (1995), and (with Lee M. Jenkins) *Locations of Literary Modernism: Region and Nation in British and American Modernist Poetry* (2000) and *The Cambridge Companion to Modernist Poetry* (2007).

Janne Stigen Drangsholt is Associate Professor at the Department of Culture and Language Studies, University of Stavanger, Norway. Her most recent publications are 'Sounding the Landscape: Dis-placement in the Poetry of Alice Oswald' in *Crisis and Contemporary Poetry* (2011), ed. Anne Karhio, Sean Crosson and Charles I. Armstrong and 'Opened Ground: Discourses of Descent in Ted Hughes and Sylvia Plath' in *The Ted Hughes Society Journal* (2011).

Terry Gifford is Visiting Scholar at Bath Spa University's Centre for Writing and Environment, UK, and Senior Research Fellow and Professor Honorífico at the University of Alicante, Spain. He the author of twelve books, including *Ted Hughes* (2009) and (with Neil Roberts) *Ted Hughes: A Critical Study* (1981), and is editor of *The Cambridge Companion to Ted Hughes* (2011).

Gillian Groszewski teaches in the School of English at Trinity College Dublin and is currently writing *Ted Hughes and America* (2015). She has published an essay on Ted Hughes and Emily Dickinson in *Ted Hughes: from Cambridge to Collected*, ed. Mark Wormald, Neil Roberts and Terry Gifford (2013). Gillian is President of The Ted Hughes Society (www.thetedhughessociety.org) and Editor of *The Ted Hughes Society Journal*.

Richard Kerridge leads the MA in Creative Writing and co-ordinates research in the Humanities at Bath Spa University, where he is a member of the Writing and Environment Research Centre. He is a nature writer and ecocritic, and was founding Chair of the UK branch of the Association for the Study of Literature and Environment. His nature-writing memoir *Cold Blood* was published in 2014. He was a lead writer in *The Face of the Earth*, a collaborative study of landscape in science and culture (2011), and has written numerous articles on environmental approaches to literature.

Joanny Moulin, Professor of English Literature at Aix-Marseille Université, France, is the author of a several books on Ted Hughes, including a biography in French, *Ted Hughes: La terre hantée* (2007), and is editor of the collection of critical essays *Ted Hughes: Alternative Horizons* (2004).

Daniel O'Connor completed his Ph.D. thesis, 'Burning the Foxes: the Dialectics of Ted Hughes' at the University of Liverpool, where he now teaches. He recently published 'Curing the Mind in the Early Poetry of Ted Hughes' in *The Ted Hughes Society Journal* (2014). He is currently researching humour in Modernism.

Iris Ralph is an Assistant Professor in the English Department of Tamkang University, Taiwan. Her most recent journal articles have appeared in *Journal of Poyang Lake* (Jiangxi Academy of Social Sciences, Jiangxi, China), *NTU Studies in Language and Literature* (National Taiwan University), *Concentric* (National Taiwan Normal University) and *Journal of Ecocriticism* (University of Northern British Columbia, Canada). She is the co-author of a chapter in *International Perspectives in Ecofeminist Ecocriticism* (2013).

Neil Roberts is Emeritus Professor of English Literature at the University of Sheffield, UK. He is the author of ten books, including *Ted Hughes: A Literary Life* (2006) and (with Terry Gifford) *Ted Hughes: A Critical Study* (1981), and editor of the *Blackwell Companion to Twentieth-Century Poetry* (2001). His latest book is *A Lucid Dreamer: the Life of Peter Redgrove* (2012).

Keith Sagar was the first major Ted Hughes scholar who became a friend and critical reader for the poet. Organizer of the first Ted Hughes conferences, he edited *The Achievement of Ted Hughes* (1983) and *The Challenge of Ted Hughes* (1994), but also wrote *The Art of Ted Hughes* (1978), *The Laughter of Foxes: A Study of Ted Hughes* (2006), *Ted Hughes and Nature: 'Terror and Exultation'* (2009), and *Poet and Critic: The Letters of Ted Hughes and Keith Sagar* (2012).

Murali Sivarmakrishnan, Professor and Head of the Department of English, Pondicherry University, India, is the author of over 100 research papers and author or editor of six books, the latest of which is *Image and Culture: The Dynamics of Literary, Aesthetic and Cultural Representation* (2011).

David Troupes holds degrees from the University of Massachusetts at Amherst, USA and the University of Edinburgh, Scotland. He has published two books of poetry, *Parsimony* (2009) and *The Simple Man* (2012), among other critical and creative work. He is currently writing a Ph.D. on Hughes at the University of Sheffield.

Usha VT, Associate Professor and Head of the Centre for Women's Studies, Pondicherry University, India, is the author of five books, including *The Real and the Imagined: The Poetic World of Ted Hughes* (1998) and *Re/Cognising Women's Studies: Issues, Texts, Contexts* (2011).

Acknowledgements

We are grateful to Seamus Heaney for allowing Keith Sagar to quote in Chapter 4 from his dedication of the memorial stone to Ted Hughes in Poets' Corner at Westminster Abbey on 6 December 2011.

Acknowledgements are also due to Faber & Faber and the Ted Hughes Estate for permission to quote from Hughes's published work.

Abbreviations

'Emory' refers to the Manuscript, Archives, and Rare Book Library (MARBL), University of Emory, Atlanta, Georgia, USA and 'BL' refers to the Ted Hughes collections at the British Library, London, UK. The following abbreviations are used for works by Ted Hughes:

CP   *Collected Poems* (London: Faber & Faber, 2003)
DG   *A Dancer to God* (London: Faber & Faber, 1992)
G   *Gaudete* (London: Faber & Faber, 1977)
LTH   *Letters of Ted Hughes* (London: Faber & Faber, 2007)
PC   *Poet and Critic: The Letters of Ted Hughes and Keith Sagar* (London: British Library, 2012)
SGCB   *Shakespeare and the Goddess of Complete Being* (London: Faber & Faber, 1992)
SPCP   *Sylvia Plath: Collected Poems* (London: Faber & Faber, 1981)
WP   *Winter Pollen* (London: Faber & Faber, 1994)

Introduction

Terry Gifford

Ted Hughes (1930–98) is a major English poet of the twentieth century whose work is read and studied at all stages of the education system, from the early years (*The Iron Wolf*), through primary school (*The Iron Man*) and secondary school (*Ted Hughes: Poems Selected by Simon Armitage*) to university (*Crow*). Few undergraduate students, for whom this book is intended, will be unfamiliar with the work of Ted Hughes.

One of the reasons why Hughes's poetry and stories are so popular with teachers at all levels is that they leave so much room for different interpretations by different readers. The texts allow for lively discussion and even disagreement amongst readers, including teachers and students. Another reason is that the ensuing discussion about what the texts are saying to readers leads to consideration of some of the most important issues of the twenty-first century: What is the nature of Nature? Is there a human nature? Have we lost an important part of ourselves that connects us to our planet and its inhabitants? What have we constructed in our culture that has alienated us from our natural environment? Do our attitudes to class, or to women, in our culture give us clues to what has gone wrong? How do we regain a connectedness with the forces at work in the ecology of which we are a part?

As we are exploring the way these questions are raised by Hughes's poetry we have also to discuss how the poetic devices used by Hughes are raising those questions in our minds. What are his poetic strategies? Why do different readers notice different strategies? How can alternative ways of reading the texts reveal quite contrasting aspects of their meaning? Many of these questions are derived from well-known theories of a variety of aspects of the way literature works and the ideas that readers bring to their reading of literature. Over the last few decades a range of literary theories has offered readers a diversity of ways of producing different readings of texts. Often these are complementary to each other, but sometimes they directly challenge each other and the reader is forced to make judgements about what seems to be an appropriate statement about the meaning of a particular text. All this contributes to the communal exploration and debate about what a poem by Ted Hughes could be taken to be saying to a reader. This book is intended to open up some of the debates that can be had about the potential meanings of Hughes's poems for those who might be new to these literary theories, or who might want to test them against their own readings of the texts. Even after several readings, the individual reader may not yet have seen all the possible meanings in a text, as, indeed, the writer may not have done. This is the stimulating, provocative and hopefully enlightening dialogue that is literary criticism in our era.

In the past, some theories tended to dominate the critical practice of their times. The history of literary criticism is a series of reactions against what had formerly been taken for granted as the appropriate approach towards reading literature. Two of the senior contributors to this volume attended the lectures at Cambridge of F.R. Leavis, as did Hughes himself briefly, and have witnessed the rejection of Leavisite criticism under the label of 'rational humanism' during the rise of structuralist and poststructuralist theory in the 1980s and 1990s. One of them, Keith Sagar, Hughes's first champion and literary critic, to whose memory this book is dedicated, was shamefully forced into early retirement by the University of Manchester because, he was told, his critical practice did not accord with that of the English Department at the time.[1] Such was the ferocity of debate about 'theory' in Britain as recently as 1995 that an internationally respected, productive scholar and teacher who might reasonably have expected to be offered a professorship could instead be offered early retirement. For this reason Keith Sagar was initially vehemently against this book, since 'theory' to him represented a requirement to toe a literary critical party line. After some correspondence he became persuaded that such inflexible conformity was in the past and that now theories, in the plural, could be used to elucidate multiple meanings in particularly rich and potent texts for open debate amongst attentive and free-thinking readers. Indeed, Sagar's contribution here is offered in the belief that this is the time when Ted Hughes's works can be opened up to a diversity of readings in dialogue with each other for the ultimate judgement of individual readers, be they students, scholars or poetry readers in general.

Ted Hughes himself disliked literary criticism, yet gave his endorsement to its most vital and important function − the making of a multiplicity of meanings in the reading of a text by a multiplicity of individual readers. As a second-year undergraduate student of English at the University of Cambridge in 1953 he had come to hate the writing of the weekly essay, 'in my usual agonising frame of mind, trying to get one word to follow another' (*LTH* 422), although, as he admitted in this letter to Keith Sagar, 'I might say that I had as much talent for Leavis-style dismantling of texts as anyone else' (*LTH* 423). These words were actually written in 1979, when seven major collections of poetry had been published, and it is the poet's defensive distortion of Leavis's practice of literary criticism that lies behind that dismissive term 'dismantling'. In his letter to Sagar, Hughes went on to recount the famous fox dream, which is so significant that it is referred to by four contributors to this book.[2] Following the fox's instruction, 'Stop this. You are destroying us' (*LTH* 422),[3] Hughes changed his studies to Archaeology and Anthropology, to the undoubted benefit of his own creativity.

Yet surely the Cambridge English Tripos had left an invaluable and undeniably influential experience of reading that came to represent, by the end of his life, what could be listed as Hughes's personal canon: *Sir Gawain and the Green Knight*, Chaucer, Shakespeare, Swift,[4] Wordsworth, Coleridge, Keats, Hopkins, Yeats,[5] Eliot, Lawrence.[6] To articulating his own idiosyncratic readings of some of these authors Hughes actually devoted months and years of his life, giving us such brilliant literary criticism as the essays of *Winter Pollen* (1994) — 'a major body of literary and cultural criticism', as its editor, William Scammell characterised it (*WP* x) — and *Shakespeare and the Goddess of Complete Being* (1992). When the academic critics, such as John Carey,[7] rejected his Shakespeare book, Hughes claimed that he was doing something different from academic literary criticism. He was an individual, widely read, reader who brought a professional poet's interest to his reading, in the manner of 'an industrial spy [...] so that I can adapt them to my own doings in different circumstances'.[8] But what he was actually undertaking in his Shakespeare book was an analysis of mythic structure underlying the major works, which he called 'the Tragic Equation'. This is the structural analysis of a social anthropologist of Hughes's era at Cambridge, much influenced by the work of Lévi-Strauss, as much as it is a poet's 'divining' of the 'riddle picture' that is 'hidden' in the texts, as Hughes explained to John Carey in a 'healing' letter just before he died (*LTH* 733). Hughes believed, as every reader is entitled to believe, that his own 'act of literary interpretation' revealed what the reader could have 'gloated on in all its 3-dimensional glaring obviousness' (*LTH* 733). Each of the twelve contributors to this book is entitled to make the same claim, as is each individual reader of Hughes's poetry.

Hughes's experience was that, in his time, university English departments did not encourage such an open attitude towards literary interpretation, and he retained scepticism about its academic practice as 'Lit Crit' (*LTH* 618). In 1994 Hughes wrote to Keith Sagar that English Studies seemed to be in crisis, 'gradually turning into something that has nothing to do with the original concern, enjoyment of books and literary works' (*PC* 241). Actually, more severely clinical 'dismantling of texts' was undertaken by the early structuralists, but without the moral dimensions that underpinned F.R. Leavis's evaluation of texts. In the spirit of Leavis, Neil Roberts and I felt that in writing *Ted Hughes: A Critical Study* (1981) our great admiration for the best work should be defined by our reservations about the weakest work. Hughes complained privately to Keith Sagar about our 'general underswell of carping, quibble & pettifogging critical remonstration' (*PC* 72), but wrote to us more graciously towards the end of a generously long letter responding to our book manuscript.[9] Hughes had joined the university archery club as a student and he explained to us a Chinese saying that says, whilst it is the knave who calls the misses, it is the good man who calls the hits. Actually, as Hughes acknowledged, our emphasis was very much more on the hits than the misses, but to Sagar he continued, 'They tend to count & analyse misses, instead of hits – which is exasperating' (*PC* 72). The reader will notice very few misses being called in this book, as the subsequent influence of theory has produced a less evaluative and more expositional critical discourse.

So in what way did Ted Hughes give his endorsement to criticism's most important function? In 1974 Hughes wrote to Sagar requesting that any comments Hughes had made to Sagar about his poems should not be acknowledged by the critic in his first book on the poet's work, *The Art of Ted Hughes* (1975), in order to avoid the misunderstanding that Hughes was attempting to impose his own interpretation of his poems upon the critic. 'Everything speculative or to do with interpretation & evaluation are anybody's own business, yours as much as mine, finally' (*PC* 43). Here Hughes the writer is clearly trying to step back from the process of literary criticism, but after having already offered the critic a sense of his artistic intentions. Then he makes a necessary and significant statement that clearly is more difficult for him, as a writer who cares deeply about the reception of his work, to accept in practice: 'Finally, poems belong to readers – just as houses belong to those who live in them & not to the builders' (*PC* 43). This is not actually a statement that endorses Barthes's idea of 'the death of the author'.[10] This author is far from dead, even in the playful, metaphorical sense that Barthes intended. But it is a recognition that each reader must make their own meaning from the evidence that the poet has provided, or not provided.[11] The practice of literary criticism is the exchange of those meanings backed by the reader's interpretation of the evidence within the text. What 'theory' did was to identify and articulate a variety of approaches to reading the text that different readers might make. What this book attempts to do is to apply twelve well-recognised different approaches to the work of Ted Hughes, to open some of the doors to the rooms in the house of Hughes's works by bringing different ideas to their readings of the poems. It is for the reader of this book to judge how useful, valid or insightful each of these approaches might be for a discussion of the achievement of Ted Hughes.

Actually, Hughes's statement that 'poems belong to readers' is in tune with one of the foundational texts of literary theory, Aristotle's *Poetics*. Aristotle argued that tragedy should charge and change its audience by means of their ability to find meaning through their own capacity for *katharsis*. Literature, for the Greek philosopher Aristotle, was essentially audience-centred in its power to move and make its deepest effects. The later Greek critic Longinus, in his treatise *On the Sublime*, elaborated a reader-response theory of literature that evaluated texts by their success or otherwise in enabling the reader to have a sense of new insights into complex experiences of conflicting energies. Both of these early theorists placed an emphasis on what we might now call the educational and the aesthetic, the moral and the emotional – at once a deepening and delightful experience of the most powerful literature. From the beginning, then, theory has been concerned to try to articulate the processes and techniques by which all this works in the triangular dynamic of writer, text and reader. But it is important to remember that, as individual readers of the elusive, charged, compelling art-speech of Ted Hughes, the contributors to this book are trying to convey their own deepening and delightful experiences as readers in the hope that this will offer a parallel, but different, experience for other readers of Hughes's works. In this exchange of readings by twelve readers we all need to keep returning to the power and pleasure of the texts, remembering that Hughes himself has reminded us that this is all about 'enjoyment of books and literary works' (*PC* 241).

So whilst this book might act as an introduction to twelve different theoretical approaches to literature, it cannot do more than briefly offer some definitions, concepts and terminology. For more extensive introductions the reader should go to the standard textbooks of literary theory that are readily available. The main focus of this book is the opening up of various ways of reading the texts of Ted Hughes and offering contrasting and complementary meanings that may be made of his texts. Indeed, the criteria for the selection of these twelve theoretical approaches has been that they are particularly productive in not only opening up new ways of reading the poetry of Ted Hughes, but in offering contrasting or alternative readings in dialogue with each other.

In the first chapter Laurence Coupe points out that Hughes writes of human alienation from the goddess of nature in mythic terms that also allow for Richard Kerridge in the final chapter to interpret this idea in ecocritical terms. In the chapters in between, the role of the goddess in Hughes's work is considered in terms of its implications for both genders by Janne Stigen Drangsholt and in terms of Indian feminism by Usha VT and Murali Sivaramakrishnan. David Troupes concludes that Hughes is both 'tirelessly mythologising' and celebrating 'moments of unmythologised, unmediated contact'. The latter, Alex Davies and Gillian Groszewski would argue, is, of course, constructed by language and therefore always mediated, in a manner which Iris Ralph's posthumanist critics would object to being necessarily human-centred. Laurence Coupe asks whether the songs of the poet can heal and both Keith Sagar and Danny O'Connor argue, from their different starting points, that they can. In the latter case Trauma Theory leads O'Connor to the brilliant observation that in *Birthday Letters* healing is made possible through the self-distancing technique of Hughes 'seeing himself through his idea of Plath'.

In terms of alternative readings of individual poems this book offers some surprising contrasts. 'Hawk Roosting', for example, can be seen as an image of the rebirth of 'Horus, the son and successor of Osiris the dying god' by Laurence Coupe and as representing the complacency of a colonial power in the postcolonial reading of the Indian critics Usha VT and Murali Sivaramakrishnan. Laughter induced by the *Crow* poem 'A Childish Prank' can be 'affirmative' for Neil Roberts, but include 'a sense of lack' for Janne Stigen Drangsholt, and a satire on Christianity for Joanny Moulin. One might ask whether this is the ambivalent laughter of the Absurd, or the defiant laughter of the carnivalesque? But some poems seem to generate agreement from whichever perspective they are read. All those readers who discuss 'The Thought-Fox' here agree that there is both a real fox present in that poem and that the poem presents itself as a verbal construct of what Joanny Moulin calls 'a fantasy fox'.

Although the organisation of the book gives the impression that these approaches are quite separate and distinctive, in current critical practice writers often draw upon several theoretical approaches in exploring the possible meanings of a text. This should be borne in mind by readers of this book, and to help them think in this way there is cross-referencing to other chapters where appropriate. Indeed, the discussion in some chapters leads to a need to refine the terms of the theory in question, as when Alex Davies, in Chapter 2, finds a need to invent the term '*post*-Modernism' to locate Hughes's work between Modernism and postmodernism.

There is intended to be a tentative progression in the book. Part I takes terms that are commonly used within cultural studies and reads Hughes's work in the context of debates within the wider culture. The book begins by considering Hughes's use of myth, as Laurence Coupe, an authority on the role of myth in literature, opens up new ways of understanding Hughes's fascination with mythic structures by considering the symbiosis of Hughes as both a writer and a reader of myth. Hughes was distinctive in seeing a link between the ancient practice of shamanism and Modernist writers such as T.S. Eliot who made use of myth and tradition. Alex Davis asks how we might read Hughes's work in relation to the historical movement of Modernism in the arts that dominated the first two decades of the twentieth century and has led to the development of postmodernism. Davis decides that Hughes's poetics is best described as '*post*-Modernist'. The extent to which Hughes's texts might be read as being in dialogue with other writers is taken up by David Troupes in an examination of Hughes's intertextual relationship with the American Transcendentalists and their poetic legacy. Keith Sagar carefully considers the European legacy of the Absurd, especially in Samuel Beckett's version, as, by contrast, it clarifies Hughes's more hopeful vision. Indeed, Hughes's mode of escape from the Absurd connects his work to another legacy of European culture, Mikhail Bakhtin's notion of the carnivalesque, used by Neil Roberts to take humour seriously in the work of Ted Hughes. Of course, much of that humour is directed at masculine hubris and Janne Stigen Drangsholt discusses the complex issue of how students of gender studies might read the poetry of Hughes, especially in relation to the figure of the goddess in his work.

Part II reads the work through the frames of six well-known current theoretical perspectives which have not, thus far, been much used to reveal new insights into Hughes's work. Gillian Groszewski clarifies the differences between structuralism and poststructuralism, showing how they each produce a quite different focus on Hughes's texts. One of the text-based approaches that has great potential for Hughes studies is explored by the French Hughes scholar Joanny Moulin, who offers a lively critique of Hughes's work deploying the influential psychoanalytic concepts of the French theorist Jacques Lacan. Largely

influenced by Lacan's work, the recent development of Trauma
Theory leads Daniel O'Connor towards new insights into Hughes's
final collection *Birthday Letters*. Demonstrating both the international
currency of literary theory and its eclectic, overlapping usage in practice, a distinctive postcolonial reading is offered by two Ted Hughes
scholars from India, Usha VT and Murali Sivaramakrishnan. Their
essay ends by suggesting that Hughes counters patriarchal hubris
by celebrating 'the posthuman energies and mysteries of nature'. In
the following chapter Iris Ralph carefully untangles posthumanism's
strands to bring current ideas in animal studies and systems theory to
bear on the poetry. Posthumanism can be considered as one aspect
of ecocritical theory, and in this book's final chapter the ecocritic
Richard Kerridge argues that Hughes's work raises important questions for the discussion of environmental issues today, and, indeed, for
the development of ecocriticism itself. Kerridge concludes this book
by pointing out that Hughes's work can itself challenge rethinking
and refinement in literary theory by posing urgent new questions that
readers need to consider.

One of the strengths of this collection of readings of Hughes's work
is its international dimension, bringing into dialogue readers who
teach in universities in the UK, the USA, Norway, Ireland, France,
Spain, Taiwan and India. So this book serves as both an introduction
to twelve different ways of approaching the reading of texts and as an
introduction to the urgent debates about what Ted Hughes has to say
to us as readers wherever we are in the world through his powerful,
mysterious and richly resonant texts themselves. The twelve specially
commissioned essays in dialogue here hope to deliver to readers a
wide-ranging theoretically informed conversation about the poetry of
Hughes that has never been attempted before.

Notes

1. Keith Sagar, *'Art for Life's Sake': Essays on D.H. Lawrence* (Nottingham:
   Critical, Cultural and Communications Press, 2011): 42.
2. See Chapters 3, 6, 7 and 11 for very different discussions of this dream.
3. This story is also told in *WP* 8–9.
4. See Ian Gadd, Terry Gifford and Lorraine Kerslake, 'A Note on Swift and
   Ted Hughes', unpublished.
5. See Rand Brandes, 'Mercury in Taurus: W. B. Yeats and Ted Hughes',
   South Carolina Review, 43(1) (Fall 2010): 198–210 and Gillian Groszewski,
   'Hughes and Yeats', *The Ted Hughes Society Journal,* 2014.
6. See Keith Sagar, '"Straight Oxygen": Ted Hughes' Debt to D.H.
   Lawrence', *Journal of D.H. Lawrence Studies,* (2:1) (2009): 71–9.

7. *Sunday Times*, 5 April 1992.
8. BL Add. 88918/6/8. Quoted by Jonathan Bate, 'Hughes and Shakespeare', in Terry Gifford (ed.), *The Cambridge Companion to Ted Hughes* (Cambridge: Cambridge University Press, 2011): 147.
9. Only part of this letter is published in *LTH* 427–9. It is in the British Library: Add 88988/1. In it Hughes wrote a long defence for the *Crow* poem 'Truth Kills Everybody', which was published as an endnote in Terry Gifford and Neil Roberts, *Ted Hughes: A Critical Study* (London: Faber & Faber, 1981): 256.
10. See Chapter 7 for a discussion of this concept.
11. In Chapter 7 Gillian Groszewski argues that Hughes at one point actually comes close to proposing a deconstructionist approach to reading poetry.

Part I
Readings through Cultural Contexts

1

Hughes and Myth

Laurence Coupe

Though it is widely acknowledged that Ted Hughes's work is 'mythic' in its breadth and depth, confusion may arise as to what exactly we mean by that word. This chapter sets out to clarify Hughes's own understanding of mythology, to demonstrate his prowess as an interpreter of specific mythic forms, and to explore the connection he makes between myth and literature.

'Blueprints for imagination'

The word 'myth' comes from the ancient Greek *mythos*, meaning 'story'. A myth is a traditional story that is handed on over the years – sometimes centuries, sometimes millennia – and keeps being retold. It is a narrative that helps human beings to make sense of themselves and their relation to one another, to the natural world and to the spiritual realm. It is a founding narrative, an essential plot, which cannot be credited to any one individual but rather belongs to the whole community. Myths combine together to form a mythology, a body of stories that define a culture. This collective narrative is not to be assessed on grounds of truth or falsity: the point is whether it has power for its community.

Perhaps Hughes's most straightforward statement on myth comes in the course of his extensive account of the mythology underlying the work of the most famous of English writers. Early on in his *Shakespeare and the Goddess of Complete Being*, he draws attention to the strongly 'mythic' strain in both the poems and the major plays. In doing so, he pauses to explain that the same word is applicable also to such diverse works as John Milton's *Paradise Lost*, William Blake's prophetic books, Samuel Taylor Coleridge's 'Ancient Mariner', W.B. Yeats's *Wanderings of Oisin* and T.S. Eliot's poetry generally, ranging from 'The Death of St Narcissus' to *The Waste Land*:

> In each of those poems listed, the whole subject matter is the image of a subjective event of visionary intensity [...] It is only when the image opens inwardly towards what we recognise as a first-hand as-if religious experience, or mystical revelation, that we call it 'visionary', and when 'personalities' or creatures are involved, we call it 'mythic'. (*SGCB* 35–6)[1]

In this light, we might say that 'mythic' for Hughes implies, first, vision, that is, the capacity to imagine that the world is charged with sacred grandeur, and secondly, a narrative unfolding of that vision.

As for Shakespeare's 'mythic' interest, Hughes is not primarily interested in the use of myth as a standard mode of allusion. What interests him is the way we can trace a dual narrative lying hidden beneath his total oeuvre:

> [he] strips the myth[s] of all identifiably mythic features, and secretes its mechanism within his plot[s], as he does with the two myths – of the Great Goddess and of the Goddess-destroying god – which are the theme of my argument here. (*SGCB* 2)[2]

Myth, for Hughes, is a mediation between the external and internal worlds, and between the material and spiritual dimensions, though often not recognisable at first reading. For Hughes, this is the basis and mode of operation of much of the greatest literature. Gods and goddesses may come in disguise, but their presence and power will always be felt.

So consistent was Hughes's interest in myth and his conviction of its importance that he wrote two essays entitled 'Myth and Education'. In the second of these, published in 1976, he argues forcefully that children should be introduced to their culture's mythology as early as possible because myths are our 'blueprints for imagination' (*WP* 151). A blueprint is a plan of action; a myth, then, is not just some dusty old text, but the indispensable format for those symbolic acts by which we keep in touch with the sources of life. For Ted Hughes the works of art which we call 'great' are those in which that contact is felt most compellingly. Myth, as blueprint for imagination, has a healing power. Whenever the inner world has become divorced from the outer we experience 'a place of demons'. Then myths demand retelling by the poets, whose function is far more than entertainment or diversion, but an imaginative reconciliation of both outer and inner worlds in a creative narrative (*WP* 151).

Kinds of myth

By my reckoning, there are four broadly different kinds of myth. They are sometimes hard to separate, but it is as well to bear them in mind as they each tell us something important. They are: *creation myth*, which tells us where we come from; *fertility myth*, which tells us how we relate to the natural cycle; *deliverance myth*, which tells us where we are going; and *hero myth*, which tells us what human qualities we value.[3] It is not to be expected that any one poet will consistently refer by name to the four categories of traditional plots just listed. For one thing, each of them has variant titles: for example, creation myth might also be known as 'myth of origins', or even 'paradise myth'; again, deliverance myth might also be known as 'salvation history'. But what I want to demonstrate here is that Hughes's use of myth is comprehensive, and that each of the four kinds I have listed does figure in his own theory of myth, which will help us understand their enactment in his poetic work.

Hughes and creation myth

Creation myth tells us how everything began. According to the late historian of religion, Mircea Eliade, humanity has been driven by the impulse of 'eternal return': we tell ourselves stories about how things were in the beginning, when the gods were in close contact with humanity. Given that it seems to be a universal conviction that the newly created world was in the beginning idyllic, human beings have always felt a deep 'nostalgia for paradise'. In other words, myth is about the regaining of 'sacred time', known to the ancient Greeks as the Golden Age; in complementary fashion, it is also about the regaining of 'sacred space', known to the Greeks as Arcadia.[4] Hughes conveys the power and beauty of this vision of the newly created world in the opening poem of his translation of *Metamorphoses*, written by the ancient Roman poet Ovid (see *CP* 865–79).

Hughes's writing on myth returns again and again to the biblical creation narrative and its momentous influence on English culture: the creation of the cosmos in six days and the serpent's role in the temptation of Adam and Eve and their subsequent fall from the Garden of Eden. In his study of Shakespeare, he is particularly interested in the way the Protestant Reformation of the sixteenth century, and the subsequent rise of Puritanism in the seventeenth, drew on the idea of a righteously omnipotent God who was not slow to take revenge on those who flouted his law. Repudiating what they saw as the pagan goddess-worship of Catholicism – with its reverence for the figure of Our Lady, mother of God, also known as the Virgin Mary – fundamentalist reformers and dissenters appealed to the masculine might of Jehovah. He was a transcendent figure whom they took to be 'far removed from the sensational, dramatic adventure of what is thought of as "myth"' (*SGCP* 13). And yet, Hughes reminds us, their God was in many ways reminiscent of Marduk, the mythic sky warrior of the Babylonians, who had defeated and destroyed the primordial goddess of the waters, Tiamat, thereby establishing cosmos and overcoming chaos. Given that the Babylonian creation myth casts its shadow over the Hebrew, Hughes surmises, 'Shakespeare was aware of the feelings behind this myth through the Bible' (*SGCP* 16). It is a bold chain of association which Hughes is forging: from the Babylonian Marduk, to the Hebrew Jehovah, and to the aggressively fundamentalist Puritan religion of the early modern world, and so to the greatest writer of that or of any other era who responds to this goddess-destroying lineage in his plays. One does not read Hughes on myth if one wants a conventionally comfortable guide. But it does offer an insight into the function of myth in his own work, where goddess-denial can lead to trouble, for example.

In offering a new perspective on the imaginative logic of Genesis, and in justifying the rough and ready approach to scriptural authority and religious orthodoxy of the protagonist of his most famous mythic volume, *Crow*, Hughes draws on an alternative mythic tradition, that of the 'trickster' tale. The mischievous male, usually priapic, protagonist of this kind of story participates in the creation of the world, but is also associated with all the disasters which plague human existence. He straddles the boundary between cosmos and chaos. Thus many of these tales feature a marginal creature who survives against the odds on the fringes of human culture: for example, crow, coyote, wolf, fox. The mythology of the Haida people of the north-western coast of North America features the exploits of 'Raven', a figure who is constantly causing trouble in his endless search for food, but whose very persistence enables him to lay out the land, establish the clan and bring light to both – all by accident. A parallel trickster is the West African (and then Caribbean) figure of 'Anansi': taking the form of a great spider, he is usually out to cause trouble but, as in all trickster myths, he inadvertently brings about the natural order of things.

Hughes is always very clear that he regards trickster mythology as a necessary corrective to the biblical narrative, which seems to present us with a thoroughly tamed nature. In his essay on his poem 'Crow on the Beach' he explains the background to his *Crow* volume and he presents the trickster as the agent of the energetic and unpredictable life-force ('his high spirits and trajectory are constant') that tests our cultural constructions to destruction ('Cultures blossom round his head and fall to bits under his feet'), and so wholly appropriate to any attempt to revitalize the mythology of our civilization (*WP* 240–1).

Hughes and fertility myth

Creation myth is implicitly cyclical. It suggests that humanity cannot help but dream of a return to the beginning, when a perfect creation emerged out of chaos. Both Hebrew and Babylonian myths are the source of 'nostalgia for paradise'. (As we shall see in due course, later books of the Bible bring a more progressive pattern into play, but Genesis certainly encourages a desire for a return to Eden.) With fertility myth, the cyclical model is emphatic, as is the role of the female deity. This kind of narrative is particularly associated with the invention of agriculture, about 12,000 years ago. Before then, there had indeed been an idea of the earth as a nurturing mother, from which human beings emerged and to which they returned at death. However, it was with the practice of sowing and reaping crops that there developed a myth based on the cycle of vegetation, with the goddess at its heart.

The pattern is as follows. The fertility goddess is immortal, but her male consort, the fertility god, has to die annually in order to ensure the renewal of the cycle. He is killed in his prime, by order of the goddess; his body is dismembered and the parts scattered across the land; he is then born again in order to fertilize the goddess once more, thus ensuring that the crops flourish for another year. This pattern persisted with the rise of urban civilizations, the goddess and god taking on different forms throughout the ancient world: Isis and Osiris (Egypt), Inanna and Thammuz (Mesopotamia, Babylonia), Aphrodite/Venus and Adonis (Greece/Rome). The very title of Hughes's second collection, *Lupercal*, refers to a Roman fertility festival, and perhaps its most celebrated lyric is 'Hawk Roosting' – a poem which Hughes has related to the Egyptian myth of Isis, the implication being that the hawk is Horus, the son and successor of Osiris, the dying god.[5]

The fertility goddess, representing the essential power of nature, necessarily has a dual identity. As the source of both life and death, light and dark, spring and winter, fruition and drought, she may be seen as both a benign and a malign force, as both lover and destroyer, both mother and murderer. This double part is well understood by those with an investment in the myth, the natural cycle making little sense to them otherwise. Hughes, we might add, was early on inspired by the poet Robert Graves's account of the complex nature of this female deity in *The White Goddess*.[6] *Gaudete* is a poetic narrative offering a variation on fertility myth, with the dying and reviving god played by one Nicholas Lumb in the village where he is vicar. Lumb is abducted into the underworld where he is asked to revive a dying goddess. The substitute wooden vicar back in the village has a rather literal idea of spreading the gospel of Love and in a comic parody gradually turns the Women's Institute into a kind of coven. The original Reverend Lumb was mistaken for a shamanic healer when he was abducted (not the role of a Church of England vicar, apparently), but when he emerges in the west of Ireland he has acquired shamanic wisdom and insight, as is revealed in the book of poems he has brought with him – the closing lyrics of the 'Epilogue' addressed to the elusive goddess.

The fertility god's death guarantees the continuity of the natural cycle, ensuring that the community survives. But also, according to Sir James Frazer in his classic work of myth theory, *The Golden Bough*, he functions as a 'scapegoat'. That is to say, by departing and disappearing into the realm of death he serves to carry off all traces of disease, corruption and pollution that might otherwise blight that community.[7]

In seeking to situate the underlying mythology of Shakespeare's body of work, Hughes is particularly interested in the Graeco-Roman version of fertility myth, given that it is the subject of one of Shakespeare's early poems. In an early rehearsal for the full-length study, namely the Introduction to his *Choice of Shakespeare's Verse*, Hughes expounds the significance of 'Venus and Adonis', which he relates to another long poem, 'The Rape of Lucrece'. Here we might pause to summarize these two works before seeing what Hughes makes of them. 'Venus and Adonis' retells the Roman (originally Greek) myth of the fertility goddess falling in love with a beautiful youth, who resists her advances, fleeing from her only to be savaged to death by a wild boar – this creature being the incarnation of Persephone, Venus's shadow-self, her underworld other. 'The Rape of Lucrece' is Shakespeare's version of another ancient Roman tale (not strictly mythic, but becoming so by association in this context). It concerns the sexual assault made by Prince Tarquin upon the chaste wife of his fellow-commander in the Roman army. Lucrece (or Lucretia) kills herself; Tarquin is banished, and the Roman monarchy comes to an end.

Hughes argues that the two texts provide the basis for the mythic 'equation' that runs through the major plays. He calls the four characters of these poems, Lucrece, Venus, Tarquin and Adonis, Shakespeare's 'four poles of energy' that provide the focus for the stages of Shakespeare's complete narrative cycle. Venus confronts Adonis, whereupon Adonis is killed by boar and is reborn as Tarquin, whereupon Tarquin destroys Lucrece, and in doing so destroys himself and all order (*WP* 116). Hughes argues that Shakespeare's plays explore these 'poles of energy' in all sorts of combinations, ultimately attempting to resist the deaths of Adonis and Lucrece.

The mythic equation is also the 'tragic' equation; and the tragedy is the result of the competing myths which were acted out in Shakespeare's era. Tarquin represents the Jehovah-worshipping Puritan, whose creation myth tells him that it is the transcendent, omnipotent God who is in charge, not the pagan goddess of nature. In his zeal he sets out to destroy her and the plays gradually tell the agonizing story of the gradual defeat of Venus and her boar. But the shifting protean puritan forces through the plays (as through the whole nation in Shakespeare's time, suggests Hughes) are ultimately self-destructive. Shakespeare's tragic hero, the puritan Adonis, is possessed by the demon he rejects. He struggles to reconcile in himself the tensions between the four principles represented by himself, Tarquin, Venus and Lucrece, and is inevitably torn apart (*WP* 116). We are not here interested in the details of Hughes's account of Shakespeare's mythic project; we are chiefly concerned with Hughes's own preoccupation with the nature of myth, and with the myth of nature. His focus is on the way the male believer in the absolute male God seeks to destroy the female principle which, according to the model of fertility, informs the whole of the natural world.

Hughes and deliverance myth

Here we need to focus mainly on the Bible, as the kind of deliverance myth relevant to Hughes's work is almost exclusively Judaeo-Christian in form and meaning. While creation and fertility myths honour the cyclical conception of time, deliverance myth offers a linear, progressive view. Jehovah may punish Adam and Eve by expelling them from the Garden, and leave them to make their way through the wilderness, but he has a grand plan for their salvation. What we know as 'the Fall' is only the beginning of a long collective adventure. In a later book of the Bible, namely Exodus, we read how Moses, guided by God, leads the Hebrews out of Egypt, where they have been enslaved, and guides them towards a 'promised land'. The Christian Gospels of the 'New Testament' extend this deliverance myth by presenting Jesus as the fulfilment of the Exodus story: through his crucifixion and resurrection he frees all humanity from the constraints of sin and death. Hughes's poem sequence *Adam and the Sacred Nine* is a moving version of the paradise/fall myth, with Adam learning from various birds how to love, and finally to be at home on, the earth.

True, some theorists of myth see Christianity as having associations with fertility myth. Jesus may be seen as a dying and reviving god, born in the winter (Christmas), sacrificed and reborn in the spring (Easter). The parallel is not coincidental: Christianity clearly has roots in some sort of nature cult. But the difference also needs emphasizing: the resurrection of Jesus is once and for all, and the result is not merely that the vegetation cycle succeeds (though we can see the link to this pagan model in various festivals of the Christian calendar), but rather that humanity is 'delivered' into the safety of the heavenly city of Jerusalem, as described in the final book of the Bible, namely Revelation. In other words, the Jesus story in its entirety belongs to that category of deliverance myth which we call 'apocalyptic' (from the Greek word for 'revelation').

Hughes throughout his work shows himself to be deeply suspicious of the biblical idea of salvation as coming about through history rather than through a renewal of our contract with nature and the goddess. If he may be said to subscribe to his own 'fall' myth, the Judaeo-Christian project is very much part of it, together with the modern cult of progress, which for him is only a secular variant of the myth of deliverance (though one that does not know itself to be mythic). In this case, a crucial moment in the protracted fall from what Hughes calls 'complete being' is that of the Reformation. For it was the funda-mentalist reading of apocalypse which inspired the Protestant reform-ers, and still more dramatically, their Puritan heirs to wage total war against the goddess. In support of Hughes's thesis, we might remind ourselves of the main scenario of the Book of Revelation. Most of the earth is laid waste, in preparation for the establishment of the heav-enly city of Jerusalem, which is built out of gold and other precious materials and which is lit neither by sunlight nor moonlight but by the light of God. Though we are told that the 'tree of life' and the 'river of life' will flourish, it is quite clear that these have a strictly symbolic existence, serving chiefly to represent the spiritual transformation of the earthly paradise depicted in the story of the Garden of Eden in Genesis. Natural trees and rivers will have disappeared, or been trans-formed beyond recognition: 'And I saw a new heaven and a new earth: for the first heaven and the first earth were passed away; and there was no more sea' (Revelation 21:1). With a fundamentalist reading of this text, the way was open for the legitimisation of a fiercely other-worldly faith, and with it that ruthless manipulation and exploitation of the earth which climaxes in modernity. So it is no surprise to find that there are several parodies of Genesis in *Crow* ('Lineage', 'A Horrible Religious Error', 'Apple Tragedy', 'Snake Hymn'). There are also ironic meditations on the crucifixion ('The Contender') and on the apocalypse ('Notes for a Little Play', 'Crow's Account of the Battle', 'Crow's Last Stand'). Interspersed with these are reflections on our abusive relationship with the great goddess ('Crow and Mama', 'Revenge Fable').

It is in the Shakespeare study that Hughes makes his case against the myth of deliverance, though not named as such. Being clear about Christianity's debt to fertility myth, he is clear also that ultimately it represents a severing of our bond with nature. It is the destruction of the goddess, first by Jehovah to preside in Heaven, then by his and her son, the Puritan Christ, that sets in train the essential tragedy of Shakespeare's narrative cycle: 'What Shakespeare goes on to reveal is that in destroying her he destroys himself and brings down Heaven and Earth in ruins' (*SGCG* 18). Christianity in this context may be seen as a religion rooted in fertility myth which eventually became divorced from those roots and began a long process of dissociation from the natural world, spurred on by an increasingly literal interpretation of its founding text, the Bible.

Hughes, then, repudiates what we are calling the myth of deliverance, and in particular its impact within modernity – early on with the Reformation and later on with the cult of progress, with unrestrained industrialisation, and what is euphemistically called 'development'. His definitive statement is 'The Environmental Revolution', his review of Max Nicholson's book of the same name. It is here that we see how his knowledge of myth and his passion for ecology inform each other. Hughes suggests that Western civilization is still dominated by Old Testament notions that 'the earth is a heap of raw materials given to man by God for his exclusive profit and use'. Because man is alienated from Mother Nature, the goddess, he is also alienated from his own inner nature. While Hughes uses the word 'quest' to describe the basic myth of the ideal life (*WP* 129), and while 'quest' is a word we would normally associate with hero myth – of which more very shortly – he is thinking primarily of that violent and destructive journey undertaken by God's chosen people, with no sense of reconciliation or return, that we have referred to as the myth of deliverance.

There is hope, however. The artist – or, by analogy, the poet – may see something else, and guide us to it, whether in images that remind us of Eden, or the world of animals, or Pan, or nature's force for regeneration even in the face of being poisoned by human activities (*WP* 130). All Hughes's writing, whether directly or indirectly related to myth, is dedicated to ensuring that the germ of nature's life not only survives but also flourishes. *River* is his celebration of the fertile natural world as the paradise (continually restored by death) that we thought we had lost – a vision of the given world as our one and only Eden.

Hughes and hero myth

I have left this category of narrative to the last because it is the most ambiguous: while it has a very specific, historically determined meaning, it can also be applied to a whole range of stories from different eras. On the one hand, then, it may be narrowly defined as that kind of myth which celebrates the rise of a warrior class in the later years of the second millennium BC. It represents the human ideal of that class, that culture. A male hero sets out on a quest, facing terrifying obstacles on the way, and proves his courage in combat, eventually returning home. Ancient Greece affords us many such tales: for instance, that of Perseus, the slayer of Medusa, the Gorgon; or again, that of Hercules (or Herakles), famous for undertaking twelve labours, which included slaughtering not only the fabulous many-headed monster, the Hydra, but also a ferocious lion and a dangerous boar for good measure. Thus does a male hero prove himself in a patriarchal culture. More complex is the figure of Prometheus, the Titan who befriends humanity and steals fire from the gods on their behalf, thus facilitating human culture. As a punishment, Zeus has him chained to a rock, where he is perpetually tormented by a giant eagle (or raven) tearing at his liver. His heroism lies in his refusal to give in or show signs of weakness. Hughes's poem sequence *Prometheus on His Crag* is a visceral retelling of the famous myth, with the emphasis on not only what the hero endures but also on what he learns about the natural order.

On the other hand, however, hero myth is the most general kind of narrative we could possibly imagine. After all, every myth that has ever been narrated has one or more central characters who we might describe neutrally as 'heroes'. Creation, fertility and deliverance myth: all are 'heroic', in that some figure, whether divine or human, achieves something. Thus, in the previous section we have noted Hughes's account of 'the Quest', which may imply hero myth but which the poet can legitimately use to refer to that collective and progressive project which derives from the biblical myth of deliverance.

Less legitimate might appear Hughes's application of the quest structure to that crucial role of every North American tribe, that of the shaman. Here again, though, he is strictly speaking accurate. For it is the shaman's function to adventure in the spirit world – the dangerous flight of the imagination – to return with the healing gift of stories and poems and songs, and thereby restore the balance between culture and nature. In so doing, he may have affinity with the fertility god, but he may also be celebrated as the archetypal hero, the soothsayer of his tribe. This, Hughes, argued, was the basic experience of the poetic temperament we call 'romantic' and would, in a shamanizing society, give the role of shaman to the authors of *Venus and Adonis*, some of Keats's longer poems, W.B. Yeats's *The Wanderings of Oisin* and T.S. Eliot's *Ash Wednesday*. The shamanic flight also 'lies perceptibly behind' many of the best fairy tales and behind myths – Hughes singles out those of Orpheus and Herakles – and behind such poetic epics as those of Gilgamesh and Odysseus (*WP* 58).

Moreover, if the shaman makes sense in terms of hero myth as well as fertility myth, the trickster makes sense in terms of hero as well as creation myth. Indeed, the trickster's endless adventures, whether in aiding the construction of the world or in wreaking havoc, seem to Hughes to conform to the pattern of the hero's journey. Taking up his idea that this is a character which represents the life-force itself, Hughes concludes that the quest of the trickster is like 'a master plan, a deep biological imprint, and one of our most useful pieces of kit'. Hughes sees trickster tales as a form of Tragicomedy in which this 'demon of phallic energy', carrying the spirit of the sperm, suffers for his misunderstandings, but is also capable of experiencing tragic joy (*WP* 241). It is not that Hughes is confusing categories of myth and blurring different mythic roles. Rather, he is demonstrating that mythology is a complex web of stories – as complex as that great web of being that we call 'nature'.

Moreover, Hughes is writing as someone who has understood that we are living in extraordinary times, having lost our bond with the earth and our sense of the sacred. Hence, any myth-making poet has, as it were, to start from scratch, building up the mythic connections as best he can. In the interview given on the occasion of the publication of *Crow*, he explained that he believed that Eliot, Joyce and Beckett were suffering and portraying the last phase of the disintegration of Christian civilization. After them came some writers who did not seem to belong spiritually to Christian civilization at all.

> In their world Christianity is just another provisional myth of man's relationship with the creator and the world of spirit. Their world is a continuation or a re-emergence of the pre-Christian world [...] it is the world of the little pagan religions and cults, the primitive religions from which of course Christianity itself grew.[8]

Cave Birds is an extension of the *Crow* myth, and a revision of the dying and reviving god featured in fertility myth, with the hero on a quest which involves the necessary disintegration of his ego before his reintegration in 'Bride and Groom Lie Hidden for Three Days' and his rebirth as a falcon. Thus it is that, in coming to write *Crow* and its extension *Cave Birds* – what we might call Hughes's gesture towards the kind of myth that might be appropriate for our desolate, alienated state of being – he finds it appropriate to redefine what we mean by 'hero'. The arrogance of the ancient warrior class, the fundamentalist conviction of the reforming Christian, the triumphalism of the modern progressive mind: these no longer suffice. Our hero must be the stripped-down figure of a creature with nothing left to lose. And finally there remains the question of whether the myth will be understood in its full healing potential. Will the newly humble, powerful, transfigured falcon, for whom 'the dirt becomes God', connect with and empower readers? 'But when will he land / On a man's wrist' (*CP* 440). Here Hughes the reader of myth becomes inseparable from Hughes the writer of myth; but in both capacities, he makes us see how much myth matters, because there is always a need for a retelling, a new version, an unanswered question about the mystery of the universe: 'At the end of the ritual / up comes a goblin' (CP 440).

Notes

1. The second revised, paperback, edition of *SGCB* (1993) is quoted in this chapter.
2. In quotations from Hughes throughout this chapter I have respected his capitalization, even where it may seem inconsistent.
3. For a fuller discussion of these categories, see Laurence Coupe, *Myth* (2nd edn, Abingdon: Routledge, 2009).
4. See Mircea Eliade, *Myths, Dreams and Mysteries: The Encounter between Contemporary Faiths and Archaic Reality*, trans. Philip Mairet (London: Fontana, 1968); Mircea Eliade, *The Sacred and the Profane: The Nature of Religion*, trans. Willard R. Trask (San Diego, CA: Harcourt, 1959).
5. Egbert Faas, *Ted Hughes: The Unaccommodated Universe* (Santa Barbara, CA: Black Sparrow Press, 1980): 199.
6. See Robert Graves, *The White Goddess: A Historical Grammar of Poetic Myth* (2nd edn, London: Faber & Faber, 1999).
7. For a comprehensive account of the role of the fertility god, including his sacrificial function, see Sir James George Frazer, *The Illustrated Golden Bough*, ed. Sabine McCormack (London: Macmillan, 1978).
8. Faas, *Ted Hughes*: 205.

2

Hughes and *Post*-Modernism

Alex Davis

A postmodern poet?

There have been relatively few interpretations of Hughes as a 'post-modernist' poet, a lacuna in his critical reception that, on the face of it, is somewhat surprising.[1] Postmodernity has been characterized by many of its theorists as denoting a seismic cultural shift against a period of modernity that, from the Enlightenment on, held fast to a belief in the demystifying power of scientific and rational thought, and the inevitable human 'progress' such empowering discourses of knowledge seemingly bring in their train. Even this thumbnail sketch gives credence to Dennis Brown's description of the discord-ant and playful registers of Hughes's *Crow* – including those of 'Fleet Street, the movies, and street talk' – as a postmodern challenge to 'the positivistic, rationalising monologism of Western master narra-tives'.[2] Charles Olson, one of the first to employ the term, writes of the 'post-modern' urge to get outside 'the Western Box';[3] and *Crow*'s irreverent polyvocality certainly lends it voice(s) to his imper-ative. Olson's comprehension of the 'modern' he sought to move beyond includes Anglo-American poetic Modernism, especially that of T.S. Eliot. Subsequent commentators on postmodernist poetry have often followed suit, perceiving in the frustrated personae and bleak landscape of Eliot's *The Waste Land* the impasse of the rational subject amid the ruins of the progressive project of modernity. In this chapter, however, I will argue that Hughes's poetics are *post*-Modernist precisely because they are informed by certain preoc-cupations regarding language's engagement with the non-linguistic world which Hughes inherits from Modernism. Moreover, in Eliot's Modernism, as we shall see, Hughes finds a 'poetic temperament' that, to his eyes, continues a tradition of 'romantic' writing that has a closer parallel in the shaman's cathartic visions than in the faded contents of 'the Western Box'.

Verbal entrapment: Hughes's poetics

'Coming down through Somerset', from Hughes's sequence of farming poems, *Moortown Diary*, begins with a night drive's encounter with a dead badger. Road-kill 'flash-glimpsed in the headlights', the animal's remains are almost reverentially recovered from the highway by the speaker, and, 'bleeding from the nose', driven to his home. There, the musteline hitchhiker lies on an old beam, his imminent putrefaction eliciting at the close of the poem the plea:

> I want him
> To stop time. His strength staying, bulky,
> Blocking time. His rankness, his bristling wildness,
> His thrillingly painted face.
> A badger on my moment of life.
> Not years ago, like the others, but now. (*CP* 524–5)

The lines possess Hughes's hallmark descriptive vividness. In 'His thrillingly painted face', for example, while the adjective ('painted') provides a sharply exact image of the animal's facial markings, the adverb ('thrillingly') conveys a sense of the speaker's exhilarated responsiveness to the badger's striking mask. Such intense *mimesis* is to be found throughout Hughes's poetry, in its memorable attempts to render in words the sensory experience that is the object of the poem. Indeed, the entry on 'mimesis' in a standard reference work on poetics, *The New Princeton Encyclopaedia of Poetry and Poetics*, employs a metaphor familiar to readers of Hughes's primer on poetic composition, *Poetry in the Making*, to describe this process. In its broadest sense, mimesis constitutes 'the verbal *capturing* or conveying of experience in such a way that the mental image or meaning created by the words is judged similar, analogous, or even identical to what we know about the world from sense-data directly'.[4]

Discussing his poem 'The Thought-Fox', from *The Hawk in the Rain*, in *Poetry in the Making*, Hughes draws a comparison between his adolescent 'capturing' of animals and his later 'capturing' of poems (*WP* 15). Hughes's emphasis on the psychic reality of this particular fox chimes with the emotiveness of the adverbial 'thrillingly' in 'Coming down through Somerset'. Both poem and prose illustrate that Hughes's is an *expressive* form of mimesis; that is, it seeks not only to render its object (a 'real' fox's movement or badger's mask) in all its physical actuality, but also the experiencing subject's (the poet's) emotional and imaginative *response* to that object. Neil Roberts sees in this the influence on Hughes of certain Romantic poets: 'Coleridge's belief in the imagination as a fundamentally creative faculty, Blake's espousal of vision, and Wordsworth's affirmation of nature as the source of his poetic gift [...] are all deeply interfused in Hughes's poetic practice.'[5] Thus, Hughes's 'Thought-Fox', as the title's compound noun suggests, is initially part of a landscape that has its origins not in any observation of the physical environment, but in the poet's initial reverie over 'this blank page where my fingers move' – spun out of his own entrails, as it were: 'I *imagine* this midnight moment's forest' (*CP* 21; emphasis added). By the middle of the poem, however, the text's powerful mimeticism –

> Two eyes serve a movement, that now
> And again now, and now, and now,
>
> Sets neat prints into the snow –

gives the strong impression that, in Roberts's words, the fox has become 'a real, autonomous creature moving in the natural world'.[6] Hughes's claim in *Poetry in the Making* that he had 'caught the real fox there in the words' implies that the verbal signs of the poem, its 'words', have securely 'captured' the referential animal, as 'with a sudden sharp hot stink of fox / It enters the dark hole of the head'. The close of the poem reinforces this sense of verbal entrapment in the analogy between the writing of the text – inferred from the closing matter-of-fact declaration, 'The page is printed' – and the tentative progress of the fox's 'prints' through the blank page of the snow. The self-consciousness of the poem to its own poetic strategy, its intense self-reflexivity, makes it almost a manifesto; and, tellingly, Hughes chose it to open his three volumes of selected poems (published in 1972, 1982 and 1995).

Yet 'The Thought-Fox' is open to another reading, one that problematizes its brief yet compelling narrative of poetic composition as a variety of, in the imagery of *Poetry in the Making*, 'hunting and the poem [...] a new species of creature' to be caught (*WP* 12). To begin with, 'the verbal capturing or conveying of experience' that is central to mimesis is, obviously enough, the *representation* in words or signs of that experience, *not* the experience itself. Hughes's commentary on 'The Thought-Fox' revealingly admits that, as an adolescent, an animal that he never succeeded in keeping alive was the fox, as, having successfully trapped the cubs, an adult stepped in either to kill or free them. The poem came, some years later, almost in compensation for his youthful frustration, the words having 'made a body for it' (*WP* 15). The thought-fox's corporeality, its 'body', is linguistic; and Hughes is determined, in this context, to emphasize the animating power of poetic language. The fox's vitality owes everything to the vividness of the language of which it is composed. Hence, in Hughes's words, 'It is [...] a fox that is both a fox and not a fox' (*WP* 14). In the background to this passage is a conception of poetic creativity owing a good deal to Coleridge's and other Romantic writers' contention that the genesis and unity of the artwork are comparable to the development and structure of an organism.[7] Whereas in Romanticism the 'organic form' of the poem is usually perceived as comparable to that of vegetable life, in Hughes it is here rendered in bestial terms: the imitative rhythm of 'And again now, and now, and now / / Sets neat prints into the snow' driving home the similarity between the fox's movement and the poet's physical act of writing the poem.[8]

However, Hughes's fox is 'not a fox' in the sense that, as the punning last line of the poem stresses, it is a 'paper being' ('The page is printed'). As Gérard Genette reminds us, 'language signifies without imitating':[9] the signification of the word *fox*, for instance, owes nothing to any vulpine quality to the sign itself, but to the sign's differential relationship with other signs within a particular language system (i.e. English). This lack of identity between word and thing, sign and referent, leads Hughes elsewhere to lament language as cripplingly unable to communicate fully the immediacy of lived experience. From this perspective, the thought-fox's 'body' is that of a verbal zombie, a kind of walking corpus.

In one of the Epilogue poems to *Gaudete*, 'I hear your congregations at their rapture', the persona forcefully makes this very point. The 'rapture' heard in the cries of birds and beasts simply 'will not chill into syntax'. So too, 'the beetling talk' of Neanderthal *Homo sapiens* has evolved into mere 'chat':

> Words buckle the voice in tighter, closer
> Under the midriff
> Till the cry rots, and speech
>
> Is a fistula
>
> Eking and deferring (*CP* 357)

Like the green anarchist John Zerzan,[10] Hughes sees language, as a mode of symbolic thought, as fully implicated in humanity's

alienation from the kind of unmediated relationship with the natural environment supposedly enjoyed by, here, the animal kingdom
and early hominids. (Zerzan argues that a similar relationship is still
present in contemporary hunter-gatherer societies; art is merely a
palliative for our loss of such non-symbolic lived experience.) In an
essay, 'Orghast: Talking without Words', justifying the largely invented
language of the collaborative dramatic venture *Orghast* – performed
in Persia in 1971 – Hughes provides a gloss on this lyric in his comment, arguing that some animals and birds seem to express in a voice
or a tone what we can recognize as a spirit or a truth that is 'under all
truths. Far beyond human words' (*WP* 124–5).[11] Writing about 'The
Thought-Fox' in *Poetry in the Making*, Hughes claims that his fox is
'both a fox and a spirit' (*WP* 14). Yet to describe language as a 'fistula',
that is, a diseased tube-shaped passageway between distinct organs,
is to diagnose the very medium of poetry as an abnormal form of
mediation. (That the word, in Latin, denotes a shepherd's or pan pipes,
as well as having its medical meaning, is perhaps not insignificant in
this context.) Both the Epilogue poem and Hughes's reflections in
'Orghast: Talking without Words' imply that what he calls 'spirit',
whether that of a material fox or that which is at 'the core of us', is
ultimately incommunicable – 'Far beyond human words'.

Hughes in the underworld: The Romantic lineage

The 'Eking and deferring' of (poetic) language, its inability to represent 'a truth under all truths', leads Paul Bentley to argue that there
is a crucial difference between 'Hughes's vision' and that of 'the more
idealistic strains of Romanticism: the imagination in Hughes is up
against something that resists, limits, oppresses and finally outflanks its
power'.[12] Employing Jacques Lacan's term for the absolute material
limit – including the pre-linguistic recourses of the body – to concep-
tualization, 'the Real', Bentley claims that the verbal pyrotechnics of
Hughes's poetry 'perpetually strive to translate experience of the Real
into human terms'; but endlessly fall short: 'The gap between word
and thing is [...] insurmountable: the more words, the more the Real
thing is "missed".'[13] Bentley is arguably over-hasty in distinguishing
Hughes from Romanticism is this respect. Psychoanalytical readings
of key Romantic texts – 'more idealistic' or less so – have identified a structure of the 'Lacanian "quest-romance" of the alienated
subject', in Jerrold E. Hogle's summary description,[14] not dissimilar to
Hughes's. But Bentley's basic point retains, I think, its validity. Hughes's

poetry can be read in the tradition of Romantic and post-Romantic 'internalised quest romance', as influentially delineated by Harold Bloom: the former's major sequences *Crow*, *Cave Birds* and *Gaudete* all conform to this pattern.[15] But the psychic romances explored in these three major works culminate in failure of one kind or another. The successful conclusion to Crow's quest, in the figure of 'the hag' transformed into 'a beautiful, lithe, naked maiden', exists only in the prose story of the poem, not the published volumes;[16] the apotheosis of the nameless avian of *Cave Birds* is qualified by the interrogative close to 'The Risen' ('But when will he land / On a Man's wrist' [*CP* 440]); and Nicholas Lumb's rebirth from the 'baboon woman' (*G* 105) in *Gaudete* is grotesquely travestied in his doppelgänger's sexual escapades in the village from which the hapless clergyman has been abducted to the underworld.[17]

To return to 'Coming down through Somerset', the dead badger looks set to undertake his own katabasis or descent to an under-world: 'Flies, drumming, / Bejewel his transit. Heatwave ushers him hourly / Towards his underworlds' (*CP* 524). As Terry Gifford states, *Moortown Diary* 'is a contemporary georgic [...] with an anti-pastoral emphasis';[18] and the sequence consequently derives, even as it defamiliarizes, much of its generic character from the example of Virgil's *Georgics* (36–29 BC). Given *Moortown Diary*'s inescapable dependence on a classical precedent that it nevertheless wrenches awry, the badger's imminent katabasis might be seen as having an unusual precedent in the inset tale of Orpheus in the underworld in the fourth book of Virgil's poem. The importance of this particular myth to Hughes's work cannot be over-emphasized; equally significant is its near-total suppression from his *oeuvre* until the very end of his career. In a late letter, Hughes wrote to Keith Sagar that the story of Orpheus's quest to recover his wife, Eurydice, from Hades 'was the first story that occurred to me after S.[ylvia] P.[lath]'s death. I rejected it: I thought it would be too obvious an attempt to exploit my situation.'[19] Aside from a radio play for children, *Orpheus*, broadcast in 1971, the myth makes no obvious appearance in Hughes's work until his late version of Euripides's *Alcestis*, in which the briefest of allusions to the myth in the original play is greatly amplified. But the myth is clearly implicit in the verse-epistles to Plath collected in *Birthday Letters*, where Hughes is cast as Orpheus to Plath's Eurydice.[20] In the encounter with a dead badger in 'Coming down through Somerset' (datelined '*8 August 1975*'), the myth's subterranean presence in Hughes's imagination during the interim arguably bubbles faintly to the surface. In Virgil's *Georgics*, as elsewhere in the ancient sources, the poet-hero

Orpheus's quest ends in failure; disobeying Proserpina's injunction not to look behind him, he loses Eurydice to the underworld as he leads her thence. His foil in Virgil is the pastoral demigod Aristaeus, the loss of whose bees is made good through his obedience to the dictates of the goddess Cyrene, his mother. In *Moortown Diary* the speaker is both a latter-day, struggling Aristaeus, whose animal husbandry is the subject of the majority of the journalistic entries, and the Orphic elegist, as in the moving series of poems in memory of his father-in-law, Jack Orchard, which close the *Diary*.[21] 'Coming Down Through Somerset' prefigures those final elegies, casting the badger as both lost object and as Orphic surrogate, his latter role further hinted at in the speaker's resistance to dismembering him – to skinning him 'Or hack[ing] off his head' in order 'To liberate his masterpiece skull' – the gruesome fate that befell the bereaved Orpheus at the hands of the Thracian women or Maenads.

After decapitation, Orpheus' head continued to sing. Philip Hardie observes that, in the context of the *Georgics*, this image suggests that 'his enduring legacy is a poetry without practical or social utility', a vehicle merely for the pathos of lost love.[22] For some readers this may well seem an appropriate description of *Birthday Letters*, particularly if one is of the persuasion that Hughes's self-depiction therein is as the victim of, in Lynda K. Bundtzen's words, 'Maenad-feminists who have hounded him over the years'.[23] But if the overwhelmingly mimetic impulse of Hughes's poetry is driven, at its roots, by a quest-romance to represent a pre- or non-linguistic otherness (something akin to Lacan's conception of 'the Real'), such an Orphic descent is clearly envisaged as socially useful. After all, for Hughes, the myth of Orpheus correlates with the experience of shamanism as a technique for moving in a state of ecstasy through spiritual realms and for dealing with spirits 'in a practical way, in some practical crisis' (*WP* 56). Furthermore, the shamanic 'technique' is for Hughes the basic experience of the poetic temperament that we call 'Romantic' (*WP* 58).

Hughes's comprehension of the Romantic poetic tradition is, as Neil Roberts remarks, 'eclectic',[24] including only one poet (Keats) whose work belongs to the literary period in question, at least as it is conventionally construed. As we have seen, Hughes's conception of the Romantic 'temperament' has at its core the basic structure of quest-romance. It is such a mentality that, in a review of Max Nicholson's *The Environmental Revolution*, he claims derives from our 'exile [...] from both inner and outer nature' (*WP* 129). As a consequence, the basic myth for the ideal Westerner's life is 'the Quest', a myth that prompts alike the despair and hubris of both spiritual romanticism and heroic technological progress, but which, just possibly, might prompt our humble recognition of the spirit of natural life (*WP* 130). It is the suppression of this 'spirit' that, in *Shakespeare and the Goddess of Complete Being* and related works, Hughes perceives Shakespeare, from *Venus and Adonis* on, as having mapped. 'The overall pattern of Goddess-centred matriarchy being overthrown by a God-centred patriarchy', as he outlines it in a letter to Nick Gammage, and which he had first discerned in the pages of Robert Graves's *The White Goddess* (*LTH* 680), is that which Shakespeare's narrative poem of Adonis's rejection of Venus allegorizes in the context of the Puritanism of Early Modern England (see *SGCB* 49–92).[25] In the same letter, Hughes makes clear that there is a 'lineage in English poetry' that, as through a glass darkly, provides a distorted glimpse of this 'terrible spirit', providing as examples 'the Sycorax figure', the monstrous Caliban's mother in Shakespeare's *The Tempest*, the fell beauty of 'La Belle Dame sans Merci' in Keats's haunting ballad, and Coleridge's 'Nightmare Life in Death' in 'The Ancient Mariner' (*LTH* 681).[26]

'Bizarre noises': Hughes and Modernism

Hughes's 'romantic'-shamanic 'lineage' of English-language poetry undoubtedly establishes, in Neil Corcoran's words, 'a line of succession from Shakespeare to himself'.[27] Hughes is the inheritor of a poetic in which the imagination is perceived to possess a therapeutic and thus social function; as he argues in his 1976 essay 'Myth and Education'.[28] However, Hughes's equally deeply held conviction that language is a 'fistula', a malignant medium of communication, threatens any such reconciliation, throwing into doubt any successful 'capture' of the Real (both 'inner' and 'outer' worlds) by poetic means. The self-awareness of Hughes's poetry to the limits (and liabilities, as he views them) of its necessarily verbal artifice arguably positions it within the matrix of Modernism – that is, contrary to the pronouncements of a number of critics, Hughes's poetics bear the impress of a similar self-reflexivity vis-à-vis the media of the arts that one finds in the Modernist movement of the early twentieth century. Michael Bell identifies this dimension to Modernism with what has come to be known as the 'linguistic turn' at this date: 'rather than describing or reflecting the world, language was now seen to form it'. Such was the conclusion, in effect, of such ground-breaking works as Ferdinand de Saussure's *Course in General Linguistics* (1916) and Ludwig Wittgenstein's *Tractatus Logico-Philosophicus* (1921).[29]

For Anthony Easthope, Hughes's poetry, unlike that of the Modernist Eliot, is seemingly unconscious of this 'turn'. Eliot's mildly surreal image of 'the sawdust-trampled street / With all its muddy feet', in his 'Preludes', draws attention to its artifice through its disorientating implication that it is the sawdust that tramples the street and that streets have muddy feet.[30] The expressive mimeticism of Hughes's poetry, Easthope maintains, instead 'aims for transparency', and in this respect is written in contradistinction to the Modernist realization that language 'Float[s] free of any supposed referent' and, as a consequence, 'textuality is thrown into prominence as we are forced to become aware of the poem *as poem*'.[31] Easthope's argument rightly identifies the *desire* for unmediated 'transparency' in Hughes's poetics; however, it ignores the nagging recognition, repeatedly raised in Hughes's poetry and prose, that language is a sign-system by means of which the referential world is constructed, and thus occluded, rather than simply accessed. Most obviously, Hughes's signature poem, 'The Thought-Fox', makes its readers acutely conscious that it is a *poem* – that the fox padding through the snow is an extended metaphor for its coming into existence as a textual or 'paper being'.

Easthope's sharp distinction between Hughes and Eliot also fails to take into account Hughes's writings on the earlier poet, especially those collected in *A Dancer to God: Tributes to T. S. Eliot*. Eliot's importance for Hughes is attested to in many contexts, but it is only in these late texts that the precise nature of that significance comes into focus. In the longest of these prose pieces, 'The Poetic Self',[32] Hughes once again considers Eliot (and Yeats) according to a shamanic paradigm. Taking his cue from the common Modernist trope of a moment of irreversible historical rupture ('the whole metaphysical universe centred on God had vanished from its place. It had evaporated, with all its meanings' (*WP* 269)), Hughes characterizes Eliot's poetic career as beginning with 'a shamanic crisis-call to regeneration' (*WP* 290). Quoting from 'Preludes', Hughes argues that the 'homeland' of the 'tribal disaster' confronting the young Eliot was that 'infinitely gentle, infinitely suffering' sprit's hold on the nature of reality, in a universe that had, 'in primitive fashion', lost its soul (*WP* 272–3). To most readers, I imagine, the 'primitivism' of this account has the ring of Hughes rather than Eliot. Yet Hughes's shamanizing Eliot cuts a less exotic figure when viewed from the perspective of an ecocritical understanding of cultural Modernism and, as a corollary, Hughes appears, at least in one respect, as Eliot's natural inheritor.[33]

Eliot clearly shares something of Hughes's preoccupation with a primeval underside to language, that to which the 'auditory imagination' alone grants access, reaching 'below conscious levels of thought and feeling [...] to the most primitive and forgotten'.[34] For the ecocritic Carrie Rohman, Eliot's 'dabbling in the discursive realm of primitivism'[35] can be heard in the 'experiments in linguistic devolution' in the infantile-cum-bestial hullabaloo of his play *Sweeney Agonistes* (in '*the bam*'s and '*the boo*'s and the 'Hoo ha ha / Hoo ha ha / Hoo / Hoo / Hoo' of the fragmentary melodrama).[36] This cacophony, argues Rohman, inscribes the dark underbelly of human animality, its instinctual drives, into the otherwise symbolic order of Eliot's play. The experimental drama, *Orghast*, as we saw above, constituted a comparable attempt to give voice to the cries of the id. In this regard, Hughes's understanding of the 'romantic' poet might be profitably interpreted as an index of his poetry's relationship to the Modernism of Eliot and others. Hughes's status as a deservedly celebrated 'nature poet', most obviously in the animal-poems on which a large part of his reputation was established, is not, as Easthope would have us believe, indicative of a writer somehow harking back to pre-Modernism. On the contrary, his work is a monumental chapter in that which Rohman describes as 'The twentieth-century eruption of animality, often encoded as the eruption of the unconscious, [which] parallels the Modernist explosion of linguistic convention'.[37]

In an introduction he gave to a reading of Eliot's *The Waste Land*, Hughes asks us to listen to the dissonance of Eliot's pocket-epic in the context of the poem's narrative of quasi-shamanic regeneration and the 'final blessing' (*DG* 16) of its closing words:

> There are many bizarre noises in *The Waste Land*: voices of water, speech of birds, and a jostling of fragments of other languages. But the unfamiliar language which finally embraces and enfolds all the voices and gathers up the whole poem is that of the Upanishads – the Sanskrit of those superhuman, ancient Hindu scriptures from which emerged Buddhism. (*DG* 15)

There are many such 'bizarre noises' in Hughes's poetry, too. The 'speech of birds' is unforgettably heard in 'Hawk Roosting', from *Lupercal*: 'There is no sophistry in my body: / My manners are tearing off heads' (*CP* 69); in the 'Squealing and gibbering and cursing' of the 'Skylarks' in *Wodwo* (*CP* 175); and, of course, in the 'Songs of the Crow'.[38] Likewise, 'voices of water' are memorably lifted in 'The Gulkana', from *River*, in the 'voice of the river' and the salmon who 'rose and sank / Like voices, themselves like singers / In its volume' (*CP* 667–8). For Eliot, the 'language' embracing and enfolding all other voices would be, subsequent to *The Waste Land*, not that of the Upanishads, but the word of orthodox Christianity. For Hughes, the 'voices of water, speech of birds' articulate an 'unfamiliar language' which, utterly incommensurate with the 'Eking and deferring' of human signification, possesses all the force of religious instruction – as the echo in 'The Gulkana' of Genesis emphasizes: 'Word by word / The voice of the river moved in me' (*CP* 669).[39]

In conclusion, Hughes's self-conscious and deep connections to the 'poetic temperament[s]' of Romantic and Modernist poetry should serve to remind us of the historicity of his work. Just as Romanticism is indelibly marked by the revolutions in America and France and Modernism by the cataclysm of the First World War,[40] 'the Real' in Hughes – the ineradicable frame to his oeuvre's attempt to 'capture' the 'otherness' of subjective and objective nature – is, in the last instance, the material history of nation, family and individual, as documented in, for instance, the regionalism of *Remains of Elmet*, the familial memories in *Flowers and Insects*, the Laureate poems and the searing confessionalism of *Birthday Letters*.[41] In 'That Morning', from *River*, the 'formations' of salmon in the glittering water proffer 'some dazzle of blessing // [...] *As if* the fallen / World and salmon were over' (*CP* 663; emphasis added). The conditional underscores the fact that the salmon's 'blessing', the 'voice of the river', can be heard only against the white noise of the postlapsarian world, or history, here audible in the drone of formations of Second World War bombers glimpsed on another dawn:

> We came where the salmon were so many
> So steady, so spaced, so far-aimed
> On their inner map, England could add
>
> Only the sooty twilight of South Yorkshire
> Hung with the drumming drift of Lancasters
> Till the world had seemed capsizing slowly. (*CP* 663)

Notes

1. An observation made by Terry Gifford in *Ted Hughes* (London: Routledge, 2009): 118.
2. Dennis Brown, *The Poetry of Postmodernity: Anglo/American Encodings* (Basingstoke: Palgrave Macmillan, 1994): 77. For an introduction to, and a selection of key texts in, the debate on postmodernity, see Thomas Docherty (ed.), *Postmodernism: A Reader* (London: Longman, 1992).
3. Charles Olson, *Selected Writings*, ed. Robert Creeley (New York: New Directions, 1966): 129.
4. Alex Preminger and T.V.F. Brogan (eds), *The New Princeton Encyclopedia of Poetry and Poetics* (3rd edn, Princeton, NJ: Princeton University Press, 1993): 1038; emphasis added.

5. Neil Roberts, *Ted Hughes: New Selected Poems* (Penrith: Humanities-Ebooks.co.uk, 2007): 25. *The New Princeton Encyclopedia* notes: 'The advent of romanticism effected a fundamental epistemological shift by reformulating [literature] not as an *imitative* but as a *constitutive* art, presenting not external reality but a fuller, partly interior version of reality which includes the feeling subject': Preminger and Brogan (eds), *New Princeton Encyclopedia*: 1039. Roberts's and the *Encyclopedia*'s understanding of Romanticism is compatible with that of M.H. Abrams's influential study, *The Mirror and the Lamp: Romantic Theory and the Critical Tradition* (Oxford: Oxford University Press, 1953).

6. Roberts, *Ted Hughes: New Selected Poems*: 26.

7. In his essay 'Shakespeare and Occult Neoplatonism' Hughes employs organic metaphors to describe the 'evolution' of Shakespeare's 'radical myth': see *WP* 309.

8. For an introduction to the notion of, and the critical debate surrounding, 'organic form', see Joel Black, 'Scientific Models', in *The Cambridge History of Literary Criticism*, vol. 5, ed. Marshall Brown, *Romanticism* (Cambridge: Cambridge University Press, 2000): 115–37. Hughes's use of 'imitative rhythm' – which is one aspect of his poetry's mimetic power – should be considered in the light of the extensive critical debate the topic has aroused; useful discussions (with further reading) include Peter Makin, *Bunting: The Shaping of his Verse* (Oxford: Oxford University Press, 1992): 337–41 and L.P. Wilkinson, *Golden Latin Artistry* (Cambridge: Cambridge University Press, 1963): *passim*.

9. Gérard Genette, *Narrative Discourse: An Essay in Method*, trans. Jane E. Lewin (Ithaca, NY: Cornell University Press, 1980): 164. The phrase 'paper being' is Roland Barthes's, and denotes the necessarily *textual* existence of characters and narrators in a literary work; see his 'Introduction to the Structural Analysis of Narrative', in *Image-Music-Text*, trans. Stephen Heath (London: Fontana, 1977): 111.

10. See John Zerzan, 'The Case Against Art', in his *Elements of Refusal* (2nd edn, Columbia, MO: Columbia Alternative Press, 1999): 63–72.

11. On *Orghast*, see A.C.H. Smith, *Orghast at Persepolis: An International Experiment in Theatre Directed by Peter Brook and Written by Ted Hughes* (New York: Viking, 1973). Hughes's essay, 'Baboons and Neanderthals: A Rereading of *The Inheritors*', in John Carey (ed.), *William Golding, The Man and His Books: A Tribute on his 75th Birthday* (London: Faber & Faber, 1986): 161–88, throws light on the poem's valorization of early hominid 'speech'; see also Keith Sagar, 'Ted Hughes and the Divided Brain', *The Ted Hughes Society Journal* [online], 1.1 (2011): 69–81, http://www.thetedhughessociety.org, accessed 22 Aug. 2014.

12. Paul Bentley, *The Poetry of Ted Hughes: Language, Illusion and Beyond* (Harlow: Longman, 1988), p. 32. Bentley is here considering Hughes's depiction of the sheer alterity of Scout Rock in a 1963 memoir of his childhood; see Ted Hughes, 'The Rock', *Listener*, 70 (19 Sept. 1963): 421–3.

13. Bentley, *Poetry of Ted Hughes*: 33. For a concise and highly readable introduction to Lacan's notoriously difficult writings, see Slavoj Žižek, *How to Read Lacan* (London: Granta, 2006).

14. Jerrold E. Hogle, 'Romanticism and the "Schools" of Criticism and Theory', in Stuart Curran (ed.), *The Cambridge Companion to British Romanticism* (2nd edn, Cambridge: Cambridge University Press, 2010): 12. Such interpretations 'expos[e] the subject and its imaginings as layers of expression and repression that lead only to signs of signs of signs that never reach ultimate objects or depths. These layers intimate, while also keeping their distance from, what Lacan calls "the Real"' (*ibid.*).

15. See Harold Bloom, 'The Internalization of Quest-Romance', in Harold Bloom (ed.), *Romanticism and Consciousness: Essays in Criticism* (New York: Norton, 1970): 3–24. Bloom's famous thesis in this essay draws upon and revises Northrop Frye's analysis of romance in *Anatomy of Criticism: Four Essays* (Princeton, NJ: Princeton University Press, 1957), and ideas presented by M.H. Abrams in, for example, 'English Romanticism: The Spirit of the Age', in Northrop Frye (ed.), *Romanticism Reconsidered: Selected Papers from the English Institute* (New York: Columbia University Press, 1963): 26–72.

16. Quotations are from the reconstructed 'Story of Crow', in Keith Sagar, *The Laughter of Foxes: A Study of Ted Hughes* (2nd edn, Liverpool: Liverpool University Press, 2006): 180.

17. The quest romances of two shorter sequences of the 1970s, *Prometheus on His Crag* and *Adam and the Sacred Nine*, end on a more hopeful note; but they are far less compelling works than the trilogy of this period. In this context, see Alex Davis, '*Crow*, Quest Romance and the Carnivalesque', in Joanny Moulin (ed.), *Lire Ted Hughes: New Selected Poems 1957–1994* (Paris: Editions du Temps, 1999): 169–87.

18. Terry Gifford, '"Dead Farms, Dead Leaves": Culture as Nature in *Remains of Elmet* and *Elmet*', in Joanny Moulin (ed.), *Ted Hughes: Alternative Horizons* (London: Routledge, 2004): 41.

19. Keith Sagar (ed.), *Poet and Critic: The Letters of Ted Hughes and Keith Sagar* (London: British Library, 2012): 275.

20. See Sagar, *Laughter of Foxes*, pp. 84–6 and Neil Roberts, *Ted Hughes: A Literary Life* (Basingstoke: Palgrave Macmillan, 2006): 172–3. On the presence of the Orpheus myth in *Birthday Letters*, see Lynda K. Bundtzen, 'Mourning Eurydice: Ted Hughes as Orpheus in *Birthday Letters*', *Journal of Modern Literature*, 23(3/4) (2000): 455–69; and Genevieve Liveley, 'Birthday Letters from Pontus: Ted Hughes and the White Noise of Classical Elegy', in Roger Rees (ed.), *Ted Hughes and the Classics* (Oxford: Oxford University Press, 2009): 216–32. (Hughes, of course, chose *not* to include the story of Orpheus and Eurydice among those he translated from the *Metamorphoses* in *Tales from Ovid*.)

21. *Moortown Diary*, it should be recalled, was originally titled *Moortown Elegies*. On the elegiac mode in Hughes's work, see Edward Hadley, *The Elegies of Ted Hughes* (Basingstoke: Palgrave Macmillan, 2010).

22. Philip Hardie, *Virgil* (Oxford: Oxford University Press, 1998): 47. The severed singing head is a theme in Hughes's major essay on Coleridge, 'The Snake in the Oak': see *WP* 399.

23. Bundtzen, 'Mourning Eurydice': 468. Bundtzen is speculating on the identity of the unspecified 'they' in the poem 'Blood and Innocence' (*CP* 1151–2).

24. Roberts, *Ted Hughes: A Literary Life*: 20.

25. A shorter, preliminary exposition of the thesis adumbrated at length in *Shakespeare and the Goddess of Complete Being* is provided in Hughes's Introduction and Note to his *A Choice of Shakespeare's Verse* (London: Faber & Faber, 1971). (Note that the 1991 reissue of this selection contains a new Introduction and Note.)

26. On the 'shamanic plane' of Coleridge's three great poems, 'Kubla Khan', 'Christabel', and 'The Ancient Mariner', see 'The Snake in the Oak', *WP* 453.

27. Neil Corcoran, 'Hughes on Shakespeare', in Terry Gifford (ed.), *The Cambridge Companion to Ted Hughes* (Cambridge: Cambridge University Press, 2011): 141.

28. The essay collected in *Winter Pollen* is entirely different from Hughes's 'Myth and Education', *Children's Literature in Education*, 1 (1970): 55–70.

29. Michael Bell, 'The Metaphysics of Modernism', in Michael Levenson (ed.), *The Cambridge Companion to Modernism* (2nd edn, Cambridge: Cambridge University Press, 2011): 16. No less than Romanticism, Modernism is subject to a wide variety of interpretations. For a lucid introduction, see Astradur Eysteinsson, *The Concept of Modernism* (Ithaca, NY: Cornell University Press, 1990).

30. T.S. Eliot, *The Complete Poems and Plays* (London: Faber & Faber, 1969): 22.

31. Anthony Easthope, 'The Poetry of Ted Hughes: Some Reservations', in Moulin (ed.), *Lire Ted Hughes*, p. 18. Easthope's critique of Hughes is very close to that made by Veronica Forrest-Thomson in her *Poetic Artifice: A Theory of Twentieth-Century Poetry* (Manchester: Manchester University Press, 1978): 146–63.

32. The essay of this title in *Winter Pollen* is a slightly revised version of the title essay of *A Dancer to God*.

33. For a detailed study of Hughes in relation to ecocriticism see Chapter 8.

34. T.S. Eliot, *The Use of Poetry and the Use of Criticism: Studies in the Relation of Criticism to Poetry in England* (2nd edn, London: Faber & Faber, 1964): 118–19. Cf. 'Poetry begins, I dare say, with a savage beating a drum in a jungle' (*ibid.*: 155). Michael Bell observes this conception of language in a number of modernists, likening it to the unknowable dark side of the moon in the 'Ithaca' episode of James Joyce's *Ulysses* and the 'Moony' chapter in Lawrence's *Women in Love*; see Bell, 'Metaphysics of Modernism': 18.

35. Carrie Rohman, *Stalking the Subject: Modernism and the Animal* (New York: Columbia University Press, 2009): 38.

36. Eliot, *Complete Poems and Plays*: 122, 126.
37. Rohman, *Stalking the Subject*: 39.
38. 'From the Life and Songs of the Crow' was the subtitle of the first edition of *Crow*.
39. Cf. 'And the spirit of God moved upon the face of the waters': Genesis 1.2 (AV).
40. Hughes draws attention to the turbulent historical context to both movements; see *WP* 269 (on Eliot, Modernism and the First World War) and *WP* 371 (on Blake, Wordsworth, Coleridge and the French Revolution).
41. I have in mind here Fredric Jameson's understanding of the Lacanian Real as the 'ground and untranscendable horizon' of history: 'History is what hurts, it is what refuses desire and sets inexorable limits to individual as well as collective praxis': Fredric Jameson, *The Political Unconscious: Narrative as a Socially Symbolic Act* (London: Methuen, 1981): 102. For a reading of Hughes that sets his work within material history, in particular that of the Cold War, see Stan Smith, *Inviolable Voice: History and Twentieth-Century Poetry* (Dublin: Gill & Macmillan, 1982): 150–69.

3

Hughes and Intertextuality

David Troupes

'Nothing is at last sacred but the integrity of your own mind.'[1] So wrote Ralph Waldo Emerson (1803–1882) in his 1841 essay *Self-Reliance*. Five years earlier the publication of Emerson's essay *Nature* had marked the beginning of American Transcendentalism, and *Self-Reliance* was his latest rearticulation of the tenets of this new intellectual movement, of which more in a moment. For now, I wish to propose the line quoted above as an apt motto for a 22-year-old Ted Hughes, asleep in his Pembroke College room in 1951, having finished for the night his struggle to write the latest weekly essay required by his University of Cambridge English degree. From this motto we might tease out other sympathies, and we will follow that thread as far as we can down the Transcendental lineage which Emerson began. This is the essence of intertextuality: the notion that implicit conversations exist between texts even in the absence of explicit direct reference. This notion will be crucial for us here, for, despite some generous common ground, Hughes had little or nothing to say about most Transcendental writers. What he wrote and what they wrote, however, have quite a lot to say to each other.

So what exactly might this motto mean? The integrated mind is not divided against itself, nor against its physical aspect, its body. The integrated mind does not suffer self-betrayal, nor the self-shame of dissipated energy. But the word 'integrated' does not describe the Ted Hughes who has abandoned his essay for bed. For Hughes, Cambridge English was a thing of critical dissections as destructive to the dissecting mind as to the dissected text. So Hughes falls asleep, and dreams of a burnt fox who tells him, 'Stop this. You are destroying us' (see Chapter 1). The 'us' for whom the fox pleads is both the natural world of creatures and the inner world of spirit and vision – everything, in short, sacred to Hughes. So what did he do? He listened to the fox. He switched his studies from English to Archaeology and

Anthropology with a fresh integrity ensuring that everything, at last, would be sacred.

The exact centre

Transcendentalism is an intellectual movement which started in New England in the early nineteenth century, related to English Romanticism but with some determinedly American twists. Emerson, ordained as a minister of the Second Church of Boston – though he resigned his post only a few years later following the death of his first wife from tuberculosis – is the undisputed father of Transcendentalist thought. He offers this somewhat daunting explanation in his 1842 essay *The Transcendentalist*:

> [T]he Idealism of the present day acquired the name of Transcendental from the use of that term by Immanuel Kant, of Königsberg, who replied to the skeptical philosophy of Locke, which insisted that there was nothing in the intellect which was not previously in the experience of the senses, by showing that there was a very important class of ideas or imperative forms, which did not come by experience, but through which experience was acquired; that these were intuitions of the mind itself; and he denominated them *Transcendental* forms.[2]

Emerson and his fellow Transcendentalists were seeking a uniquely American form of philosophy. For them this Kantian idealism combined with an appreciation of the wild and unhistoried enormity of the North American continent to produce a rejection of European modes of order and civilization, and an assertion that nature does not depend on culture for its intrinsic truth. Each individual, by becoming aware of the 'Transcendental forms' which mediate experience, can become master of his own perceptions, freeing the mind of stale patterns. Often, this meant the experience of divinity unencumbered by religion:

> Standing on the bare ground,—my head bathed by the blithe air and uplifted into infinite space,—all mean egotism vanishes. I become a transparent eyeball; I am nothing, I see all; the currents of the Universal Being circulate through me; I am part or parcel of God.[3]

Emerson's sublime transport is saved from the charge of solipsism by its dependence on environment and the deprecation of ego – the 'transparent eyeball'. The self is essentially given over to nature, an experience as joyful as any homecoming. At the same time, Transcendentalism is above all an individualist philosophy, as enshrined in another of Emerson's great aphorisms: 'Whoso would be a man must be a nonconformist.'[4]

Emerson thus set the challenge, but it fell to his friend and pupil, Henry David Thoreau (1817–1862), to take it up and report on the drama of its living form. For two years Thoreau lived in a one-room cabin by a lake in the woods of Concord, Massachusetts, following his own commandment of simplification while theorizing on culture and rhapsodising on nature. The document of his experience is the book *Walden; or, Life In the Woods* (1854). Scarcely noticed in Thoreau's lifetime, it has since become an eccentric masterpiece of world literature, a gospel of countercultural angst married to ecstatic receptivity to the natural world.[5] Just as Emerson quit his religious orders to pursue his thought outside Christian orthodoxy, so did Thoreau quit the town and its social orthodoxy to pursue his thoughts under the trees. And so, we might add, did Hughes quit Cambridge English to pursue his thoughts outside the orthodoxy of criticism led by F.R. Leavis.

'We need to witness our own limits transgressed',[6] writes Thoreau. But how? And to what end? The answer to both questions is 'nature': a meditation on nature through which the meditating mind is restored to a state of ignorance; it is from this ignorance – we might say 'innocence' – that the transcendental forms arise. But this is a very abstract way of speaking, and Thoreau and Hughes both offer a more concrete means of engagement with nature: fishing. Thoreau calls this 'the true industry for poets', and writes with arresting beauty and mystery of what it is to fish at night.

> Sometimes, after staying in a village parlor till the family had all retired, I have returned to the woods, and, partly with a view to the next day's dinner, spent the hours of midnight fishing from a boat by moonlight, serenaded by owls and foxes, and hearing, from time to time, the creaking note of some unknown bird close at hand. These experiences were very memorable and valuable to me,—anchored in forty feet of water, and twenty or thirty rods from the shore, surrounded sometimes by thousands of small perch and shiners, dimpling the surface with their tails in the moonlight, and communicating by a long flaxen line with mysterious nocturnal fishes which had their dwelling forty feet below, or sometimes dragging sixty feet of line about the pond as I drifted in the gentle night breeze, now and then feeling a slight vibration along it, indicative of some life prowling about its extremity, of dull uncertain blundering purpose there, and slow to make up its mind. At length you slowly raise, pulling hand over hand, some horned pout squeaking and squirming to the upper air. It was very queer, especially in dark nights,

when your thoughts had wandered to vast and cosmological themes in other spheres, to feel this faint jerk, which came to interrupt your dreams and link you to Nature again. It seemed as if I might next cast my line upward into the air, as well as downward into this element, which was scarcely more dense. Thus I caught two fishes as it were with one hook.[7]

We are almost spoiled for choice in seeking a Hughes passage to place alongside Thoreau's, such was his enthusiasm for fishing, but the most apt must be the fishing passage from *Poetry in the Making* (*WP 19*), which displays the absolute centrality of its sentiments to both the Transcendentalist perspective, and Hughes's own – which, in time, I hope to refer to as one. Hughes's association of the fish with 'those inevitable facts' is an appeal to modes of truth independent of human culture or experience, akin to Thoreau's 'Nature', which he sets against the 'vast and cosmological themes in other spheres' occupying his thought. We cannot fail now to turn to Hughes's deservedly famous poem 'Pike', which closes with a scene of night fishing every bit as mysterious as Thoreau's:

The still splashes on the dark pond,

Owls hushing the floating woods
Frail on my ear against the dream
Darkness beneath night's darkness had freed,
That rose slowly towards me, watching. (*CP* 85–6)

We find hints that Hughes's speaker is slipping into a realm of fantasia and projection: 'still splashes', for instance, and 'the dream / Darkness beneath night's darkness had freed', which correspond to the air Thoreau finds nearly as dense as the black and moonlit water, and the second fish he caught there. And just as Thoreau observes that the strike of an actual fish serves 'to interrupt your dreams', so we note that the dream which approaches Hughes's speaker out of the second darkness comes without a strike. It is a presence only, an approaching form without a name summoned by the meditation of fishing; but it is not a fish. However tempted we may be to hold that 'Pike' is concerned with capturing a pike, we must admit that the poem culminates in the arrival of something altogether different.

Can we define this approaching form, this dream? Hughes seems unable to, and his recollection, 'I was all for opening negotiations with whatever happened to be out there',[8] is an honest statement of the tentative state of his poetic project early in his career. Indeed, it is the *opening* of negotiations which concerns Hughes throughout *Lupercal*, as he makes clear in a letter from the time: '*Lupercal* seems to me to suffer from the lack of natural flow of spirit & feeling which it takes as its subject' (*LTH* 178). Much of *Lupercal* was written whilst Hughes and his first wife Sylvia Plath were living in Massachusetts, and many commentators have remarked on the complete lack of American scenery in spite of this. For Hughes, 1950s America was a cellophane world of suburban conformity, and clearly his imagination still resided in the soil (and ponds) of his native Yorkshire. Yet here, too, we find sympathies, in the first true poet of the American Transcendental tradition, Walt Whitman (1819–1892). Here is Whitman in the centrepiece poem of his career, 'Song of Myself':

> Houses and rooms are full of perfumes, the shelves are crowded with perfumes,
> I breathe the fragrance myself and know it and like it,
> The distillation would intoxicate me also, but I shall not let it.

> The atmosphere is not a perfume, it has no taste of the distillation, it is odorless,
> It is for my mouth forever, I am in love with it,
> I will go to the bank by the wood and become undisguised and naked,
> I am mad for it to be in contact with me.[9]

We can see immediately how Whitman sets up a schematic that accurately reflects Hughes's own aversions and aspirations, with the perfumed interiors standing for all of stifling civilization, and the odourless atmosphere standing for that unnameable *something* – Hughes's 'whatever happened to be out there'. This madness for 'contact' – a term I will return to often – was shared by both men; yet there is a difference, and to see it we must cast an eye back to a line in Hughes's 'Pike' about his pond: 'It was as deep as England.' More than nationalistic, this is a pronouncement of cultural ancientness, of land constituted in part by its long human association, which the speaker will neither abandon nor regret. Whereas the American Transcendentalists were only too glad to jettison their European cultural baggage, Hughes maintains that deep, recovered culture has a part to play, leading to his career-long engagement with biblical reference, alchemy, shamanism and ancient religions. When we return to 'Song of Myself', we can almost feel an argument brewing:

> Have you reckon'd a thousand acres much? have you reckon'd the earth much?
> Have you practis'd so long to learn to read?
> Have you felt so proud to get at the meaning of poems?

Stop this day and night with me and you shall possess the origin of all poems,
You shall possess the good of the earth and sun, (there are millions of suns left,)
You shall no longer take things at second or third hand, nor look through the eyes of the dead, nor feed on the spectres in books,
You shall not look through my eyes either, nor take things from me,
You shall listen to all sides and filter them from your self.[10]

We can read Whitman's mocking lines about reckoning the earth as a derision of all existing systems of knowledge, including those Hughes would deploy in his own negotiations. Whitman's 'nor look through the eyes of the dead' might have become a direct challenge to Hughes the archaeologist, folklorist and occultist. This argument could be the end of our chapter, except that Hughes is not so unwavering in his position, admitting – both intentionally and despite himself – the merit of a view such as the Transcendentalist perspective.

Hughes followed *Lupercal* with *Wodwo*, which concludes with its title poem ('wodwo' is a Middle English word meaning 'wild man' or 'troll'). The poem perfectly encapsulates the Transcendentalist perspective, and these are the crucial lines: 'I suppose I am the exact centre / but there's all this' (*CP* 183). Whitman's instruction to 'listen to all sides and filter them from yourself' is relevant here, but even more so are the following passages from Emerson and (getting ahead of ourselves for a moment) Wallace Stevens:

The eye is the first circle; the horizon which it forms is the second; and throughout nature this primary figure is repeated without end.[11]

*

When the blackbird flew out of sight,
It marked the edge
Of one of many circles.[12]

The wodwo's pondside pondering humanizes and contextualizes these abstract passages, just as Emerson and Stevens corroborate the wodwo's instinct to figure itself as the centre of a tentative world. In thinking this over, much will depend on our attitude towards 'Wodwo' the poem. Is it merely fugitive, a curiosity? Is it in some sense ironic? Certainly, scantily punctuated, heavily enjambed and with uncapitalized line-beginnings, it resembles nothing else Hughes wrote. Yet it gives its name to the book in which it appears, and enjoys pride of place as the closing piece in the book's 'single adventure' structure which charts the reintegration and empowering of a disintegrated individual. In this context the wodwo is a creature returned to origins, and speaks with special authority of the centrality of the self. From the lines quoted above, the poem concludes:

> what is it roots
> roots roots roots and here's the water
> again very queer but I'll go on looking ...

There is much significance in the wodwo's extrapolation of 'all this' – which might include nature, culture and the deep past – into 'roots roots roots'. Roots of what? Feeding what? These are the roots of the world, yes, but also of the wodwo itself, feeding and creating the wodwo, connecting it with the whole of creation while granting it special status as – for the moment – the culminating blossom of that creation. Thus aware of itself, it stares at the water in which its reflection floats, an emblem of the self given over to nature and created by nature.

However casual it may appear on the page, 'Wodwo' is a vital next step in the development of Hughes's vision, and the surest sign yet that his art is Transcendentalist in its aspirations. Indeed, the poem immediately preceding 'Wodwo', 'Full Moon and Little Frieda', is scarcely less Transcendentalist in flavour, the final three lines enacting that ecstatic rushing of the self into the not-self, which then reciprocates with an inrush of nature to the individual: 'The moon stepped back like an artist gazing amazed at a work // That points at him amazed' (CP 183). And the poem preceding that, the intoxicating 'Gnat Psalm', is yet another turn on the same Transcendentalist impulse:

> My hands fly in the air, they are follies
> My tongue hangs up in the leaves
>
> My thoughts have crept into crannies
>
> Your dancing
>
> Your dancing
>
> Rolls my staring skull slowly away into outer space. (CP 182)

The poem vividly dramatizes Emerson's head 'bathed by the blithe air and uplifted into infinite space', as well as Thoreau's absorption into 'vast and cosmological themes in other spheres'. And it approaches, through its humorous and only slightly ironizing gnat-focus, the affirmative life-love which proliferates in Whitman's verse. To be sure,

'Wodwo', 'Full Moon and Little Frieda' and 'Gnat Psalm' conclude what has been a largely grim book full of harrowing encounters; but climactically conclude they do, successfully providing an escape route from such darker pieces as 'Ghost Crabs', 'Heptonstall' and 'Pibroch'.

So what next? Does the Transcendental vision continue in Hughes's poetry? Immediately, it does not. Things get complicated. For reasons difficult to trace in *Wodwo* (book or poem), Hughes turns from that culminating vision, and descends into the very different world of *Crow*. The reason may well originate, however, in an event outside poetry: Sylvia Plath's suicide in 1963. Of the Transcendental *Wodwo* poems discussed above, 'Full Moon and Little Frieda' and 'Wodwo' were both written before her death, and the man who emerged from the three-year poetic block which followed the death of his first wife was perhaps simply incapable of sustaining such a vision. Whereas the wodwo saw only roots, Crow adventures though a bloody carnival of despised culture and messy metaphysics, antagonizing the religious referents on which it depends, updating Hughes's poetry by one sudden jerk into postmodernism. In 1969 the deaths of Hughes's partner Assia Wevill and her daughter Shura brought further trauma, followed quickly by the death of his mother. Works such as *Prometheus on His Crag* and *Cave Birds* are possessed of a palpable hankering for transcendence of the sort accessible to the younger Hughes, and there are occasional successes to report, though these are often so encumbered by ritualistic detail as to make a reader long for the wodwo's parsimonious freedom, and little Frieda's uncomplicated transactions with the moon. But is there any hope of returning to such a vision outside wild men and children?

I touched the universe

Among the many and varied books Hughes published during the 1970s, we may be surprised to find it is the oddball volume *Gaudete* which returns us most deliberately and completely to the realm of Transcendentalism, and in a way which almost eerily parallels our continuing succession of American writers. Though I would not want to spare anyone the delights of reading this book cover to cover (for which Faber's *Collected Poems* is insufficient), here's the gist: Lumb, an Anglican clergyman, is abducted into the spirit world to find that he is expected to heal a female figure. While away, he is replaced in this world by a changeling who reorganizes the local Women's Institute into a farcical pagan love-cult so that he might conceive the next Messiah. The men realise what's going on and kill the changeling, while the real Lumb is finally returned to our world by a lough in Ireland, where he fills a notebook with poems to a 'nameless female deity'; the text of these poems forms the book's Epilogue. The changeling's misadventures form the largest portion of the text, and serve mostly to dramatize the inability of ritual to guarantee meaningful effect. In spite of Hughes's brilliant descriptive technique, little of lasting interest happens in the changeling narrative, and we must turn to the Epilogue poems to find the gatherings of the real meaning of the book.

But first let us detour into the next of our Transcendental writers, Emily Dickinson (1830–1886). Dickinson is the first of the Americans discussed here about whom Hughes had anything to say, and in fact he said a good deal about her, all of it extremely positive. In letters from 1960 he calls her 'America's greatest poet' (*LTH* 169) and says that her poetry is 'the most unself-conscious poetry ever, the most intensely occupied with her thought,—Shakespearean language and genuine. Makes Crowe Ransom etc seem like Museum pieces' (*LTH* 166). The more significant compliment comes several years later, when he edits a selection of her verse for Faber, supplying an introduction which offers an illuminating condensation of her life and art; and, as with the commentary of all strong writers on other writers, Hughes illuminates his own work by what he writes about Dickinson's (*WP* 156–7). His suggestion of the reclusive Dickinson as cultural crucible may be difficult to swallow, but it comes as no surprise from Hughes. He is fitting her into the role of tribal shaman, a visionary spokeswoman for her people, just he does for Eliot in *A Dancer to God* and Shakespeare in *Shakespeare and the Goddess of Complete Being*. Clearly this was a role of great importance for Hughes, and his strong impulse in discussing poets he admires is to translate them into his own preferred terms.

He writes: 'She was devoted, she led the life of a recluse and she wore white, proper for a bride of the spirit, and she daily composed poems that read like devotions. But she was first of all true to herself and her wits' (*WP* 157). Gillian Groszewski discusses objections raised to Hughes's characterization of Dickinson, especially as regards the casting of her as 'spiritual wife' to a masculinized universe. She defends Hughes, arguing that later in the Introduction he 'presents Dickinson's self-characterization of herself as "wife" as a metaphorical tactic'.[13] I agree, and would add that it is a tactic deployed by Hughes himself. For both poets the marriage metaphor provides an artistically productive means of dramatizing the Transcendental movement from self to not-self: the giving of the self to nature in a way which does not destroy the self, but confirms it as part of a larger and (at the moment of experience) new whole. This movement finds a natural symbol in idealized marriage: just as Hughes accepts the presentation of Dickinson as a woman married to God, he casts his own Lumb as a reverend-poet devoted to a goddess.

What of the poems themselves? In manner and content, the *Gaudete* epilogue poems bear a strong resemblance to Dickinson's verse. Compare, for instance, the *Gaudete* poem 'I said goodbye to earth' (*CP* 365) with Dickinson's poem 378:

> I saw no Way – The Heavens were stitched –
> I felt the Columns close –
> The Earth reversed her Hemispheres –
> I touched the Universe –
>
> And back it slid – and I alone –
> A speck upon the Ball –
> Went out upon Circumference –
> Beyond the Dip of Bell –[14]

Both poems journey in a realm of chilling vision; both use short lines and dense imagery; both resolve nothing – they merely confront. Contact here assumes very dark shades indeed, and in Hughes's comments on Dickinson we see the continuing inability to describe the object of that contact, those vast and cosmological themes, the dream freed by darkness beneath night's darkness: 'In this condition, there opened to her a vision – final reality, her own soul, the soul within the Universe – in all her descriptions of its nature, she never presumed to give it a name' (*WP* 158).

There are, of course, many earthier tones to be found from both Dickinson and Hughes's Reverend Lumb, but never without a complicating sense of religious mystery, and never without the awareness that plants and animals are, by their very existence, a source of metaphysical revelation. Death is for both poets a constant preoccupation, as when Lumb writes 'The spider clamps the bluefly – whose death panic / Becomes sudden soulful absorption' (*CP* 358) and 'Am I killed? / Or am I searching?' (*CP* 373). To be alive in this world is to be searching ('very queer' said the wodwo, 'but I'll go on looking'), and to have found the object of one's search is to be dead – just as Hughes says of Dickinson, 'Death obsessed her, as the one act that could take her the one necessary step beyond her vision. Death would carry her and her sagacity clean through the riddle. She deferred all her questions to death's solution' (*WP* 159). The sort of spiritual marriage read by Hughes into the details of Emily Dickinson's inner life and his own male protagonists' adoration of goddess figures provides a symbolic and poetic means of stepping beyond mere vision. Finally, the entire shamanic flight motif folds into an elaborate metaphor for a Transcendental type of contact.

In that one eye

There remains a final Transcendentalist to consider: Wallace Stevens (1879–1955). As with Dickinson, Hughes was familiar with Stevens's poetry and commented upon it. These comments, however, are few and negative. Sylvia Plath was an enthusiastic admirer of Stevens, but it is an enthusiasm her husband seems never to have shared. Here is a passage from a letter the 26-year-old Hughes wrote to Plath, after four months of marriage, in 1956: 'Last night I began to read Wallace Stevens aloud, starting from the back because I've recently read all the poems in the beginning. I like Stevens continually, but every poem lets you down' (*LTH* 52). In April of the following year in a letter to a friend he floats the following theory of perception to Stevens's disadvantage, noting that

> [P]eople like Wallace Stevens house their demon where the eye-nerve enters – so that everything is arbitrary & colourful & partial & question-able. Whereas Wyatt & Crowe-Ransome [*sic*] house theirs where their ear enters – so that in them everything is inevitable & final & bottomless & unquestionable as the response of glands or the harmony of moving muscles. (*LTH* 97)

This to me suggests a young poet impatient for revelation, con-cerned that his own art should lead somewhere 'final & bottomless & unquestionable' (Crowe Ransom was one of Hughes's favourites). A third remark worth considering comes in a 1977 interview with Ekbert Faas: 'But all along, though with a growing scepticism, she [Plath] preserved her admiration for Wallace Stevens. He was a kind of god to her, while I could never see anything at all in him except magniloquence.'[15] 'Magniloquence' (high-flown or bombastic speech) suggests that Hughes's aversion was stylistic rather than substantial. I have no wish to criticize Hughes's tastes; however, as an enthusiast of both Hughes and Stevens, I have long wanted to justify my suspicion that profounder sympathies exist between their work than Hughes recognized or acknowledged, and I proceed, now aided by the con-viction that Hughes's poetic vision was essentially Transcendental.

Transcendentalism in Stevens achieves a culminating self-reflexiveness, elaborating endlessly on its own imaginative procedures. His is a poetry about poetry – that is, about the Transcendental impulse – and this has led to charges that his art is arid, cerebral and disembodied. Nothing, I maintain, could be further from the truth: like all Transcendentalists Stevens relies on the physical world, on nature, as the only adequate house for the searching spirit, and his poems teem with the opulence and earthiness of the natural world, refracted through a tirelessly dissatisfied imagination. The implications of this are dramatized in one of Stevens's most famous poems, 'The Idea of Order at Key West', in which a woman sings as she walks by the sea:

> It may be that in all her phrases stirred
> The grinding water and the grasping wind;
> But it was she and not the sea we heard.[16]

Put plainly, although the woman may truly and beautifully relate the sea in her song, we will never have direct access to the sea. The imagination must mediate between the self and the not-self, and her song is the fruit of that mediation.

Of course, Hughes's favourite metaphor for Transcendental contact was not singing, nor even marriage, but fishing. Does Stevens offer us any fishermen for comparison? He does indeed, in a poem with the typically Stevensian title 'Thinking of a Relation Between the Images of Metaphors', which presents us with a man fishing for bass while a dove coos overhead. The fisherman is described as being both 'all one ear' and 'all / One eye',[17] taking a different view from Hughes's dualistic eye/ear theory: the true poet, Stevens tell us, attends entirely to both. The poem concludes:

> In that one eye the dove
> Might spring to sight and yet remain a dove.
>
> The fisherman might be the single man
> In whose breast, the dove, alighting, would grow still.

Just as in Hughes's 'Pike', Stevens's fisherman is not really here for the fish. Searching for a bass, he succeeds in summoning a dove, just as Hughes's fisherman, searching for pike, succeeds in summoning his dream. For Stevens to say that in the fisherman's eye 'the dove / Might spring to sight and yet remain a dove' is to suggest that the capable poet might summon for his reader not just the appearance of nature, but nature itself, authentic and credible. This reminds us of Hughes's statement on his famous poem 'The Thought-Fox' (*WP* 15). It is striking that Stevens should refer to a fisherman as 'the single man' capable of summoning an authentic dove – and doubly striking when we consider that Hughes chose to end his 1995 *New Selected Poems* with 'A Dove', as it now concludes his *Collected Poems*, making this bird a culminating vessel for his poetic energies.

Despite this confluence of imagery, however, Hughes and Stevens own such different aesthetic sensibilities that we might assume their poetry is fundamentally at odds – that Stevens's meta-imaginative play undermines the seriousness of Hughes's rituals. Certainly this may explain Hughes's personal aversion. Yet, when we return to the poetry itself, there is no real disagreement. The tentative nature of shamanic transport is admitted frequently in Hughes, most succinctly in the 'Finale' to *Cave Birds* (*CP* 440), which Hughes repeats in an interview:

> We go on writing poems because one poem never gets the whole account right. There is always something missed. At the end of the ritual up comes a goblin. Anyway within a week the whole thing has changed, one needs a fresh bulletin. And works go dead, fishing has to be abandoned, the shoal has moved on.[18]

This process accounts for the long parade of Hughes's myth-making, and it is the process which Stevens describes again and again. The crucial difference between Stevens and Hughes can be accounted for by Hughes's insistence on a ritualistic context for these flights. But even in the sheer variety of his poetry, we can see that Hughes understood these as halting, subjective experiences – that we are, as Stevens wrote in the late poem 'July Mountain', 'Thinkers without final thoughts / In an always incipient cosmos'.[19] For his part, Stevens surely would have understood the necessity of Hughes's tireless mythologizing, his insistence on Pennine landscapes and Devon rivers, and his assertion of the depth of England. We see this clearly in another late poem by Stevens, '"A mythology reflects its region…"', which beautifully articulates the spirit of Hughes's entire poetic opus, declaring that a mythology 'must be of the nature of its creator':

> Wood of his forests and stone out of his fields
> Or from under his mountains.[20]

This is Stevens's final statement on the proper structure of poetry, earth-bound and place-bound, a thing of youth and of myth. He wrote it not long before his death in 1955, two years before the publication of *Hawk in the Rain*, in which Hughes, if not with the stone then certainly with the mud of his fields, began to strive toward this very ideal.

Ted Hughes stands always in uncertain relation to the Transcendentalists: most obviously because of his stated admiration for poets such as John Crowe Ransom and T.S. Eliot, whose own work, full of dark vistas and funeral energies, positions itself well apart from – even in opposition to – the Transcendentalist programme. Hughes's neglect of Stevens and the tradition he capped may have much to do with Hughes's desire to credit the myths and folk tales he pursued, cultural tokens which Transcendentalism habitually disregards. Whatever his stated aims, however, one of the organs of Hughes's poetic genius is surely an instinct for Transcendental freedom of a piece with Whitman, Dickinson and Stevens – those moments of unmythologized, unmediated contact: just the one line, the dark water, and the shapes rising.

Notes

1. Ralph Waldo Emerson, *Selected Essays* (Harmondsworth: Penguin, 1982): 178.
2. *Ibid.*: 246.
3. *Ibid.*: 39.
4. *Ibid.:* 178.
5. It has become the most frequently taught text in the American education system.
6. Henry David Thoreau, *Walden; or, Life in the Wood and On the Duty of Civil Disobedience* (New York: Signet, 1980): 211.
7. *Ibid.*: 121.
8. Ekbert Faas, *Ted Hughes: The Unaccommodated Universe* (Santa Barbara, CA: Black Sparrow Press, 1980): 201.
9. Walt Whitman, *Leaves of Grass* (New York: Modern Library, 1921): 25.
10. *Ibid.*
11. Emerson, *Selected Essays*: 225.
12. Wallace Stevens, *The Collected Poems of Wallace Stevens* (New York: Vintage Books, 1990): 94.
13. Mark Wormald, Neil Roberts and Terry Gifford (eds), *Ted Hughes: From Cambridge to Collected* (Basingstoke: Palgrave Macmillan, 2013): 166.
14. Emily Dickinson, *The Complete Poems of Emily Dickinson* (London: Faber & Faber, 1970): 180.
15. Faas, *Unaccommodated Universe*: 210.
16. Stevens, *Collected Poems*: 129.
17. *Ibid.*: 356–7.
18. Fass, *Unaccommodated Universe*: 204.
19. Wallace Stevens, *Opus Posthumous* (New York: Vintage Books, 1990): 140.
20. *Ibid*: 141.

4

Hughes and the Absurd

Keith Sagar

The Absurd

When we think of the Absurd as a literary term, we think primarily of drama, and specifically of such continental writers as Samuel Beckett, Eugène Ionesco and Albert Camus. We do not think of Ted Hughes. This is partly because Hughes himself rarely used the term, and spoke of Beckett only disparagingly. But many poems from the first third of Hughes's career seem to me to be purer manifestations of the Absurd than we can find in any other British writer of the period. The only acknowledgement of this I am aware of is a passing comment by Elaine Feinstein: 'Hughes grappled with a darkness that few English poets of the time felt any necessity to allow into their poetry. His vision is comparable only to Beckett's in its bleakness.'[1]

The Absurd first entered the consciousness of English theatregoers and the majority of critics on 3 August 1955, when Peter Hall's production of Beckett's *Waiting for Godot* opened at the Arts Theatre in London. It was greeted with bafflement and derision. Peter Bull, who played Pozzo, recalled the reaction of that first-night audience:

> Waves of hostility came whirling over the footlights, and the mass exodus, which was to form such a feature of the run of the piece, started quite soon after the curtain had risen. The audible groans were also fairly disconcerting [...] The curtain fell to mild applause, we took a scant three calls and a depression and a sense of anti-climax descended on us all.[2]

Several smug reviewers seized on the line, 'Nothing happens, nobody comes, nobody goes, it's awful'[3] as their verdict on the play itself. In fact, of course, a boy comes and goes twice; Pozzo and Lucky come and go twice. We also have the putting on and taking off of hats and boots, the eating of carrots and radishes, a suicide attempt, a dance and a 'think' from Lucky, and an oration from Pozzo. Estragon is bitten and Lucky kicked. A tree comes into leaf. One could almost say, 'All human life is here.' What these critics meant was that nothing happened which they recognized as dramatic. Yet in saying that, they were betraying their ignorance of a great deal of what is most important in modern drama (including all the contributions of Chekhov and Pirandello).

Two more receptive reviewers, Harold Hobson and Ken Tynan, saved the production from early closure. But even those critics, who were aware that something both dramatic and important was going on, showed no signs of understanding what the play was actually about. The *Evening Standard* Drama awards were inaugurated in 1956. When some of the judges proposed *Waiting for Godot* as Best New Play, others, led by Sir Malcolm Sargent, threatened to resign. An English compromise was worked out by awarding *Godot* a prize as Most Controversial Play of the Year, a prize that has never been awarded since. The plays of Eugène Ionesco would shortly be received with similar incomprehension.

Ted Hughes, who wrote most of the poems in his first collection, *The Hawk in the Rain*, in 1955–56, saw that first production and recommended it to his sister Olwyn, who from 1959 worked for the theatrical agency in Paris which represented Ionesco. He also saw the English premiere of Ionesco's *Rhinoceros* at the Royal Court Theatre in 1960, directed by Orson Welles and starring Laurence Olivier. Olwyn later gave him her copy of Ionesco's complete plays in French. In Hughes's library at his death were several plays and several novels by Beckett, Deirdre Bair's biography, Linda Ben-Zvi's *Samuel Beckett* and Paul Foster's *Beckett and Zen*. However, I am not concerned here with any possible influence. The Absurd element in Hughes would have been there if he had never heard of Beckett or Ionesco. What concerns me is their shared vision and ancestry.

English culture and the Absurd

There are many varieties of the Absurd, but the one essential and definitive characteristic is that an Absurd work, or element in a work, should testify to the meaninglessness of 'life, the universe and everything'. It is not to be confused with the general angst of modern literature, which expresses the failure to discover meaning. The

Absurd has abandoned that search as futile and often ridicules those who persist in it. From the perspective of the Absurd, all human striving is futile, all beliefs delusions, all claims to superiority over other animals laughably pretentious. Men are, in Beckett's phrase, 'bloody ignorant apes'.[4]

For millennia, many thinkers and writers worldwide have argued that human reason has no answer to the largest and ultimate questions, and that if the universe itself is meaningless, so is everything within it. Literature and philosophy on the Continent have never lost touch with this tradition (or with each other). It was central to Existentialism, which influenced the great works of Sartre in the 1930s, Camus in the 1940s, and Beckett and Ionesco in the 1950s. But English consciousness has remained largely impervious to this tradition.

I can suggest some reasons for this. First is a wilful ignorance among supposedly educated English readers about classical and continental literature, myth and folklore. Second, is a more forgivable lack of interest in philosophy. Third, perhaps, is a problem with the word 'absurd' itself. I have used an initial capital throughout this chapter to distinguish the Absurd from 'absurd' as used in common English parlance, where its meaning has drifted from the original meaning of 'not accessible to reason' to become synonymous with 'ridiculous'. The 'ridiculous' is by definition that which cannot be taken seriously. In the context of continental or global myth, folklore and literature, nothing is more serious than the Absurd. What could be more disturbing than the conviction that life is without meaning, and therefore without value? A fourth reason is our desire to keep tragedy and comedy in clearly labelled compartments. We do not take kindly to being at a loss to know when we are supposed to laugh.

In 1954 Ionesco wrote of a world which seemed to him 'a baseless and ridiculous sham'

> in which all human behaviour tells of absurdity and all history of absolute futility; all reality and all language appear to lose their articulation, to disintegrate and collapse, so what possible reaction is there left, when everything has ceased to matter, but to laugh at it all?[5]

But what kind of laughter is this? In *Waiting for Godot* Estragon's trousers fall down − a classic circus jape. Is it still funny when we know that he has removed the cord holding them up in order to try to hang himself with it? Beckett spoke of 'the laugh at that which is unhappy'.[6] In 1958 Ionesco eliminated the distinction between tragedy and comedy altogether:

> There are no alternatives; if man is not tragic, he is ridiculous and pain-
> ful, 'comic' in fact, and by revealing his absurdity one can achieve a sort
> of tragedy. In fact I think that man must either be unhappy (metaphysi-
> cally unhappy) or stupid.[7]

The Absurd is far beyond satire or farce in its mockery not of deviant human foibles, but of humanity itself, and life itself. It is darker than tragedy – tragedy without catharsis, irredeemable loss.

A fifth factor is the misleading but long-lasting effect of Martin Esslin's very influential 1962 book *The Theatre of the Absurd*, where Esslin undertook to educate the English-speaking public on the meaning of the Absurd. He airbrushed the global tradition, dating absurdism from Nietzsche's announcement of the death of God in 1882, and crediting Alfred Jarry with its first theatrical manifestation in *Ubu Roi* (*Ubu the King*) in 1896. He defined the Absurd as 'the literature of verbal nonsense',[8] and made the extraordinary claim that the Absurd is comic because we cannot identify with its characters. When *Waiting for Godot* was performed at San Quentin jail in 1957, the inmates had no difficulty in identifying with the tramps who represent Everyman, just as Berenger, the main character in several of Ionesco's best plays, is obviously Everyman.

The only English absurdists Esslin could come up with were Harold Pinter and N.F. Simpson. Simpson used the absurd for social satire. Much of his work is like more intellectual versions of Goon Show scripts. Pinter, though he learned a great deal from Beckett in terms of theatrical technique, had no interest in the philosophy which underpinned the genre on the Continent. Even in his most apparently absurd plays, such as *The Birthday Party*, the absurdity is a thin veneer over meanings which are resolutely psychological, social and political. The antecedents of the Absurd, Esslin claimed, were clowning and *commedia dell'arte*, Punch and Judy and *Alice in Wonderland*. His book created the lasting impression that the Absurd was an escape from intolerable reality into surrealism, the fantastic and the nonsensical. He claimed that the Absurd dissolves 'unease', anxiety and despair in laughter. For some of the minor dramatists he discusses this may have been true, but for the major ones, especially Beckett and the later Ionesco, it was exactly the opposite – a way of confronting reality open-eyed. 'The Theatre of the Absurd', Edward Albee wrote, 'is the Realistic theatre of our time.'[9]

Four routes to the Absurd

I have avoided using the terms Absurdist and Absurdism since these
suffixes suggest a mode of writing, or group, or manifesto, or fashion
with which a writer might choose to associate himself. Writers do
not choose the Absurd. Far from being an escape route from intolerable reality, the Absurd is a dark cul-de-sac which most writers would
much prefer not to find themselves driven into. And what drives
them? I shall outline four of the commonest routes in Western culture
that are also to be found in the work of Hughes.

The first route is driven by a loss of faith in science and rational
intelligence as having any purchase on reality, other than a destructive or reductive one. Hughes inherited from Blake, Nietzsche and
Robert Graves's *The White Goddess* an early hatred of the scientist and
rationalist: the subject of the early poem 'Egg-Head', the Master in
The Tiger's Bones, St George in *Crow* and Socrates in *Cave Birds* (which
Hughes at one point subtitled *The Death of Socrates and his Resurrection
in Egypt*). Hughes later, but long before the science of neurology
caught up with him, developed his own version of the split between
the two hemispheres of the human brain: the left hemisphere, which
is rational, analytical and orderly, having in the modern Western world
come to silence almost completely the right hemisphere, which is
holistic, imaginative and creative.[10] He believed that the responsibility of the poet was to give voice to that gagged hemisphere. But
'everything among us is against it'.[11]

The second route is summed up by Beckett: 'All I regret is having
been born, dying is such a long, tiresome business.'[12] Actually this
notion has a long history. Nietzsche wrote:

> An old legend has it that King Midas hunted a long time in the woods
> for the wise Silenus, companion of Dionysos, without being able to catch
> him. When he had finally caught him the king asked him what he con-
> sidered man's greatest good. The daemon remained sullen and uncom-
> municative until finally, forced by the king, he broke into a shrill laugh
> and spoke: 'Ephemeral wretch, begotten by accident and toil, why do you
> force me to tell you what it would be your greatest boon not to hear?
> What would be best for you is quite beyond your reach: not to have been
> born, not to *be*, to *be nothing*. But the second best is to die soon.'[13]

The spirit of this legend is identical with the spirit of much Greek
myth and literature, as in the ending of *Oedipus the King*:

> Count no man happy till he dies, free of pain at last.[14]

In the Christian tradition, life is frequently referred to as a 'vale of tears'. In 1580 the French Catholic essayist Michel de Montaigne wrote:

> Is it possible to imagine any thing more laughable than this pitiful, wretched creature – who is not even master of himself, but exposed to shocks on every side.[15]

Nietzsche used the word 'absurdity' about such a view of existence:

> The truth once seen, man is aware everywhere of the ghastly absurdity of existence, comprehends the symbolism of Ophelia's fate, and the wisdom of the wood sprite Silenus: nausea invades him.[16]

Suffering, vulnerability and exposure are recurrent themes in Hughes from the beginning. 'Mayday on Holderness' suggests that only the 'dead and unborn are in God comfortable' (CP 60). The old woman in 'Pibroch' who hangs on only 'because her mind's gone completely' (CP 180) might also be the 80-year-old woman of the poem 'On the Slope' 'with the stone agony growing in her joints / And eyes dimming with losses, widening with losses' (CP 125). Hughes suffered more than his share of losses. The typical human response to suffering is either to grin and bear it (the grin in Hughes's poems is a rictus of suffering) or to retreat into delusions of grandeur. The attraction of animals as poetic subjects for Hughes is partly that they bellow the evidence. His poetic response to the loss of his wife Sylvia Plath in 1963 was two poems, 'Song of a Rat', an articulated screech, and 'The Howling of Wolves', followed by a two-year silence. When Crow, Hughes's most famous alter ego, alights in this world, he shivers 'with the horror of Creation' (CP 220). Hughes's response to the loss of his partner Assia Wevill and her daughter in 1969 was to abandon *The Life and Songs of the Crow* (at the very point where Crow was about to escape from the Absurd),[17] to write *Prometheus on His Crag* – 'a numb poem about numbness' (PC 29) – and 'Existential Song', where the tenet of Existentialism that man is free to defy Fate is bitterly mocked. The speaker claims that he is more than 'some dummy hare on a racetrack', only to be torn to pieces by the dogs, too late for him to realize 'That he was, in fact, nothing / But a dummy hare on a racetrack // And life was being lived only by the dogs' (CP 203).

    Thirdly, far from regarding death as the one sure release from intolerable life, many writers see it as cancelling all possibility of meaning and value in life. *Troilus and Cressida* is Shakespeare's most Absurd play: 'What's past and what's to come is strew'd with husks / And formless ruin of oblivion' (4.5.165–6). According to Jaques in *As You Like It,* since 'from hour to hour, we ripe and ripe, / And then from hour to hour, we rot and rot / [...] Motley's the only wear' (2.7.34).

The Jacobean dramatists like John Webster were obsessed with death. For them the image of Hamlet with a skull in his hands said everything. In Eliot's words: 'Webster was much possessed by death / And saw the skull beneath the skin'.[18] This form of the Absurd has not changed over the centuries. For Hopkins, whatever man thinks he has learned or achieved 'death blots black out':[19]

> since, no, nothing can be done
> To keep at bay
> Age and age's evils, hoar hair,
> Ruck and wrinkle, drooping, dying, death's worst, winding sheets, tombs
> and worms and tumbling to decay.[20]

As he sank into a 'womb-of-all, home-of-all, hearse-of-all night',[21] he came close to Eliot's 'Birth and copulation and death. / That's all, that's all, that's all, that's all'[22] and to Beckett's 'They give birth astride of a grave'.[23] Without the 'comfort of the Resurrection' he felt that he would be no more than a 'Jack' and a 'joke'.[24] Hopkins's belief in resurrection was his only shelter from the Absurd, but in several of the last poems he could no longer hold on to that.

At the beginning of his career Hughes claimed that his only theme was the battle between vitality and death. It was an unequal battle, since death had all the weapons. Nature, for early Hughes, was sink not source. In the first poem of his first collection, *The Hawk in the Rain*, rain does not bring fertility, but drowns, converts ploughland into the clay of graves and hacks the poet's head to the bone. The wind – a traditional symbol of inspiration and renewal – 'kills these stubborn hedges' and throws his breath. Hughes admires the hawk's ability to hang still at the 'master-fulcrum of violence', but even the hawk is doomed at last to be smashed, to 'mix his heart's blood with the mire of the land' (*CP* 19). Nature can miraculously light a fox in the dripping ground in the poem 'Crow Hill' (*CP* 62), but that fire will soon be extinguished by the persistence of rain, erosion and decay.

The process of Nature devouring itself is even clearer in the sea. In 'The Dry Salvages' Eliot had written of 'the beaches where it tosses / Its hints of earlier and other creation: / The starfish, the horseshoe crab, the whale's backbone'.[25] In 'Relic' Hughes echoed this with less emphasis on creation:

> Jaws
> Eat and are finished and the jawbone comes to the beach:
> This is the sea's achievement; with shells,
> Vertebrae, claws, carapaces, skulls. (*CP* 78)

But the horror of existence is outweighed by the horror of non-existence. Hughes believed that we are programmed to survive at all costs.[26] Philip Larkin seized on work, the 'old toad', to take his mind off death in 'Toads Revisited': 'Give me your arm, old toad; / Help me down Cemetery Road'.[27] Hughes admired 'Aubade' as Larkin's best poem. Here Larkin confronted death: 'the total emptiness for ever, / The sure extinction that we travel to / And shall be lost in always'.[28] In 'I Said Goodbye to Earth' Hughes attempted to repudiate all the trappings of earthly life, to project himself into space. But when he meets the snowflakes 'crucified / On the nails of nothing', he realizes that it is better to be a man on a cross than not to be a man at all (*CP* 278).

The fourth route to the Absurd is driven by questions about a savage god. After seeing a performance of Alfred Jarry's play *Ubu the King*, Yeats wrote: 'After us the savage god.'[29] Yet he must have known the much older tradition of savage gods who, far from investing existence with meaning, were themselves the authors of its absurdity. The obvious answer to the question, 'Why is creation so horrible?' has to be that it is the fault of whoever created it.

The gods of the ancient world (including the God of the Old Testament) had no inkling of morality. Their behaviour is like the worst of human behaviour. When the Olympian gods defeated the rebellious Titans, Zeus devised excruciating and eternal tortures for them, nailing Prometheus to a rock and sending a vulture to tear out his liver every day. Hughes wrote a whole sequence of poems titled *Prometheus on His Crag* (*CP* 285–96). Camus took the fate of Sisyphus, pushing a huge boulder to the top of a mountain, whence it invariably rolled down again, for ever, as an image of the absurdity of all existence. Much of Beckett's dark comedy consists of such futile repetition. When Prometheus stole fire from the gods as a gift for mankind, Zeus punished mankind by putting every conceivable ill into Pandora's box, which she was forbidden to open. He knew that she would be unable to resist, and took the precaution of adding Hope to prevent men from taking the easy option of suicide, thus depriving him of the pleasure of watching their torments.

The God of the Book of Job boasts that the chief of his ways is the monstrous Behemoth. In order to win a wager with Satan, he casually gives Satan permission to kill all Job's children and servants. In *King Lear* Gloucester gives voice to the same vision of divine tyranny: 'As flies to wanton boys are we to th' Gods; / They kill us for their sport' (IV.i.36). This tradition was still very much alive for Thomas Hardy in 1891, who ended *Tess of the d'Urbervilles* with his heroine, a 'pure woman', on the gallows: 'The President of the Immortals, in Aeschylean phrase, had ended his sport with Tess.'[30] Just a few years later, in 1903, Bertrand Russell gave the inevitability of extinction memorable philosophical weight:

> That Man is the product of causes which had no prevision of the end they were achieving; that his origin, his growth, his hopes and fears, his loves and his beliefs are but the outcome of accidental collocations of atoms; that no fire, no heroism, no intensity of thought and feeling, can preserve an individual life beyond the grave; that all the labours of the ages, all the devotion, all the inspiration, all the noonday brightness of human genius, are destined to extinction in the vast death of the solar system, and that the whole temple of Man's achievement must inevitably be buried beneath the debris of a universe in ruins – all these things, if not quite beyond dispute, are yet so nearly certain, that no philosophy which rejects them can hope to stand.[31]

There is a direct line of descent from this to Lucky's big 'think' in *Waiting for Godot*. Lucky starts from the standard model of 'a personal God quaquaquaqua with white beard quaquaquaqua outside time without extension', who 'loves us dearly with some exceptions for reasons unknown' and suffers with those who suffer, but finds it difficult to reconcile this God with the one who plunges many in fire, and 'whose fire and flames [...] will fire the firmament'. He continues by summarizing 'the labours of the age [...] the whole temple of Man's achievement' as establishing beyond doubt only that 'man wastes and pines'.[32] His 'think' peters out with a repetition of the word 'skull'. Lucky is at the mercy of Pozzo, who carries a worn-out whip and makes Lucky carry bags of sand, with obvious echoes of the labours of Sisyphus devised by cruel gods. For most modern writers the confident faith of a writer like John Donne is now impossible.[33] In *Endgame*, when Hamm's prayers produce 'Sweet damn all!', he complains, 'The bastard! He doesn't exist.'[34]

For Hughes, the non-existence of such a Pozzo-like God is some-thing devoutly to be wished. In 1959 he wrote to his sister Olwyn:

> An entire vision of life seems to have grown up for me around the notion of God as the devourer – as the mouth & gut, which is brainless & the whole of evil, & from which we can only get certain concessions. (*LTH* 148)

Hughes's alter ego, his own grandfather, Crag Jack, prays to be able to see God in more than 'a wolf's head' or 'eagles' feet' (*CP* 84). In 'Karma' we find the God 'Of the world / Made of Blood' (*CP* 168). The 'Ghost Crabs' of the poem of that title which 'tear each other to pieces' are 'God's only toys' (*CP* 150). The God of *Crow* owes much to Blake's tyrant Urizen. In 'Crow's Song About God', what is left of a ravaged man is sitting at the gatepost of heaven. He is like a much further-gone Estragon in *Waiting for Godot*:

> Head fallen forward
> Like the nipped head of somebody strung up to a lamp-post
> With a cheese-wire, or an electric flex,
> Or with his own belt,
> Trousers round his ankles. (*CP* 271)

He is waiting for God to take life back as unliveable in the given conditions.[35]

Beyond the Absurd

Beckett was content to remain in the Absurd, placing great value on the lucidity of unblinkered defiance. He wrote:

> I am the cow, which, at the gates of the slaughterhouse, realizes all the absurdity of pastures. A pity she didn't think of it sooner, back there in the long, lush grass. Ah well. She still has the yard to cross. No one can take that away from her.[36]

To Hughes, however, in the poem 'The Contender', for example, it seemed that such defiance was merely the hubris of a doomed con-tender in a senseless trial of strength (*CP* 267).

In the poems I have cited so far Hughes is, indeed, as bleak as Beckett. But there is an essential difference. Bleakness was Beckett's consistent and permanent mode (not lightened by his comedy). There are, as we have seen, many Hughes poems in which death appears to be unconquerable; but there are others in which vitality holds its own, at least survives to fight again.

Vitality is defeated only in two phases of Hughes's career, the years in which he was stricken by the personal tragedies of 1963 and 1969. For example, in 'Childbirth', written in 1955, the birth of every new child is a miracle which can right 'the stagger of the earth' (*CP* 40); but in 'Logos', written in 1966, 'within seconds the new-born baby is lamenting / That it ever lived' (*CP* 136). Apart from those two phases, the horror is qualified by its opposite: an admiration for the persistence and the beauty of nature. The pike, though 'killers from the egg', have a grandeur and delicacy to offset the horror (*CP* 84). In 'Still Life', first published in 1961, miserly stone

> expects to be in at the finish.
> Being ignorant of this other, this harebell,
>
> [...] in which – filling veins
> Any known name of blue would bruise
> Out of existence – sleeps, recovering,
>
> The maker of the sea. (*CP* 147–8)

Hughes was anxious that his poems should not spread his bleakness to his readers. He was careful to structure his collections to end in an upbeat mood, *Lupercal* with 'Lupercalia', *Wodwo* with 'Wodwo' itself, *Crow* with 'Littleblood', *Moortown* with 'The Sole of a Foot'. Even *Prometheus on His Crag* ends with the release and rebirth of Prometheus. In 1967 Hughes spoke of being for several years 'dominated by a long nightmare' of subjectivity from which he hoped the arrangement of poems in *Wodwo* would 'work powerfully to bring me back to the objective world where my talent really belongs' (*LTH* 274).

Though he soon transformed his divinity from god to goddess, she remained ugly, an ogress, until Crow and then Lumb came to the painful realization that her ugliness is a result of their blinkered preconceptions and the wounds they have themselves inflicted on her. Tennyson had seen her ugly, 'red in tooth and claw'.[37] Eliot had dismissed nature as 'dung and death',[38] Beckett as 'the whole bloody business'.[39] Hughes, without discounting predation, sought, through the 1970s, to discover nature's laws, and how it might be possible to live by them.[40]

Towards exultation

It would be easy to give an Absurdist reading of *Crow*, but as misleading as interpreting a Shakespeare play on the strength of the first three acts alone. The ideas that initiated *Crow* are important and are not easily identified from the published text. In 1966 Leonard Baskin suggested that Hughes should write some poems to accompany his drawings of crows. The project rapidly grew into an 'epic folk-tale', *The Life and Songs of the Crow*, where Crow recapitulates all the errors both in Hughes's personal life and in the whole history of mankind in man's relationship with the female. The female, that is, in all her manifestations – wife, mother, Nature. Crow comes, after all his horrible errors, and with the help of an Eskimo shaman, to recognize and pay for his guilt, to become a man, and to become reconciled with his former victim, now his bride, in the lovely poem from *Cave Birds* 'Bride and Groom Lie Hidden for Three Days'. *Crow* (1970) is a selection of poems from the first two-thirds of this unfinished story. *Cave Birds* (1978) is a retelling of the same story, but this time carried through to its 'upbeat' ending. When reading Crow poems Hughes invariably set them in the larger far-from-absurd framework. The story of Crow was, in fact, Hughes's first systematic attempt to escape from the Absurd.[41]

In 1968 Hughes dissociated himself explicitly from the Absurd. Speaking of the Eastern European poets, he wrote:

> In a way, their world reminds one of Beckett's world. Only theirs seems perhaps braver, more human and so more real [...] At bottom, their vision, like Beckett's, is of the struggle of animal cells and of the torments of spirit in a world reduced to that vision. But theirs contains far more elements than his. It contains all the substance and feeling of ordinary life. And one can argue that it is a step or two beyond his in imaginative truth, in that whatever terrible things happen in their work happen within a containing passion – Job-like – for the elemental final beauty of the created world. [...] They have got back to the simple animal courage of accepting the odds. (WP 221–2)

In his 1970 interview, Egbert Faas reminded Hughes that he had described *Wodwo* as 'a descent into destruction', and suggested that he had gone beyond Eliot in his portrayal of the waste land of modern civilization. Hughes replied:

> What Eliot and Joyce and I suppose Beckett are portraying is the state of belonging spiritually to the last phase of a Christian civilization, they suffer its disintegration. But there are now quite a few writers about who do not seem to belong spiritually to the Christian civilization at all. In their world, Christianity is just another provisional myth of man's relationship with the creator and the world of spirit. Their world is a continuation or a re-emergence of the pre-Christian world.[42]

Beckett is at his furthest from the later Hughes in his scorn of nature:

> The crocuses and the larch turning green every year a week before the others and the pastures red with uneaten sheep's placentas and the long summer days and the new-mown hay [...] and the apples falling and the children walking on the dead leaves [...] and of course the snow and to be sure the sleet and to be sure the sleet and bless your heart the slush [...] and the endless April showers and the crocuses and then the whole bloody business starting all over again. A turd.[43]

In *Season Songs* (1974) and his farming poems *Moortown Elegies* (*Moortown Diary*) (1978) Hughes was able to celebrate all these things as miracles, without deviating from his precept that 'everything must be paid for'.[44] In 1974 he wrote that working on the land and with animals made him 'feel to be waking up for the first time in my life'; that it had reconnected him 'to the only world I belong to in any way' (*LTH* 345, 365).

For Beckett death cancels birth. The midwife doubles as gravedigger. In *Endgame* Hamm's parents are confined to dustbins. He reviles his father as 'accursed progenitor!'[45] In the Bible, Ham's father is Noah, who ensured the survival of life on earth. Hamm's project is to bring about its extinction by ensuring that there are no more births. In Hughes birth gradually gains the ascendancy over death. At last winter succumbs to spring. In April it produces a single last snowflake:

> Solitary signal
> Of a storm too late to get in
>
> Past the iron bar's leaf
>
> Through the window
> Of the salmon's egg
> With its eager eye. (*CP* 313–14)

Probably that unborn salmon is doomed all too soon to become the 'shroud in a gutter', 'death's puppet' of 'October Salmon': 'This was inscribed in his egg. / This chamber of horrors is also home'. But this doom cannot cancel his epic role 'in the machinery of heaven' (*CP* 679). Finally, for Hughes, '*only birth matters*' (*CP* 681), which is as far from Beckett as it is possible to get.

In 'A Reply to My Critics', written in 1981,[46] Hughes defended *Crow* as 'Trickster literature',[47] from misleading attempts to relate it to its opposite, the Absurd (which he calls 'Black Comedy'):

> In Black Comedy, the despair and nihilism are fundamental, and the attempts to live are provisional, clownish, meaningless, 'absurd'. In

Trickster literature the optimism and creative joy are fundamental, and the attempts to live, and to enlarge and intensify life, however mismanaged, fill up at every point with self-sufficient meaning. (*WP* 239)

But, as Neil Roberts has pointed out, this is a far from accurate description of the 1970 figure Crow, who is 'not portrayed as a sexual being at all'.[48] It is closer to being a description of the hero of the poems Hughes was writing in 1981, the cock salmon, dressed in death's 'clownish regimentals' (*CP* 678), whose entire epic life-purpose is the fertilization of salmon eggs.

'A Reply to My Critics' is not so much a defence of Crow as an unconscious defence of the Hughes of the 1960s against the charge of writing black comedy, against, that is, any association with the Absurd, which now, from the perspective of all he had achieved in the 1970s (in the opinion of most Hughes scholars a decade of wonders), seemed to him entirely sterile. Hughes had by then come close to Bakhtin's carnivalesque,[49] which is indeed the opposite of the Absurd, claiming, as it does, that even when reduced to its most basic and sordid, to Eliot's 'dung and death' and to Beckett's 'a turd', life is still irreducibly worth having and capable of generating joy.[50]

As I have demonstrated elsewhere, in the chapter 'From World of Blood to World of Light' which is in both *The Laughter of Foxes* and *Literature and the Crime Against Nature*, and at greater length in *Ted Hughes and Nature*, in the 1970s Hughes had dragged himself, painfully, and with huge setbacks, from a nihilism indistinguishable from that of the Absurdists to an exultation as far removed from them as we can conceive.

As Seamus Heaney said in his address at the dedication of the memorial stone to Hughes in Poets' Corner at Westminster Abbey on 6 December 2011, the later Hughes 'sang the glory of creation':

Ted's poems belong in the same two dimensions as Caedmon's, in this world of earth and creatures of earth, and the world of the shining cosmos. What he created is a phantasmagoria, an ark of animals and elementals, an almanac of seasons and astrological signs; in their own way all of these are representations of a reality we know through our senses, but at the same time they manage to have the otherness of vision. It's as if he took William Blake's oracular statement that eternity is in love with the productions of time and tried to view the planet and all that lived and moved on it from that perspective.[51]

Hughes believed that in the visible, tangible world there is a great deal worthy of reverence. In *River* (1983), in some of the finest poems in the language, he transformed what Camus called 'the unreasonable silence of the world'[52] into perpetual music.

Notes

1. Elaine Feinstein, *Ted Hughes: The Life of a Poet* (London: Weidenfeld & Nicolson, 2001): 184.
2. Peter Bull, *I Know the Face, But ...* (London: Peter Davies, 1959): 171–2.
3. Samuel Beckett, *Waiting for Godot* (London: Faber & Faber, 1965): 41.
4. *Ibid*.: 13.
5. Eugene Ionesco, *Notes and Counter-Notes* (London: Calder & Boyars, 1964): 170.
6. Samuel Beckett, *Watt* (London: John Calder, 1998): 47.
7. Toby Cole (ed.), *Playwrights on Playwriting* (London: McGibbon & Kee, 1960): 283.
8. Martin Esslin, *The Theatre of the Absurd* (London: Eyre & Spottiswoode, 1962): 243.
9. 'Which Theatre is the Absurd One?', *New York Times*, 25 Feb. 1962.
10. See Keith Sagar, 'Ted Hughes and the Divided Brain', *The Ted Hughes Society Journal* [online], 1(1) (2011): 69–81 at http://www.thetedhughes society.org.
11. Ekbert Faas, *Ted Hughes: The Unaccommodated Universe* (Santa Barbara, CA: Black Sparrow Press, 1980): 206.
12. Samuel Beckett, *No's Knife* (London: Calder & Boyars, 1967): 142.
13. Friedrich Nietzsche, *The Birth of Tragedy and The Genealogy of Morals* (New York: Doubleday Anchor, 1956): 29.
14. Sophocles, *The Three Theban Plays*, trans. Robert Fagles (Harmondsworth: Penguin, 1984): 251.
15. Michel de Montaigne, *Apology of Raymond Sebond* (Harmondsworth: Penguin, 1987): 13.
16. Nietzsche, *Birth of Tragedy*: 51–2.
17. See 'The Story of Crow', in Keith Sagar, *The Laughter of Foxes: A Study of Ted Hughes* (2nd edn, Liverpool: Liverpool University Press, 2006): 170–80.
18. T.S. Eliot, *Collected Poems 1909–1962* (London: Faber & Faber, 1963): 55.
19. Gerard Manley Hopkins, *Poems and Prose*, ed. W. H. Gardner (Harmondsworth: Penguin, 1953): 66.
20. *Ibid*.: 52–3.
21. *Ibid*.: 59.
22. Eliot, *Collected Poems*: 131.
23. Beckett, *Waiting for Godot*: 89.
24. Hopkins, *Poems and Prose*: 65–6.
25. Eliot, *Collected Poems*: 205.
26. See Hughes's story 'Snow', in *Wodwo*: 71–81.
27. Philip Larkin, *Collected Poems* (London: Faber & Faber, 1988): 148.

28. *Ibid.*: 208.
29. Quoted in Michael Benedikt and George E. Wellwarth (eds), *Modern French Theatre* (New York: E.P. Dutton, 1964): xiii.
30. Thomas Hardy, *Tess of the d'Urbervilles* [1891] (London: Macmillan, 1957): 446.
31. Bertrand Russell, 'A Free Man's Worship', in Louis Greenspan and Stefan Andersson (eds), *Russell on Religion* (London: Routledge, 1999): 32.
32. Beckett, *Waiting for Godot*: 42–4.
33. Compare, for example, Donne's reliable God with the non-appearance of Godot: 'We ask our daily bread, and God never sayes you should have come yesterday, he never says you must come againe tomorrow, but today if you will heare his voice, today he will heare you' (*John Donne: Complete Poetry and Selected Prose* (London: Nonesuch Press, 1945): 586); 'Mr Godot told me to tell you he won't come this evening but surely tomorrow' (Beckett, *Waiting for Godot*: 50).
34. Samuel Beckett, *Endgame* (London: Faber & Faber, 1958): 38.
35. See Sagar, 'Story of Crow': 173.
36. Samuel Beckett, *Eleutheria* (London: Faber & Faber, 1996): 20.
37. Alfred Lord Tennyson, *Poems of Tennyson* (London: Henry Frowde, 1904): 389.
38. Eliot, *Collected Poems*: 197.
39. Samuel Beckett, *Watt* (London: Calder & Boyars, 1963): 45.
40. I have told that story at length in Keith Sagar, *Ted Hughes and Nature: 'Terror and Exultation'* (Clitheroe: Fastprint, 2009).
41. For a full account of this story see Sagar, 'The Story of Crow'.
42. Faas, *Unaccommodated Universe*: 205.
43. Beckett, *Watt*: 45.
44. See e.g. *LTH* 365–7.
45. Beckett, *Endgame*: 15.
46. The full text of the original article is in *PC* 304–7. The text revised for *WP* is quoted here. See Chapter 8 for another use of this text.
47. See Jarold Ramsey, '*Crow*, or the Trickster Transformed', in Keith Sagar (ed.), *The Achievement of Ted Hughes* (Manchester: Manchester University Press, 1983): 171–85.
48. See '*Crow* in its Time: Trickster Mythology and Black Comedy', in Neil Roberts, *Narrative and Voice in Postwar Poetry* (London: Longman, 1999): 42, where Roberts demonstrates how close Hughes came in *Crow* to the black comedy of playwright Joe Orton.
49. See Chapter 5.
50. The later Hughes had a habit of disingenuously misinterpreting his own bleak early work in order to bring it into line with the more upbeat vision which he had come through to. This is also evident in the 1992 essay 'Poetry and Violence', in *WP* 251–67. See Sagar, *Ted Hughes and Nature*: 55–6.
51. Quoted by kind permission of Seamus Heaney.
52. Albert Camus, *The Myth of Sisyphus* (London: Hamish Hamilton, 1955): 29.

5

Hughes and the Carnivalesque

Neil Roberts

Bakhtin's carnivalesque

Ted Hughes studies, and modern interest in literary theory which was initiated by structuralism, made each other's acquaintance late in the day, and among the first theoretical texts to be thought useful were the Russian critic Mikhail Bakhtin's (1895–1975) writings about carnival. This is not surprising. Mainstream poststructuralist thought typifies the rational scepticism that was anathema to Hughes and to many of his most sympathetic early critics, and Bakhtin himself was hostile to what he called 'theoreticism': 'Being cannot be determined in the categories of non-participant theoretical consciousness – it can be determined only in the categories of actual communion, i.e., of an actually performed act.'[1] Above all Bakhtin's notion of carnival, with its hostility to all forms of dogma, its valuation of the transgression of boundaries, and its idealization of folklore and a pre-modern, pre-scientific social order, has seemed in tune with Hughes's poetry and ideology.

Perhaps the first critic to link Hughes and carnival, glancingly, was Neil Corcoran in 1993. More substantial considerations were offered later in the 1990s by Paul Bentley and Alex Davis.[2] I shall be examining these contributions later, but first I want to consider Bakhtin's own writings on carnival, which are somewhat problematic both in themselves and for any project of appropriating them to the discussion of modern texts. The most frequently cited text is *Rabelais and His World*, which was first published in English in 1968 and was Anglophone readers' first introduction to Bakhtin. The concept of carnival also figures prominently in Bakhtin's *Problems of Dostoevsky's Poetics*, the revised and extended version of his 1929 study of Dostoevsky, produced in the 1960s. The long essay 'Forms of Time and of the Chronotope in the Novel', published in the

1981 translated collection *The Dialogic Imagination*, also discusses Rabelais at length, including a number of characteristics associated with carnival, though the term 'carnival' itself does not appear in this essay. One of the pitfalls of appropriating the concept for criticism of other writers is that Bakhtin's emphasis is notably different in each of these three texts.

Bakhtin's central contention is that in the Renaissance, and above all in the writing of Rabelais, we see a resurgence of life-affirming laughter, and celebration of the body in all its messy physicality, in reaction against the religiously imposed solemnity and suppression of the physical in the Middle Ages. (To an Anglophone reader his dating may seem dubious, and there is not a single mention of Chaucer in *Rabelais and His World*.) This spirit derives from folk culture, from the market place (the place where people mingle, not the hypostasized god of modern capitalism) and above all from carnival itself. Carnival is in Bakhtin's view 'non-official',[3] a site where hierarchies are collapsed or reversed, where nothing is sacred – or, rather, where the sacred may be subjected to mockery and parody. Carnival laughter, often taking the form of abuse and obscenity, is ambivalent in the sense that it 'revives and renews' at the same time as it mortifies and humiliates.[4] In *Rabelais and His World* Bakhtin argues very emphatically that the 'sacred parody' of carnival is completely different from what he calls 'the negative and formal parody of modern times' – one of the complicating factors for any attempt to appropriate carnival in criticism of modern literature.[5] Along with laughter, the dominant principle of Bakhtinian carnival is what he called the 'grotesque body'[6] – the body that is not (like a classical statue) sealed off from the world, but which is represented with an emphasis on the orifices and protuberances – the sexual organs, anus, mouth, breasts and nose – through which the body is linked to the world. Eating, defecation, sex and death are dominant in this representation, which has had a profound influence on postmodern thought about the body in literature.

Bakhtin's central interest is in the influence of carnival on literature, but *Rabelais and his World* betrays an attraction bordering on obsession for the actual institution of carnival as it was practised especially in the early Renaissance. As a result, this book, while being one of Bakhtin's most influential, has been subjected to quite severe criticism, even among his admirers. Prominent among these are Gary Saul Morson and Caryl Emerson in their major study *Mikhail Bakhtin: Creation of a Prosaics*. Morson and Emerson draw attention to Bakhtin's idealization of carnival, ignoring the dangers of the violence and exclusion (such as anti-Semitism) that were often intrinsic to it.[7] They also point out that, whereas Bakhtin's other influential writings, especially on the novel, emphasize the importance of a multiplicity of voices in dialogue, the argumentative structure of *Rabelais and His World* is rigidly binary, with the values of carnival always accorded priority over those of the Church and official morality.[8] One criticism that is especially pertinent to the consideration of Bakhtin in relation to Hughes is that the Russian writer adopted a false position of 'neglect and apparent disdain for modernism' while writing from within the conditions to which modernism responds.[9]

A very significant feature of Bakhtin's writings on carnival, to which Morson and Emerson draw attention, concerns the difference between *Rabelais and His World* and the other texts, especially *Problems of Dostoevsky's Poetics*. In the Rabelais book Bakhtin is scathing about the decline of the carnivalesque spirit after the Renaissance, and especially about what he calls the 'reduced laughter' of the Romantic period. The German comic writer and theorist Jean Paul Richter, for example, knows, according to Bakhtin, only 'a reduced form of laughter, a cold humour deprived of positive regenerating power'.[10] When Bakhtin came to revise the book about his other favourite novelist, Dostoevsky, it is understandable that he would have wanted to credit his great compatriot with one of the qualities that he most valued. Nevertheless, few could have predicted that he would find carnivalesque qualities, as described in *Rabelais and His World*, in the author of *Crime and Punishment*. True, Bakhtin's emphasis has shifted from carnival itself to 'carnivalization' – the disruption of rigid generic categories – and his use of the term in the Dostoevsky book is much more strictly literary and less historically nostalgic than in *Rabelais*. But it does entail a significant revaluation of 'reduced laughter', which is no longer the mere negative that it was in his discussion of Jean Paul Richter. In Dostoevsky's great novels 'laughter is reduced almost to the minimum', but in all his novels 'we find a trace of that ambivalent laughter, absorbed by Dostoevsky together with the generic tradition of carnivalization, performing its work of artistically organizing and illuminating the world'. Above all, reduced laughter 'excludes all one-sided or dogmatic seriousness and does not permit any single point of view, any single polar extreme of life or of thought, to be absolutized'.[11] As we shall see, this difference between the two accounts is of the utmost importance when considering carnival in relation to Ted Hughes.

Hughes and the carnivalesque

Bakhtin's revaluation of 'reduced laughter' is relevant to Hughes's only published mention of Rabelais, when he was defending the *Cave Birds* poem 'After the First Fright' against the charge of crudity. In this poem the speaker engages in a 'disputation' in which (like some of Hughes's critics) he invokes 'Civilization' and 'Sanity and again Sanity and above all Sanity', in response to which his opponent chops off his fingers and disembowels himself (*CP* 420). Hughes writes:

> The basic situation in this poem, as you'll have seen, is one of those medieval disputations – but as in Rabelais and in some folk-tales one side is a pedagoguic (that can't be spelt right) fool and the other is a wise clown. One comes out with theological riddles, in crushing scholastic terms, and the other replies with obscene caperings, ludicrous non-sequiturs, profane body-talk, which turn out to be superior sense. (*LTH* 396)

There is no evidence that Hughes read *Rabelais and His World*. There are no books by Bakhtin in his library held at Emory University, but he did possess two translations of Rabelais's novel, and this account obviously corresponds to the carnivalesque in a number of ways: the 'decrowning' (as Bakhtin calls it) of official ideology, the positive function of obscenity, the body as a signifier and above all 'reduced laughter': beneath the horror of the wise clown's self-mutilation is a profound and satirical comedy of incongruity which paradoxically affirms the life of the body.[12]

However, the carnivalesque in Hughes is usually identified in *Crow*, and specifically in the well-known influence of Trickster mythology on that sequence. Paul Bentley writes:

> Hughes uses the figure of the comic, bungling and irrepressible Trickster in *Crow* as a carnivalesque device; that is, the Trickster grants a licence to improvise, to combine 'the sacred with the profane, the lofty with the low, the wise with the stupid': Crow is as much as anything else the incorrigible prankster of poems like 'A Childish Prank' and 'Crow Blacker than ever', his perverse meddlesomeness affording the poet the means to question and tinker with received theological wisdom.[13]

In this connection Bentley cites the perceptive early comment of Jonathan Raban on *Crow*, that a great deal of the energy and violence of the poems 'springs from the tension that they tap between the permitted and the forbidden. Their language, far from being post-Christian, post-civilized, is a language obsessed by institutional rules.'[14] Exactly the same can be said of carnival, whose *raison d'être* is the temporary release from 'institutional rules'.

From an anthropological point of view, the parallel between Trickster mythology and carnival is problematic. As Bakhtin writes, 'at the early stages of preclass and prepolitical social order [i.e. tribal societies] it seems that the serious and the comic aspects of the world and of the deity were equally sacred'. In other words, sacred clowns and tricksters were part of the 'official' religion. In what he calls 'the definitely consolidated state and class structure', however, 'such an equality of the two aspects became impossible. All the comic forms were transferred [...] to a comic level.'[15] There is in carnival, therefore, a potential for subversion which doesn't exist in tribal comic expression. However, if there is not strictly a parallel between the two, the carnivalesque (to which, as we have seen, Hughes was attuned through Rabelais even if he hadn't read Bakhtin) could mediate, even unknowingly, Trickster mythology for a modern writer.

Bentley is certainly right to draw attention to similarities between *Rabelais and His World* and Hughes's attempt to expound the influence of Trickster mythology on *Crow*. Bentley cites Bakhtin's contrast between the 'indestructible vitality' of the carnivalesque and 'the negative and formal parody of modern times', and parallels it with Hughes's contrast between Trickster mythology and 'Black Comedy'.[16] In his essay 'A Reply to Critics' Hughes writes:

> In Black Comedy, the lost hopeful world of Trickster is mirrored coldly, with a negative accent. In Trickster Literature, the suffering world of Black Comedy, shut off behind thin glass, is mirrored hotly, with a positive accent. It is the difference between two laughters: one, bitter and destructive; the other zestful and creative, attending what seems to be the same calamity.[17]

Elsewhere I have made a detailed criticism of this essay of Hughes's, and what I consider its false polarity between Trickster mythology and black comedy.[18] What interests me in the present context is the parallel between Hughes's rigid separation of the modern from the primitive, and Bakhtin's similarly rigid separation of modern parody and irony from carnival (compare Bakhtin's use of the word 'cold' in his critique of Jean Paul Richter). The two writers share a disavowal of their present cultural context and an idealization of a defunct cultural form.

Alex Davis's essay, published in 1999, does not cite Bentley, but could be considered an implicit refutation of Bentley's 'carnivalesque' *Crow*. Davis acknowledges that several aspects of Bakhtin's character-ization seem applicable to *Crow*, notably 'images [...] opposed to all that is finished and polished, to all pomposity, to every ready-made solution in the sphere of thought and world outlook'.[19] Davis also points out that Paul Radin (author of *The Trickster*, the text that definitively influenced Hughes), Carl Jung and Karl Kerenyi all drew parallels between Trickster mythology and carnival. However, Davis goes on to remind the reader of Bakhtin's low opinion of modern humour, specifically the distinction between true carnival laughter and what he calls the 'existentialist grotesque' in which 'the satirist whose laughter is negative places himself above the object of his mockery'. This, Davis argues, is the category to which *Crow* belongs. Bakhtin, Davis points out, takes issue with the German philosopher Wolfgang Kayser, author of *The Grotesque in Art and Literature*, for whom 'the essential trait of grotesque is "something hostile, alien and inhuman" [...] The gay, liberating and regenerating element of laughter, which is precisely the creative element, is completely absent.'[20] According to Davis, Hughes appropriates and interprets Trickster mythology in the same way that, according to Bakhtin, Kayser interprets carnival. For Davis *Crow* manifests at best 'pseudo-carnivalism', and the grotesque in a poem such as 'In Laughter' is 'light-years away from that of the tales one encounters in Radin's *The Trickster*'.[21]

Yet, as we have seen, the opposition on which Bakhtin bases his critique of Kayser disappears when he discusses the carnivalesque in Dostoevsky, and Hughes explicated a *Cave Birds* poem 'After the First Fright' (similar in style to *Crow*) in terms that strongly echo the 'reduced laughter' of Bakhtin's Dostoevsky. The opposition of carnival and the modern grotesque, like Hughes's opposition between Trickster mythol-ogy and Black Comedy, is not adequate to investigate the possible rele-vance of carnival to *Crow*.

Before discussing some of the poems I want to introduce two more pieces of evidence. As is well known, Hughes originally conceived of *Crow* as an 'epic folktale' with poems embedded in a prose narrative, numerous fragmentary drafts of which can be found in the archives at the British Library and Emory University. These fragments don't tell a consistent story, and I have argued elsewhere (unlike Keith Sagar in Chapter 4) that they can't be used to supply an explanatory framework for the published poems.[22] Nevertheless it is fascinating to see that one of the episodes takes place in a fairground with a giant vagina and penis and doors shaped like vaginas, where Shakespearean

heroes engage in a sheep-eating contest, a brothel is fitted with 'cop-
ulometers' and adulterers afflicted with satyriasis (what is today called
'sex addiction') couple with crocodiles.[23] There is nothing idealized
about this carnival, which is a place of random and horrific violence,
but the influence of Rabelais is obvious. The exaggeration of bodily
parts is a feature of Rabelais's *Gargantua and Pantagruel* that Bakhtin
particularly relishes: 'The material bodily element has here a positive
character. And it is precisely the material bodily image that is exag-
gerated to disproportionate dimensions: the monastic phallus as tall
as a belfry, the torrents of Gargantua's urine, and his immeasurably
large, all-swallowing gullet.'[24] Another episode that Bakhtin quotes
with approval involves the use of vaginas to build a wall. Panurge
says: 'I have observed that the pleasure-twats of women in this part
of the world are much cheaper than stones.' Bakhtin's determination
to represent Rabelais in a celebratory light is shown in his comment
on this: 'It is clear that the cheapness of Paris women is merely a
secondary theme, and that even here there is no moral condem-
nation. The leading theme is fecundity.'[25] It may be that Hughes is
striving for a similar bypassing of morality and sexual politics with the
copulometer and adulterers coupling with crocodiles, though even
Rabelais stops short of celebrating bestiality, and the introduction of
mechanical measurement is likely to be satirical. The sheep-eating
contest is unmistakably Rabelaisian. Eating to excess is one of the
most distinctive features of *Gargantua and Pantagruel*, and for Bakhtin
is a key element in the carnivalization of genres, eroding the boundary between the elevated zone of tragedy and the familiar zone of
everyday life, above all the 'lower bodily stratum'. (This is, of course,
already present in Shakespeare, whom Bakhtin credits with a certain
degree of carnivalization.)

However, we must be cautious in using this material to reflect on
the poems. There is little, if any, of this kind of socially grounded folk
humour in the published *Crow* which, despite its author's generic tag,
is more myth than folk tale. However, it is evidence that Hughes was
at least dabbling in Rabelaisian humour, and aspiring to something
literally carnivalesque.

My second piece of evidence is more nugatory, but perhaps takes
us deeper into the carnivalesque character of *Crow*. One caricature
view of the collection and its relation to Hughes's life is that it is a
dark, 'nihilistic'[26] book testifying to its author's state of mind after the
suicide of Sylvia Plath. Undoubtedly, as Hughes himself has stated
(*LTH* 719), one aspect of *Crow* is an indirect response to that tragedy, but it is important to realize that it was the fruit of a period of

renewed creative energy – he didn't begin it until three years after Plath's death, a time of creative sterility – and that it was brought to an end by the second tragedy, the deaths of Assia Wevill and her daughter Shura in March 1969. Creatively, this was the happiest time in Hughes's life, the only time when he seems to have been completely satisfied with what he was writing, and that he looked back on nostalgically, lamenting his inability to recapture the 'free energy' that he had at that time (*LTH* 718). This 'free energy' may be connected with the sense he had of some taboo about what he was writing.[27] It may also be the result of his determination, as he later put it, 'to re-simplify my language but simultaneously to break out of dependence on a sacred object for subject […] to include a broader play of a more liberated music'. (By 'sacred object' he means images such as the hawk and pike on which he 'got into such a state of fixated concentration that I felt myself sinking like a stone beyond words'.) In the same letter he writes that 'the scabby foal [his metaphor, in the 1970 Ekbert Faas interview, for the style of *Crow*[28]] was a way of finding a mount outside my own self-respecting socially responsible ego' (*LTH* 632, 629) – a very carnivalesque idea.

Carnivalesque in the *Crow* poems

Now turning to the poems themselves, I will illustrate some of the more obvious ways in which the Bakhtinian carnivalesque illuminates the *Crow* poems, but also look for signs of the 'free energy' that Hughes experienced, and try to meet some of Davis's objections. Perhaps the most obvious candidates for carnivalesque status are those poems which parody, or otherwise 'decrown', religious and specifically Christian stories and ideas. One such poem is 'A Childish Prank', cited by both Bentley and Davis, which parodies the biblical account of Creation. There are a number of obviously carnivalesque motifs: God is 'decrowned' by being portrayed in an exhausted sleep throughout the poem, having failed to endow man and woman with souls; Crow's response is laughter; Christ and Satan are identified in the phrase, 'the Worm, God's only son'; Crow's 'prank', biting the worm in half and stuffing the ends into man and woman, so waking them by creating sex, epitomizes what Bakhtin calls 'the essential principle of grotesque realism', namely 'degradation […] the lowering of all that is high, spiritual, ideal, abstract, it is a transfer to the material level, to the sphere of earth and body in their indissoluble unity'.[29] But is Hughes's handling of these motifs an example of what Bakhtin calls 'the pure satire of modern times' in which 'The satirist whose

laughter is negative places himself above the object of his mockery'?[30]
There is, it is true, a certain thinness and sharpness about the language
of *Crow,* which couldn't contrast more with the richly overflowing
humour of Rabelais. But it is Crow, not the transcendent author,
who is laughing, and he is laughing not just at God but at man and
woman – including, we must suppose, the author. Sex represented as
being dragged by a worm trying to bring its severed halves together
is as far removed from romantic love as it could be, just as this image
of creation is far removed from the breathing of life into man by God.
To that extent the poem is clearly a satire on the biblical story. But is
the laughter merely negative and satirical?

> Man awoke being dragged across the grass.
> Woman awoke to see him coming.
> Neither knew what had happened.
>
> God went on sleeping.
>
> Crow went on laughing. (*CP* 216)

Is it not possible to detect a wry but affirmative note in this laughter?
Man and woman may not have been awakened by having immaterial
souls breathed into them, but they have been awakened. God is sleeping,
but they are obeying a power greater than themselves which may be the
Worm, but is also God's only son. The poem's determination to identify
the spiritual with the animal is not necessarily nihilistic.

Another poem that manifests Bakhtin's notion of 'degradation' is
'Crow Communes'. Once again God is 'exhausted with Creation',
unable to respond to Crow's chirpy questions about what to do now
that Creation has been accomplished. Frustrated by this, Crow tears
off and eats a mouthful of the 'great carcase' of the sleeping God (*CP*
224). He jokingly asks himself if it will 'divulge itself to digestion',
but is surprised to find that it does make him feel stronger. The pun
in the poem's title is obvious, but the poem isn't just a cheap satire on
transubstantiation. The traditional doctrine that the bread and wine of
the communion are literally the body and blood of Christ insists that
Christ's bodily life was not a mere accident, and that the communi-
cant is strengthened by it. Crow, it is true, is 'Appalled' by this discovery, but this is the shock of realizing that God isn't going to wake up
and answer his question 'Which way?' With the strength from eating
God's body comes the responsibility of finding the way himself.

Bakhtin rather programmatically categorizes the grotesque motifs
in Rabelais into a number of 'series' such as sex, death, eating and
drinking, and crucially notes that these series 'intersect' on what he

calls 'a grotesque and clownish plane'.[31] One can easily construct such 'series' in *Crow*: 'Lineage', 'That Moment', 'A Disaster', 'Crow Tyrannosaurus', 'Crow and the Birds', 'A Horrible Religious Error' (eating); 'A Childish Prank', 'Crow's First Lesson', 'Lovesong' (sex); 'That Moment', 'A Disaster', 'Crow Tyrannosaurus', 'Criminal Ballad', 'In Laughter' (death). One might add to these a 'series' in which laughter is explicitly a theme: 'A Childish Prank', 'Criminal Ballad', 'In Laughter'. It will be immediately obvious that these series 'intersect', as Bakhtin says of Rabelais, and in particular that incongruous series such as death and eating, death and laughter, intersect in a 'grotesque and clownish' way. Bakhtin adds that Rabelais will frequently 'intertwine his eating and drinking series with religious concepts and symbols', and again we do not have to search far for examples in *Crow*: 'Lineage', 'Crow Communes', 'A Horrible Religious Error', 'Apple Tragedy', 'Crow's Song of Himself'.

The poem in which death and eating 'intersect' most powerfully is perhaps the least obviously Rabelaisian in the whole of *Crow*: 'That Moment'. The first twelve of this poem's thirteen lines (a single sentence) constitute a solemn and poignant meditation on absolute loss. It is one of the poems that most obviously answer to Hughes's avowal that *Crow* was a creative response to Plath's death, above all in the piercing lines, 'the only face left in the world / Lay broken / Between hands that relaxed, being too late' (*CP* 209). The haunting and bereft sentence is completed with the line, 'Crow had to start searching for something to eat'. For one perfectly arguable reading of the poem this is the final turn of the screw: the triumph of brute survival over meaning-bestowing grief. The words 'had to' suggest that this time even Crow, who normally eats with unthinking gusto, is compelled contrary to his higher feelings. It would surely be special pleading to claim even the most 'reduced' laughter for a poem such as this. But let us recall Bakhtin's claim that reduced laughter 'excludes all one-sided or dogmatic seriousness and does not permit any single point of view, any single polar extreme of life or of thought, to be absolutized'.[32] This is precisely the function of the final line of 'That Moment': the poem tears itself away from the fixity of grief, in a way that is, in Jarold Ramsey's words, 'at once macabre and eminently practical' – what, ultimately, makes the difference between mourning and melancholia.[33]

The function of eating in *Crow* may even challenge 'one-sided or dogmatic seriousness' on the part of the author himself. Keith Sagar's *The Laughter of Foxes* includes a 'Story of Crow' that he published with Hughes's approval, and that is largely drawn from fugitive statements, including public readings, by Hughes. An important part of the story is that Crow is searching for his creator, whom he constantly misrecognizes because she is female. 'It's seemingly monstrous and enigmatic. He misinterprets it. He tries to destroy it ("A Horrible Religious Error"). He mismanages his opportunity to find whatever it might be that this thing holds for him. So it's a disaster.'[34] 'A Horrible Religious Error' is one of the most finely wrought *Crow* poems, one of Hughes's several versions of the Fall, in which an ambivalent, chthonic and celestial serpent reduces God to a shrivelled leaf, and man and woman to prostrate tearful worship. At the end Crow 'Grabbed this creature by the slackskin nape, // Beat the hell out of it, and ate it' (*CP* 231). Leaving aside the question of how the reader is supposed to recognize the serpent as female, this is a possible reading of the poem, but is it the only plausible one? The serpent is beautiful and powerful ('flexing on that double flameflicker tongue / A syllable like the rustling of the spheres'), but if Crow's response is a mismanagement, what of man and woman's? The line 'Their tears evacuated visibly' doesn't invite the reader to identify with their emotion. Crow's eating is predominantly positive throughout the poems, and the simple, unliterary vigour of this poem's concluding lines is one of the sequence's strongest values. Hughes's exposition, via Sagar, reminds me of his commentary on 'After the First Fright': 'One comes out with theological riddles, in crushing scholastic terms, and the other replies with obscene caperings, ludicrous non-sequiturs, profane body-talk, which turn out to be superior sense' (*LTH* 396). Except that, in this case, the crushing scholastic terms are the author's, and the profane body-talk Crow's.

Alex Davis chooses the poem 'In Laughter' to illustrate his critique that the humour of *Crow* 'can hardly be glossed as "liberating" and "regenerating"'.[35] He quotes these lines:

In laughter
People's arms and legs fly off and fly on again
In laughter
The haggard mask on the bed rediscovers its pang
In laughter, in laughter
The meteorite crashes
With extraordinarily ill-luck on the pram. (*CP* 233)

Davis comments, 'The grotesque in these lines is light-years away from that of the tales one encounters in Radin's *The Trickster*', and quotes Neil Corcoran's comment that such laughter 'insist[s] on the way violence comes to us ready-processed, already assimilated, in contemporary media, and therefore hardly properly assimilable at all [... such as] the

Vietnam War, whose atrocities were being edited for nightly television viewing'.[36] But is this really so? In the examples here, the first seems to me a cartoon image, the second a highly internalized representation of pain (not violence) and the third a sick joke, dependent entirely on its ironically inappropriate expression, that one can't imagine 'being edited for nightly television viewing'. (These last lines preoccupied Hughes for years before he wrote *Crow*: they occur twice in a note-book of *Hawk in the Rain* drafts.[37]) The violence in *Crow* is nothing compared to some passages of Rabelais that Bakhtin quotes from with equanimity. One episode is set on the island of Catchpoles who 'earn their living by letting themselves be thrashed'. Bakhtin quotes:

> they whacked with lusty gauntlet, knocking their enemy dizzy [...] bruising his whole frame [...] making one eye like nothing so much as a poached egg with black-butter sauce [...] smashing eight ribs, staving in his chest, and cleaving his shoulder-blades in four [...] breaking his jaw into three separate parts [...] and accomplishing the whole amid good-natured laughter (*et le tout en riant*). (Book 4, Chapter 12)[38]

As Bakhtin's citation of the French indicates, the good nature of the laughter appears to be a translator's queasy emendation. Bakhtin's comment on this passage is 'The carnivalesque nature of this chastise-ment is obvious.'[39] His notion of liberating and regenerating laughter is capacious.

However, I would agree that 'In Laughter' doesn't completely correspond to Bakhtin's carnivalesque, not so much because of the nature of its violence, but because of the way it ends. The personified laughter is 'only human' and eventually, exhausted, is compared to 'somebody the police have come for'. The poem is a mirror image of 'Criminal Ballad'. In that poem every moment of creaturely ful-filment in a man's life – being breastfed, childhood play, making love, enjoying his children – is shadowed by somebody else's suffering until

> His hands covered with blood suddenly [...]
>
> And under the leaves he sat weeping
>
> Till he began to laugh (*CP* 229)

The capacity of laughter and guilt to turn into their opposite, the exhaustibility of extreme feeling, is a dimension of psychological sub-tlety absent from the treatment of laughter and violence in *Rabelais and His World*.

'Free energy'

I want, finally, to reflect on the experience of reading *Crow* – at least
my own reading, which I don't think is unique. I have never found
Crow depressing or nihilistic, and I have always thought this was
because of its style. I tentatively suggest that this may be related to the
'free energy' that Hughes experienced when he was writing it. I will
just cite a few examples of carnivalesque conclusions to poems, all of
which, as it happens, involve eating.

I have already cited 'A Horrible Religious Error', in which Crow,
responding to God's, man's and woman's submission to the serpent,
'Grabbed this creature by the slackskin nape, // Beat the hell out of it, and
ate it'. The vigorous verbs beginning each line with an aggressive voiced
consonant and monosyllabic action, the inventive economy of 'slackskin
nape', the humorous colloquialism and simple final action combine to
epitomize a 'free energy' of style which alone makes me want to resist
Hughes's own account of Crow's action as a religious crime.

'Lineage' is a parody of the biblical form that culminates in Crow

> Screaming for Blood
> Grubs, crusts
> Anything
>
> Trembling featherless elbows in the nest's filth ... (*CP* 218)

The last line is perhaps the most stylistically accomplished in *Crow*,
and epitomizes what I find invigorating about the book. The transitive
use of 'trembling', the humanizing touch of 'elbows', the rhythmic
shift from mimetic dactyls to emphatic spondee, the collapsing of the
consonants of the trisyllabic 'featherless' into the monosyllable 'filth'
combine in a seemingly casual mastery to create this image of vora-
cious creatureliness.

In similar vein perhaps the most carnivalesque line of the book
is the last one of 'Crow and the Birds': 'Crow spraddled head-down
in the beach-garbage, guzzling a dropped ice-cream' (CP 210). This
elongated and ramshackle alliterative line, hinging on the alliteration
of the two words around the caesura, with a lexical reach from the
dialect 'spraddled' to the American-inflected 'garbage', follows a series
of perhaps parodically but certainly poetically invoked birds, in such
a way as to seem a manifesto for the *Crow* project. As such it recalls
Hughes's avowal of his desire 'to re-simplify my language but simultaneously to break out of dependence on a sacred object for subject
[...] to include a broader play of a more liberated music' (*LTH* 632).

As we might expect, an investigation of the carnivalesque in *Crow* is complex and multi-faceted. Hughes shares with Bakhtin a questionable tendency absolutely to privilege pre-modern cultural forms. More positively, he cites Rabelais as a model for subversive challenge to orthodox nostrums, specifically the retort of bodily expression to verbal formulae, and the figure of Crow, especially his eating, functions in a way similar to the 'decrowning' effect of the Bakhtinian grotesque. Bakhtin's more positive account of 'reduced laughter' in his Dostoevsky book is particularly congenial to the tone of *Crow*. Bakhtin's tendency to idealize carnival is tolerant of sometimes horrific violence, at least as disturbing as that of *Crow*. But none of this would be important if it were not for the stylistic freedom and energy of the 'little scabby foal'. This is the most carnivalesque quality of all in *Crow*.

Notes

1. Mikhail Bakhtin, *Toward a Philosophy of the Act*, trans. Vadim Liapunov (Austin: University of Texas Press, 1993): 13.
2. Neil Corcoran, *English Poetry Since 1940* (London: Longman, 1993):118–19; Paul Bentley, *The Poetry of Ted Hughes: Language, Illusion and Beyond* (London: Longman, 1998): 39–54; Alex Davis, '*Crow*, Quest Romance and the Carnivalesque', in Joanny Moulin (ed.), *Lire Ted Hughes* (Paris: Editions du Temps, 1999): 169–87. Admittedly none of these is an example of the critic who shares Hughes's hostility to rationality.
3. Mikhail Bakhtin, *Rabelais and His World*, trans. Hélène Iswolsky (Bloomington: Indiana University Press, 1968): 6.
4. *Ibid*: 16.
5. *Ibid*: 14, 11.
6. See especially *ibid.*: 303–67.
7. Gary Saul Morson and Caryl Emerson, *Mikhail Bakhtin: Creation of a Prosaics* (Stanford, CA: Stanford University Press, 1990): 470.
8. *Ibid.*: 445.
9. *Ibid.*
10. Bakhtin, *Rabelais and His World*: 42.
11. Mikhail Bakhtin, *Problems of Dostoevsky's Poetics,* trans. Caryl Emerson (Minneapolis: University of Minnesota Press, 1984): 165.
12. As one of the authors of the criticism to which Hughes was responding, I must confess myself to have been implicitly an object of this satire.
13. Bentley, *Poetry of Ted Hughes*: 40, quoting Bakhtin, *Problems of Dostoevsky's Poetics*: 123.
14. Bentley, *Poetry of Ted Hughes*: 42, citing Jonathan Raban, *The Society of the Poem* (London: Harrap, 1971): 166.
15. Bakhtin, *Rabelais and His World*: 6.
16. Bentley, *Poetry of Ted Hughes*: 40–1.

17. 'A Reply to Critics (1979)', in A.E. Dyson (ed.), *Three Contemporary Poets: Thom Gunn, Ted Hughes & R.S. Thomas* (Basingstoke: Macmillan, 1990): 110. Originally published in *Books and Issues*, 3 (1979), as 'A Reply to My Critics'. Dyson's text is 'approved by the poet as the correct version'.

18. See Neil Roberts, *Narrative and Voice in Postwar Poetry* (Harlow: Longman, 1999): 36–47, also referred to in Chapter 4.

19. Davis, '*Crow*, Quest Romance and the Carnivalesque': 180, citing Bakhtin, *Rabelais and His World*: 3.

20. Davis, '*Crow*, Quest Romance and the Carnivalesque': 181, citing Bakhtin, *Rabelais and His World*: 12.

21. Davis, '*Crow*, Quest Romance and the Carnivalesque': 182.

22. See Neil Roberts, *Ted Hughes: A Literary Life* (Basingstoke: Palgrave Macmillan, 2006): 71–80.

23. Emory, Box 62, ff 55. There are also extensive, though fragmentary drafts of the *Crow* saga in BL, Add 88918/1/23. See Keith Sagar's 'Story of Crow', quoted below.

24. Bakhtin, *Rabelais and His World*: 312.

25. *Ibid.*: 313.

26. Calvin Bedient, *Eight Contemporary Poets* (London: Oxford University Press, 1974): 101.

27. Ekbert Faas, *Ted Hughes: The Unaccommodated Universe* (Santa Barbara, CA: Black Sparrow Press, 1980): 207.

28. *Ibid.*: 208.

29. Bakhtin, *Rabelais and His World*: 19–20.

30. *Ibid.*: 12.

31. Mikhail Bakhtin, 'Forms of Time and of the Chronotope in the Novel', in *The Dialogic Imagination: Four Essays*, trans. Caryl Emerson and Michael Holquist (Austin: University of Texas Press, 1981): 194.

32. Bakhtin, *Problems of Dostoevsky's Poetics*: 165.

33. Jarold Ramsey, '*Crow*, or the Trickster Transformed', in Keith Sagar (ed.), *The Achievement of Ted Hughes* (Manchester: Manchester University Press, 1983): 180. For the distinction between mourning and melancholia see Sigmund Freud, 'Mourning and Melancholia' [1917], in *The Standard Edition of the Complete Psychological Works of Sigmund Freud, Volume XIV (1914–1916): On the History of the Psycho-Analytic Movement, Papers on Metapsychology and Other Works*, ed. James Strachey (London: Vintage, 2001): 237–58.

34. Keith Sagar, *The Laughter of Foxes: A Study of Ted Hughes* (2nd edn, Liverpool: Liverpool University Press, 2006): 176.

35. Davis, '*Crow*, Quest Romance and the Carnivalesque': 181.

36. *Ibid.*: 182, quoting Corcoran, *English Poetry Since 1940*: 119.

37. Emory, Box 57, ff 1, 3.

38. Bakhtin, *Rabelais and His World*: 196.

39. *Ibid.*: 200.

6

Hughes and Gender

Janne Stigen Drangsholt

Traditionally, Ted Hughes has not had a great reputation among feminists. The gap that was created by the death of Sylvia Plath and opened up by the more partisan of her 'supporters' was never quite bridged during his lifetime. Whether criticized for self-protective and defensive motives in his administration of Plath's literary estate, or, in the most extreme case, identified as a 'one-man gynocidal movement' in Robin Morgan's poem 'Arraignment', Hughes was invariably cast in the role of the misogynist by American feminists in particular.[1]

Hughes's reputation was not solely created by the Plath controversy, however. Numerous critics have noted that the ambiguity associated with the female figures presented in his poetry, as well as his representation of the feminine, have contributed to the difficulties in forging an alignment between Hughes's name and feminism.[2] Both Tracy Brain and Nathalie Anderson have commented extensively on this, and Anderson refers to Hughes's female figures as 'double-edged emblems' that emerge as largely negative for women looking to find a vision of themselves in the poems.[3] In similar terms, Paul Bentley notes that Hughes's notions of the feminine come dangerously close to damaging essentialist stereotypes.[4]

The latter point is especially relevant to one of Ted Hughes's central tropes, that is, the figure of the 'the goddess', capitalized in Hughes's study of Shakespeare, *Shakespeare and the Goddess of Complete Being.* Most readers have placed this figure in the context of writings by Robert Graves and Carl Jung, who are well known for the gendered metaphors of 'white goddess' and *anima*, respectively. Thus, Joanny Moulin refers to Hughes's early poem 'Song' as a 'declaration of love' to the *anima,* while also calling attention to the likeness between Jung's concept and Graves's 'white goddess'.[5] Similarly, in *Ted Hughes: Form and Imagination*, Leonard Scigaj renders the feminine presences in

Gaudete and *Cave Birds* as a 'white goddess' and *anima* figure, respectively,[6] with whom the male protagonist hopes to unite in order to achieve a sense of spiritual and psychological wholeness.

From a feminist perspective, such a merging of Jung's and Graves's gendered metaphors is challenging. For one thing, while Jung frequently stressed that his concept of the anima is only symbolically feminine and should not be confused with the female or, indeed, woman, the concept of 'femininity' in itself raises a lot of questions. Among feminists it has been established usage to view 'feminine' and 'masculine' as social and cultural constructs that refer to patterns of sexuality and behaviour imposed by patriarchal norms, while 'female' and 'male' refer to the biological aspects of sexual difference. From such a viewpoint, 'femininity' and 'masculinity' are problematic because they impose certain reductive features of femininity on all biological women and masculinity on all biological men.

The problem with associating these goddess figures with femininity, then, is that they can end up reinforcing certain essentialist ideas of what it means to be female. An example of this is found in Graves's 'white goddess', whose female configuration can both seem to play into the Romantic positioning of the woman as 'other' *and* continue the patriarchal conflation between womanhood and marginalized elements of human life such as chaos, nature and irrationality. Similarly, the danger of collapsing Jung's feminine *anima* archetype with the female is also inevitably present. As noted by Demaris S. Wehr, Jung's own discussions of the feminine *anima* frequently turn into deliberations on the psychology of women, resulting in a blurred agenda where it is unclear whether one or the other is being portrayed.[7]

Similar challenges are also to be found in terms of Hughes's feminine and female figures. Paul Bentley particularly emphasizes *Cave Birds* as an example, saying that Hughes's portrayal of the *anima* as a mouthpiece for the unconscious in poems like 'After There was Nothing There Was a Woman' and 'Bride and Groom Lie Hidden for Three Days' is fraught with ambiguity.[8] And while Hughes wrote literature that celebrated femininity in the form of the nurturing, loving goddess in poems like 'Take What You Want But Pay For It', such images can also be experienced as oppressive to all those women readers who do not feel at home in the role of the Earth Mother.

At first sight, then, Hughes's representations of the female and feminine stand in danger of regurgitating the cultural and social misogyny that is still cast over women, and with which feminist criticism is still concerned. At the same time, it would be a mistake to view Hughes's gendered metaphors as a static representation of Jungian or Gravesian ideas. While Hughes was clearly influenced by both of these thinkers, there are aspects of his work that actually have more in common with the thoughts of Hélène Cixous, or even Jacques Derrida. In *Ted Hughes: A Literary Life*, Neil Roberts notes that it is unlikely that Hughes ever read Derrida, but says that his poetry nevertheless displays linguistics concerns that echo those of the French theorist.[9] Like Derrida, Hughes was immensely critical of the metaphysical thinking that governs our culture, and ultimately aimed to rethink human subjectivity and rebuild the moral and ethical relationship between self and other. As noted by Joanny Moulin, Hughes saw the radical rationalism of the Western world as the disease of civilization and sought to challenge this poetically.[10]

This chapter will investigate these poetic concerns, which are particularly relevant in the experimental volumes of the 1970s, where the arrogance and iniquity of a male subject – represented by Hughes in *Cave Birds* as an 'imbecile innocence' (*CP* 423) – prevents him from establishing a relationship with an 'other' who is both gendered as feminine in a challenging sense and as female in a biological sense. While the male, or masculine, subject attempts to incorporate the female, or feminine, other into the hegemony of all-powerful self-hood, the poetic discourse signals that such an approach is flawed and can only lead to self-destruction and death.

Powerful energies

Hughes's reputation as a poet was established with the poetic collections *The Hawk in the Rain, Lupercal* and *Wodwo*. In this early work, his imagination largely centres on the idea of unity and wholeness. As he explains in an interview with Ekbert Faas, he initially set out to capture an energy so powerful that it 'will destroy an impure nature and serve a pure one'.[11] In this, Hughes positioned himself against the Movement poets, who were mainly interested in 'the cosiest arrangement of society'.[12] Hughes, who was all set for communicating with 'whatever was out there', referred himself to a number of iconic creatures, such as jaguars, hawks and pike, that had 'real summoning force', rendering them powerful symbolic structures that were also potentially dangerous because he saw them as difficult to manage.[13]

While Hughes saw these creatures as 'invocations of the Goddess',[14] many readers thought them provocative, partly because they were associated with primitive masculine values. As a consequence, poems like

'Hawk Roosting' (*CP* 68) and 'The Jaguar' (*CP* 19) quickly resulted in Hughes being viewed as a 'poet of violence'.[15] In the interview referred to above, however, Hughes protests against such a designation, saying that if his poetry is, indeed, 'violent', it is only so in the sense of belonging to the same kind of field that 'Shakespeare found the fable for in his "Venus and Adonis"'.[16]

'Venus and Adonis' is a key text in understanding Hughes's poetry, even for his earliest work. For one thing, it is a mythological text that deals with transformation and rebirth, two central themes in Hughes's poetic universe. What is more, Hughes saw the myth of Adonis's rejection of Venus as an emblem for Western civilization's failure to communicate with the same kind of powerful energies that he himself evoked in his poetry, powers that had since been replaced by rationality and science. For Hughes, poetry is a way of reconnecting with these energies (cf. *WP* 226), as can be seen in poems like 'The Jaguar', 'Pike' and 'Hawk Roosting'.

Another example of Hughes's handling of this theme is 'The Thought-Fox', where the poet sits at his desk, trying to compose a poem, when 'something else' suddenly appears (*CP* 21). Significantly, this 'something else' occurs in 'this midnight moment's forest', that is, in a time and place when the human being is most exposed to those elements that transcend the rational mind. It seems that when the poet uses his imagination, he opens himself up to an otherness, which proceeds to enter the 'dark hole of the head' in a manner whose violence is emphasized through the alliteration and cacophony of the phrase 'a sudden sharp hot stink of fox' (*CP* 21), but whose presence is nevertheless a blessing as it allows the poet to complete his poem.

As has been noted on several occasions by Keith Sagar, the fox is Hughes's totem animal, holding 'the unquenchable flame' of life itself.[17] If we look at Hughes's work, we can find numerous examples of his calling upon the fox for strength or advice, something that is also suggested in the fragment 'The Burnt Fox', where Hughes refers to the dream in which a fox tells him to abandon his studies in English literature because it is 'killing us' (*WP* 9).

While the lyrical 'I' in 'The Thought-Fox' is seen to welcome the fox, however, the poet in a *Birthday Letters* poem, 'Epiphany', refuses the fox cub, rationalizing to himself that it is not possible to fit such a creature into the domestic framework of a marriage: 'How would we cope with its cosmic derangements / Whenever we moved?' (*CP* 1116). In the final stanza, however, he comes to view that the offering of the fox was a test and blames himself for having failed it.

A spiritual challenge

The theme of failing to accept a challenge is a recurring element of Hughes's poetry from *Wodwo* onwards. In a letter to János Csokits Hughes describes how, at the time of writing *Wodwo*, he received a spiritual demand or a challenge 'from a subjective world' which he refused (*LTH* 273–4). It could well be argued that this spiritual demand comprises the vital difference between his two early poetic collections and those that were to follow in the late 1960s and 1970s. While poems like 'The Thought-Fox', 'Hawk Roosting' and 'Pike' represent a subjectivity which is in balance with its own sense of self and is able to open up to the hot stink of fox, the sequence of collections that begin with *Wodwo* satirically (in *Crow*) or critically (in *Cave Birds*) expose an alienated being who fears such otherness more than anything.

As in the earlier two collections, the presence referred to as '[t]he maker of the sea' (*CP* 147) in *Wodwo* is not directly referred to as feminine. Rather, it is presented as an overwhelming nothingness which sleeps and recovers in 'Still Life', or is registered as a '[t]hickness of silence', pressing itself between 'us' in 'Ghost Crabs' (*CP* 149). But from *Crow* onwards, the energy represented by animals such as the fox, hawk and jaguar in the early collections, and by a nothingness in *Wodwo*, acquires a clear female (and feminine) shape. What is more, this female figure is set up against a male being that Hughes has referred to as an 'imbecile innocence' (*CP* 423) or as a 'mad-innocent' (*CP* 559). This being is saturated by a sense of guilt that originates in a failure to accept the challenge, which seems to amount to what Hughes, in his essay 'Myth and Education', refers to as the rejection of our 'inner world' for the sake of the singular vision of the rational 'objective' eye of consciousness (*WP* 144). As a result of this self-inflicted blindness, the inner world becomes 'elemental, chaotic, continually more primitive and beyond our control' and is eventually transformed into 'an animal crawling and decomposing in a hell' (*WP* 149).

The spiritual challenge that Hughes refers to is directly connected with the feminine entity, or 'goddess'. She is the other side of the fox, 'the unquenchable flame' that is both destructive and healing at the same time. In poems like 'Crow and Mama', 'Revenge Fable' and 'Song for a Phallus', Hughes describes the male self rejecting the challenge in the form of Crow physically attacking the mother in order to break free from what he perceives to be her suffocating interior. Whatever he does to escape, though, Crow still awakes 'Under his mother's buttocks' (*CP* 220). As signalled by 'Crow's Undersong' (*CP* 237), his struggle to ignore the primordial mother is both futile and harmful, and sends him on a trajectory towards utter self-destruction.

In the poetic discourses following the publication of *Crow,* the focus is increasingly placed on the male being's rejection of the goddess, and several critics have noted the similarity in the narrative of the volumes from this period. In *The Laughter of Foxes*, Keith Sagar declares that *Orghast, Prometheus on His Crag, Gaudete, Cave Birds* and *Adam and the Sacred Nine* are all parallel versions of the same story, which traces a process towards healing an inherently divided selfhood.[18] In *Re-Making Poetry: Ted Hughes and a New Critical Psychology*, Nick Bishop makes a similar assertion, saying that *Crow, Gaudete* and *Cave Birds* are narratives recounting a psychic drama directed towards realizing the repressed *anima* archetype.

In the subtitle for *Cave Birds: An Alchemical Cave Drama*, Hughes explicitly signals to the reader that he is exploring a Jungian process of individuation which, in Platonic terms, will lead the subject from a shadowy existence (*nigredo*) into illumination (*conjunctio*).[19] As signalled by the reference to Plato,[20] however, the project exceeds that of a Jungian psychological process. As Keith Sagar noted, Hughes blamed Socrates and Plato for the philosophical dualism that continues to plague Western civilization.[21] In a letter to Terry Gifford and Neil Roberts, he refers to *Cave Birds* as 'a critique of sorts of the Socratic abstraction and its consequences through Christianity to us' (*LTH* 395), whilst in a letter to Craig Raine he says that the sequence mediates the 'execution of the anti-feminist ironist, & his restitution as a child of Isis, living in the sun' (*LTH* 480).

Opening up to otherness

In both *Cave Birds* and *Gaudete* this process of execution and restitution is undertaken on a spiritual, psychological and physical level. Poems like 'At the top of my soul' (*CP* 358) from the *Gaudete* Epilogue poems and 'The Scream' (*CP* 419) from *Cave Birds* display a poetic subject who is closed off in his own solipsism. He sees the world as a 'thrilling weapon' (*CP* 358) and himself as riding 'the wheel of the galaxy' (*CP* 419), evoking Luce Irigaray's description of the affliction of the Western man, who 'in wanting to act like the universe in its most violent aspect, and not with it in its beauty and wisdom, [...] has forgotten this world, has forgotten himself'.[22] Through this affiliation, man has also forgotten his other, who is left behind in the cave, groaning incomprehensibly (*CP* 358).

The poetic subject's world-view is thwarted, however. In 'The Scream' (*CP* 419), a cry suddenly forces its way through the male being's throat, while the *Gaudete* poem 'In a world where all is temporary' presents us with a subject who has been discarded himself and left at the road's edge (*CP* 359–60). In other poems, like 'In These Fading Moments I Wanted to Say' and 'Something was Happening', the lack of relationship between self and other leads to the other's death. The way that both of these poems relate themselves structurally and thematically to W.H. Auden's 'Musée des Beaux Arts'[23] could seem to suggest that the lacking acknowledgement of the female other presents an *a priori* ethical problem. Hughes, however, chooses to emphasize that we are in a state of forgetfulness in terms of our responsibility for our neighbour. This stand is evocative of Emmanuel Lévinas, who, in *Of God Who Comes to Mind*, looks at the Hebrew *kamokhah* ('yourself') in the Christian imperative 'to love your neighbour as yourself' (Leviticus 19.18) and postulates that 'yourself'' refers to all the words that precede it, rendering the meaning of the commandment as 'Love your neighbour; all that is yourself; this work is yourself; this love is yourself.'[24] This definition of 'yourself' points directly to the problems that the male subject faces in these two poems. He is not only blind to the sufferings of the female other, but also to central aspects of selfhood. His consistent focus on shallow features such as 'the leather of my shoes' and the 'silence of the furniture' signals that the love that is necessary is lacking both in relation to 'you' and to 'self'. In the same way as the 'you' is hidden, covered by a numbing snow, or concealed by thin webby rain, the eye is also closed on the depths of his own being.

Interestingly, however, many of the early poems from this period signal that this lack is an affliction that can plague both male and female counterparts in a love relationship. The love poems in *Crow*, for instance, are based in an equivocal, aimless desire which represents an attempt to eradicate an internal void for both beings. In 'A Childish Prank', the bodies of Adam and Eve lie 'dully gaping, foolishly staring, inert' until Crow introduces the libido. The way in which Adam and Eve become aware of their own lack after Crow's intervention renders 'A Childish Prank' a parodic enactment of the Fall. Through the libido, the human being gains an awareness, a knowledge, that it is lacking, and calls upon the other part to 'join up quickly, quickly / Because O it was painful' (*CP* 215). Tragically, however, the desire that is installed with them only enhances the sense of lack.

This twisted, moronic underside of love is the only relation available in the universe of *Crow*, as is also signalled in poems like 'The

Lovepet' and 'Lovesong', where two lovers desperately feed on each other in order to survive psychologically and spiritually, making the love relationship a negative act of appropriation of the physical body of the other. This hunger is the only reason for the subject's interest, and, like Narcissus, the lovers are in a state of self-deception, hoping to lay hold on something that does not exist: 'Look away and what you love is nowhere' (*CP* 920). *Eros,* the enactment of the erotic, it seems, is solely an act of self-assertion, depending on the other only as an object that may be devoured and assimilated into the self.[25]

A new kind of lover's prayer

With the exception of the post-apocalyptic poem 'Notes for a Little Play', there is no gesture towards accepting otherness in *Crow.* In the Epilogue poems of *Gaudete,* however, there are attempts towards opening up, as Lumb re-emerges into the world from his abduction into the spirit world and starts composing 'hymns and psalms to a nameless female deity' (*CP* 1200). In *The Laughter of Foxes,* Keith Sagar holds that these poems represent an attempt to imagine what it would be like to accept the goddess in her totality, which amounts to accepting life unconditionally.[26] This is not an easy task. In poems like 'Who are you?', 'In a world where all is temporary', 'Trying to be a leaf' and 'A primrose petal's edge', the goddess comes as a violence, leaving the subject electrocuted or empty. In 'A primrose petal's edge', the male speaker, Lumb, attempts to overcome his fears by posing a question intended to name, and thereby place, the 'you' addressed by these poems: 'Who is this?' (*CP* 364). Here, the male speaker seeks an answer that fits in with what Joanny Moulin refers to as 'the total-itarian scientific spirit of the West',[27] which means that he intends to categorize her within the pattern of binary opposites, where one cannot conceive 'I' if there is no 'you', and where one of two opposites always assumes a role of dominance over the other. What he fails to understand is that the complexity of otherness explodes such a paradigm and that the expectation of an answer amounts to an act of closing oneself off in isolation.

In 'The dead man lies, marching here and there', however, the male subject comes close to recognition. Here, his stillness is shot to pieces by the imposition of an other, who arrives 'Invisible as a bullet' (*CP* 373). The arrival of the goddess transforms the body into a con-centrated effort of worship. Stanza four portrays how the powers of 'that moment' when the invisible bullet hits the man, cause an unceas-ing effort to praise the other: 'from that moment / He never stops trying to dance, trying to sing' (*CP* 374). Here, as in the negative love poems of *Crow*, the physicality of the body is emphasized. Unlike the commodification of the body in 'Lovesong' and 'The Lovepet', however, the body of the dead man now is transformed and becomes a vital part in generating the senseless joy and praise (*gaudete*) referred to in the title of the book as a whole.

What is brought to life seems to be what Hughes refers to as the 'inner world', embodying everything that the empirical gaze previously perceived as a void or an emptiness. The importance of the body in this process furthermore lies in its ability to be absolutely present, rendering it more alert to the question as an openness rather than as a way to confirm the concreteness of 'who'. In this poem, the body does not delay the moment in order to rationalize, but is able to let something happen. The movement of the dance and the poetry of the song seem to comprise true thought, that is, thought not as intellect alone, but what one might refer to as 'unconditional reason', which is the kind of inclusiveness that the chorus refers to towards the end of *The Oresteia*, where that which has been divided and in conflict is finally brought together to form a 'marriage', or a 'single mind, a whole mind'.[28]

Interestingly, there are suggestions of a similar recognition as early as *Crow*. The poem 'Notes for a Little Play' presents us with an apocalypse or a holocaust that strips being down to 'two survivors' who are subsequently married through 'a strange dance' that takes place 'in the darkness of the sun, // Without guest or God' (*CP* 212). Like the dead man, the two beings are fully present in the spatial movements of the dance, which is a celebration of their marriage. The suggestion of a performance implicit in the title's use of 'play' is, moreover, negated in the final verse's confirmation that they are dancing 'Without guest or God'. The two beings are there as pure, genderless presence, which can be seen as a gesture towards healing.

In his centenary tribute to T.S. Eliot, entitled 'The Poetic Self', Ted Hughes renders dancing a ritual through which transcendence might be achieved, as in shamanism, where the shaman dances to the beat of the drum in order to achieve ascension to the spirit world (*WP* 279). This is one of the reasons why Hughes views 'The Death of St Narcissus' as T.S. Eliot's most essential work. Here, he says, Eliot's poetry remythologizes itself as the voice of Eros who, through sufferings and death, finally becomes rejuvenated and unified (*WP* 290). In this context, the act of dancing becomes an alternative mode of communication where the subject proceeds to move, not according to rigid rationalities or culturally spawned dogmas, but in accordance with being itself.

This echoes the process presented in 'Notes for a Little Play', where the dance appears to comprise a true speech of love. To love means to form a relation to an other which is not characterized by subjugation, consumption or annihilation in terms of gender or binary oppositions. As such, it also involves sustaining a space in which both individuals are able to maintain their autonomy and alterity, and where the 'I' is not allowed to sacrifice 'otherness' for the sake of 'sameness'. It comprises what Sarah Coakley refers to as a 'mutual *ecstasis*' based on a fundamental respect for the other, an equality of exchange, and a recognition of the other's desire as distinct, as other.[29] As such, this poem emerges as the complete opposite to the devouring *eros* presented in poems like 'Lovesong', where the goal is to completely eradicate difference and incorporate the other within what is understood as the self.

Bodies that matter: The reciprocal reflection of the bride and groom

While 'Notes for a Little Play' comprises a hopeful gesture towards an encounter, however, the apocalyptic setting within which this wedding takes place taints it with a dystopic atmosphere, signalling that within the universe of *Crow,* hope can only emerge as a black sun or a flickering of light, in the form of a 'note'.

In terms of the relationship between the male and female counterparts, it is not until *Cave Birds* that a true hope emerges. Interestingly, Neil Roberts has characterized *Cave Birds* as Hughes's 'only fully integrated narrative sequence'.[30] While Roberts sees *Crow* as a 'loose assemblage in which poems could easily be differently ordered' and with a 'narrative background that could not be construed from the poems', *Cave Birds* takes 'the reader through the stages of a story'.[31] Here, Roberts points to an essential difference, not only between *Cave Birds* and *Crow*, but also between *Cave Birds* and sequences such as *Wodwo* and *Gaudete*. While the latter texts are characterized by repetitive and concurrent structures of regeneration, suspended moments and a prevalence of cyclical time, *Cave Birds* presents us with a trajectory that continuously brings the male subject to new insights, the greatest of which is openness.

In several letters to Keith Sagar, Hughes emphasizes an aversion against the sequence, saying 'there's a funny atmosphere about them that I really dislike' (*PC* 61). He was more favourably inclined towards the group of poems that have 'a more human progress', however, that functioned as counterpoints to those featuring bird-spirits (*PC* 50).

Among Hughes's favourite poems in this sequence are 'His Legs Ran About' and 'Bride and Groom Lie Hidden for Three Days' (*LTH* 61).

The reason for Hughes's preference for the former could lie in the way that this poem fulfils a process that goes all the way back to early *Crow*. The title, suggesting that the legs are somehow severed from the rest of the body and act of their own accord, echoes 'Crow Wakes' (*CP* 258), where the consciousness tries to disentangle itself from the rest of the body and is consequently hunted down by the various parts from which the 'I' feels completely alienated. Here, however, the male being is tripped over by the body of an other, and is caught in 'a single tangle' (*CP* 436). This 'single tangle' of legs suggests a simultaneous sense of autonomy and unity, an indication which is developed in the following lines where his arms feel their way 'through dark rooms' until finally his hands catch her hands and become 'enwoven'. Then the chest meets the breast and the navel fits over the other navel 'Like a mirror face down flat on a mirror'. Here, there is no need to eradicate the other for the sake of unity. Instead, the pecular process is abolished by the fulfilment of the touch. What we see in this poem is a community of bodies which are in proximity, rather than in a process towards amalgamation. It is a kind of proximity that was suggested as early as *Wodwo*, through the question 'Where are you heading?' and the attendant answer that 'Everything is already here' (*CP* 177). The truthfulness in this has, however, not entered the subject's being until the very point when his running is intercepted by the other. The lip, throat, belly, chest, all push towards the limit where it weighs upon, and is weighed upon by, the other, having nothing to deliver, nothing to deliberate, beyond a letting be.

The touch and the weight of the other body seem to make room for difference, as arms, navels and breasts traverse space in order to expose themselves. As suggested in the final verses of the poem, moreover, the peace and truth that descend on the being do not signal stasis, but a new-found ability to explore. The 'vast astonishment' of the final verse points to a transformed human perception of the world, characterized by openness and enthusiasm.

This insight is taken even further in 'Bride and Groom Lie Hidden for Three Days' which, in Jungian terms, represents *conjunctio*, that is, the symbolic marriage between self and other, reconciling the feminine and masculine elements. The poem is not merely a celebration of a perfected process of Jungian individuation, however. The way in which the two beings remain autonomous throughout the process confirms an understanding of them as incommensurable entities. In this, it is also important to note the spiritual context in which this encounter takes place. When faced with the female other's difference, the male being is also faced with the difference of the goddess. What takes place resembles what Heidegger refers to as reciprocal reflection, that is, a mutual presence where '[o]ne comes over to the other, one arrives in the other'.[32]

This reciprocity is also laid out in the mythical foundation of the poem, where Crow carries the hag across the river. In a letter to Keith Sagar, Hughes specifically identifies the poem as an answer to the question 'Who gives most, him or her?', which was put 'provisionally in the Cave-bird sequence' (PC 49). Seen thus, the poem from the very outset inscribes a radical transformation in the relationship between the male/female and masculine/feminine elements, from one demanding sacrifice to one underpinned by a radical togetherness. While an early poem of transformation like 'Crow's Song of Himself' is structured as a witches' duel, placing it in the negative setting of a contest, the bride and groom of this poem complement each other in their use of the imagination to bring each other to fulfilment. In a reflection of their own history in the sequence as such, the two beings employ objects that have been discarded as 'rubbish', or that have gone unnoticed, and award them with new life. While 'she' finds his eyes 'Among some rubble', 'he' pulls her skin 'down out of the air' (CP 437–8). These acts of creation are associated with ecology, ingenuity and magic, as suggested in epithets such as 'assemble', 'perfect', 'order', 'puzzle', 'fashion', 'fittings'. Seen thus, the poem attempts a reinvention of technology, transcending the techno-scientific materialism of 'Crow's Account of St George' and the narcissism of 'Lovesong', where the other is either made into a monster, or objectified in order to claim mastery. The focus is not placed on the subject, but on the process itself. The joy that the beings take in each other's inventiveness is indicated in the verses describing how they continuously test 'each new thing at each new step' (CP 438).

Restoring the rift

'Bride and Groom Lie Hidden for Three Days' is not only the apex of *Cave Birds,* but also marks the fulfilment of the period of suffering that was inaugurated with the challenge, or call, received in *Wodwo*. In the sense that this poem comprises an acceptance of the call, its quest leads to the uncovering of a grail which is a continuous movement of reaching out to and returning from the sun. The way in which the two beings keep taking each other to the sun signals the irrevocable postponement of meaning and conclusion, at the same time as the process towards the sun is a celebration of the imagination as a site in which meaning 'came on, came on, and kept on coming' in a past that is also present and future (*CP* 663). Although this process could be seen to keep up the framework of binaries in the sense that the vision of fulfilment remains underpinned by a duality, the continued focus on 'gathering' in 'Bride and Groom Lie Hidden for Three Days', as well as the 'vast astonishment' in 'His Legs Ran About', emphasizes the heterogeneous and dynamic nature of the process.[33] The creation of the one leads into the creation of the other as a process that never reaches its conclusion, in the same manner as the poetic utterance always gives rise to renewed speech. We can also see this in the way that 'Bride and Groom Lie Hidden for Three Days' is not the final poem of *Cave Birds*. The epigrammatical poem 'Finale' both ends and opens the sequence, by overthrowing everything that has been achieved.

What we see here, then, is a poetry that never stops questioning, deepening and challenging the ways in which we think about and interact with ourselves, each other and the world of other around us, complicated as it is by our experiences and notions of masculinity and femininity, expressed inevitably in our culturally gendered language. The emphasis on regeneration and touch in poems like 'Dead man lies, marching here and there', 'His Legs Ran About' and 'Bride and Groom Lie Hidden for Three Days' almost conjures the experience of a child before it is introduced to language, at the same time as they are poems of healing: of restoring the rift between self and other, feminine and masculine, masculine and feminine, seen from a multitude of perspectives. Throughout his life, Hughes continuously strove towards a poetry which would speak with the hot stink of fox rather than to 'chill into syntax' (*CP* 357), creating a clearing, or a space, which would allow for an open encounter between a self and an other and simply let them engage. This is an achievement that will outlive the dualities and divisiveness of the culture in which it was produced.

Notes

1. Robin Morgan, *Monster: Poems* (New York: Vintage, 1972): 76.
2. See Tracy Brain, 'Hughes and Feminism', in Terry Gifford (ed.), *The Cambridge Companion to Ted Hughes* (Cambridge: Cambridge University Press, 2011): 94–106.
3. Nathalie Anderson, 'Ted Hughes and the Challenge of Gender', in Keith Sagar (ed.), *The Challenge of Ted Hughes* (London: Macmillan, 1994): 91 and Brain, 'Hughes and Feminism'.

4. Paul Bentley, *The Poetry of Ted Hughes: Language, Illusion & Beyond* (London and New York: Longman, 1998): 97.

5. Joanny Moulin, 'The Problem of Biography', in Gifford (ed.), *Cambridge Companion to Ted Hughes*: 21.

6. In Robert Graves's book *The White Goddess* (London: Faber & Faber, 1961) the title refers to a figure who has a strong resemblance to the archetypical Mother, or Moon-goddess or Muse, which occurs in most of the world's mythological heritage, whereas the Jungian concept of the *anima* can be defined as the feminine aspects of the male (and female) unconscious. For Jung, a balance between the masculine and feminine aspects of self is the key to harmonious being.

7. Demaris S. Wehr, *Jung and Feminism: Liberating Archetypes* (London: Routledge, 1988): 104.

8. Bentley, *Poetry of Ted Hughes*: 95.

9. Neil Roberts, *Ted Hughes: A Literary Life* (Basingstoke: Palgrave Macmillan, 2006): 99.

10. Moulin, 'Problem of Biography': 24.

11. *Ibid.*: 199.

12. *Ibid.*: 201.

13. *Ibid.*: 199.

14. *Ibid.*

15. *Ibid.*: 197.

16. *Ibid.*

17. Keith Sagar, *The Laughter of Foxes*, 2nd edn (Liverpool: Liverpool University Press, 2006): 40.

18. *Ibid.*: 129. Hughes describes them as overlapping in a letter to Sagar (*PC* 57).

19. Jung employed alchemy as a symbolic representation of the individuation process, through which the conscious and unconscious aspects of self finally become united.

20. The 'cave' in the title is a reference to Plato's allegory of the cave, as presented in *The Republic*. This is a mythical narrative through which Plato explains that what we see as reality is, in fact, only shadows on a wall. He also describes the challenges facing someone with true knowledge. While Hughes rejects the kind of philosophy that Plato represents, he seems to sympathize with Plato's vision in the allegory of the cave, in terms of the difficulties we have with accepting true knowledge. This can also be seen in the first poem of the sequence, 'The Scream', where Hughes's subject's imperfect consciousness only allows him to take in 'the sun on the wall' (*CP* 419), that is, shadows rather than the true form of reality.

21. Keith Sagar, 'Ted Hughes and the Classics', in *Ted Hughes and the Classics*, ed. Roger Rees (Oxford: Oxford University Press, 2009): 5–6.

22. Luce Irigaray, *To Be Two* (London: Routledge, 1991): 71.

23. Like Auden's poem, 'In These Fading Moments' is divided into two parts, reflecting the theme of the moral challenge that the split between self and other represents. In contrast to Auden's poem, as well as Peter

Brueghel's painting *Landscape with the Falling Icarus*, however, Hughes's subject does not go about his business, but appears devastated at the sight of the distant shape of Icarus falling into the ocean. While Auden presents the 'human position' as an ontological fact, Hughes emphasizes the moral sin in failing to take heed of one's immediate neighbour.

24. Emmanuel Levinas, *Of God Who Comes to Mind*, trans. Bettina Bergo (Stanford, CA: Stanford University Press, 1998): 91.

25. The theologican Karl Barth defines *eros* as a rapacious need, which is 'hungry and demands the food that the other seems to hold out'. This hunger is the only reason for its interest in the other, and Barth compares the lover to the wolf who swallows and consumes both Red Riding Hood and her grandmother. While union with the beloved is the overarching goal, the result of such a union would be that the object of love is 'taken to himself' so that 'even in the event he alone remains'. Karl Barth, *Church Dogmatics IV.2: The Doctrine of Reconciliation*, trans. G.W. Bromiley (Edinburgh: T. & T. Clark, 1958): 734.

26. Sagar, *Laughter of Foxes*: 144.

27. Moulin, 'Problem of Biography': 24.

28. Ted Hughes, *The Oresteia: A New Translation by Ted Hughes* (London: Faber & Faber, 1999): 198.

29. Sarah Coakley, 'Living into the Mystery of the Holy Trinity: Trinity, Prayer, and Sexuality', *Anglican Theological Review*, 80(2) (1998): 231.

30. Roberts, *Ted Hughes*: 115.

31. *Ibid*.

32. Martin Heidegger, *Identity and Difference*, trans. Joan Stambaugh (Chicago: Chicago University Press, 2002): 69.

33. The concept of 'gathering' is here used in a Heideggerean sense, meaning that it refers to an act of re-collecting that which the Cartesian ego fails to take into account. See Martin Heidegger, 'What Calls for Thinking?', in *Basic Writings: Revised and Expanded Edition*, ed. David Farrell Krell (London: Routledge, 1993): 365–92.

Part II
Readings through the
Frames of Theory

7

Structuralist and Poststructuralist Readings

Gillian Groszewski

Structuralism and poststructuralism

The structuralist method of textual interpretation that emerged in the 1950s and 1960s advocated an objective, quasi-scientific way of reading texts. Heavily influenced by French theorists in the fields of linguistics and philosophy, structuralists concentrated on the closed system of oppositions and parallels contained within a text that revealed a comfortable 'solution' for, or interpretation of, that text. In the wake of modernist experimentations with narrative and language, and a mid-century existentialist trend in French philosophy, poststructuralism later questioned these supposedly stable structuralist interpretations, exploring instead the instability of language, texts and the oppositions that could be invoked to interpret a text. This chapter provides a brief introduction to these movements followed by structuralist and poststructuralist readings of some of Ted Hughes's poems. Hughes's work has frequently been interpreted with reference to contexts such as his biography or his geographical location at the time of writing. During his lifetime, critics often wrote to Hughes to ask for explanations of certain lines from his poems that they felt they could not interpret without further information. Although always generous in answering these questions, Hughes also emphasized the importance of a text-based approach to interpreting writing that was similar in approach to that of the structuralist and poststructuralist methods. A structuralist or poststructuralist approach to interpreting Hughes's work is, in fact, a novel one because it does not depend on familiar contexts that are regularly used to explain his texts. A structuralist or poststructuralist method also works well as a strategy for interpreting Hughes's frequent, often complex, use of oppositions or parallels to establish narratives within his poetry. A structuralist reader may choose to schematize scientifically the oppositions or parallels within a poem by Hughes in order to consider systematically the symbolic story that is being told. A poststructuralist will consider the ways in which Hughes's use of opposing or parallel words or images perform inter-actively or suggestively in relation to one another in order to create meaning within a poem or to destabilize a particular meaning that appears to be suggested by a poem.

Structuralism is grounded in the linguistic work of Ferdinand de Saussure, particularly his *Course in General Linguistics* (1916), a post-humously published book based on his lectures at the University of Geneva. Before Saussure, linguists only considered the historical derivation of languages and their influences on each other. Seeking to move away from this historical approach, and to define language as a self-contained, objective, scientific system, Saussure claimed that 'linguistic structure seems to be the one thing that is independently definable and provides something our minds can satisfactorily grasp'.[1] His ideas had an enormous influence on linguistic and literary studies in the twentieth century.

Saussure began by explaining that each linguistic sign has two parts, a 'signified', which designates the concept of the thing that is being described, and a 'signifier', which is 'the hearer's psychological impression of a sound'.[2] Saussure also asserted that there were two main principles of linguistics. The first was that signs are arbitrary. That is, there is no 'natural connection' between a word and the thing represented by the word.[3] For example, there is no reason why the word 'sister' should represent a female sibling or the word 'chair' should describe an object with a seat, back and legs. Saussure illustrated this idea by noting that there is a different word for 'ox' in each language.[4] Saussure's second principle stated that words take their place in a chain of differential meaning. For example: stool chair armchair throne. Each word in the chain takes on meaning because of its relation to the word placed before and after it. What was happening *between* words in the chain was not explored by Saussure but would later be considered by French philosopher Jacques Derrida to form the basis of deconstruction. Importantly, Saussure also emphasized the relationship between *langue* and *parole*. *Langue* represented all of the rules and conventions of a language while *parole* denoted a specific instance of language use.[5] In order to understand a sentence in German (*parole*), for example, we must understand German grammar and all its conventions (*langue*).

Taking Saussure's work as its model, structuralism emerged in 1950s France in the work of literary theorist Roland Barthes and anthropologist Claude Lévi-Strauss, who both explored the history and sign-systems of narratives. Structuralism advocates a mode of analysis that considers the oppositions and parallels – man and woman, good and bad, night and day, for example – in a work. In doing so, structuralists suggest a system that explains the work. However, structuralism can be criticized for its inability to work *outside* the system which it attempts to analyse. In its attempts at objectivity and its refusal to consider elements outside the text, structuralism tends to ignore any social dimension that is implicit in the writing, or interpretation, of a work. By suggesting that a text contains the oppositions of man and woman and good and bad, for example, one structuralist reader might align the man with good and the woman with bad, while a different structuralist reader could suggest the converse. In *Image-Music-Text* (1977), Barthes began to acknowledge that many different meanings could be suggested by different readers, based on the same set of oppositions and parallels that depended on the position adopted by each reader:

> The variation in meanings is not [...] anarchic; it depends on the different kinds of knowledge – practical, national, cultural, aesthetic – invested in the image [...]. It is as though the image presented itself to the reading of several different people who can perfectly well co-exist in a single individual.[6]

It is the reader's sociocultural background (an element outside the text) that determines the hierarchy by which the parallels or oppositions in a text may be identified and interpreted. The text itself, however, suggests multiple possible interpretations based on limited sets of oppositions or parallels. The implication that there is a clear system and hierarchy of signs (which was actually the result of a social evaluation on the part of the reader) within structuralist criticism was later explored and criticized by Derrida and Barthes, forming the basis for deconstruction.

The deconstructionist approach to interpreting texts was initiated by Derrida in the mid-1960s. In a lecture given at Johns Hopkins University in 1966 entitled 'Structure, Sign and Play in the Discourse of the Human Sciences', Derrida outlined his objections to Saussure's definition of writing as subsequent, and subservient to (spoken) language and considered the tensions in the structuralist approach that could be found in the writings of Lévi-Strauss. Derrida also objected to the idea that there was a *certain* 'origin' of language, a claim that he believed was implicit in Saussure's theory.[7] These ideas were elaborated in three books on deconstruction published by Derrida in 1967: *Writing and Difference, Speech and Phenomena* and *Of Grammatology*. In *Of Grammatology*, Derrida used the work of Lévi-Strauss and Jean-Jacques Rousseau to provide examples of two writers who at times appeared to acknowledge the limitations of Saussure's concept of the linguistic system, but who chose, nonetheless, to continue working *within* it. Acknowledging these problems, while also reasserting the importance of writing to language formation, Derrida's pivotal deconstructionist statement that 'there is nothing outside the text' demonstrated his belief that examining the text itself, rather than suggesting structures that might be used to explain it, reveals everything about it.[8]

Defining his deconstructionist approach, Derrida coined the term *différance* and encouraged the focus on what he called 'play' within texts. Derrida's use of the term *différance* came about through his consideration of the French verb 'to differ', which can mean both 'to differ' and 'to defer'.[9] Invoking Saussure, who claimed that 'in language there are only differences *without positive terms*',[10] Derrida suggested *différance* as belonging 'neither to the voice nor to writing in the ordinary sense, and it takes place [...] *between* speech and writing'.[11] If Saussure's definition posited that a sign took its meaning from 'the other signs that surround it', then Derrida emphasized the importance of what was happening *between* each sign:

> Every concept is necessarily and essentially inscribed in a chain or a system, within which it refers to another and to other concepts, by the systematic play of differences. Such a play, then – *différance* – is no longer simply a concept, but the possibility of conceptuality, of the conceptual system and process in general.[12]

In our attempts to define the meaning of any word, we always find ourselves in an in-between space in which we are remembering the previous word and waiting on the next word in the chain. This process is what led Derrida to include the idea of deferral in *différance*. Derrida also related the idea of *différance* to Freud's explanation of the 'facilitation' between 'conscious and unconscious'.[13] With this idea in mind, examining *différance* within a text reveals to us many aspects of the text which may not be overtly explored by the author – aspects which are being unconsciously suggested. This means that a deconstructionist approach often involves considering what a text *does not explicitly say*. The reader is required to look *behind* what the text does say to uncover latent meanings and to question how (and why) these latent meanings may undermine, or interact with, more obvious explanations of a text.

Derrida's method of deconstruction also departed from structuralism in his interrogation of the system of oppositions that formed the basis of the structuralist approach. Derrida claimed that structuralists 'neutralized' the 'binary oppositions' that they used to interpret a text.[14] Structuralists could take for granted the idea that, in the opposition between night and day, for example, day takes precedence over night without questioning why this is so and ignoring the fact that there might be instances when day does not take precedence in this opposition. In a poem about aerial bombardment in the Second World War, for instance, night would take precedence over day in the day/night opposition as the darkness of night allows for stealth and concealment. According to Derrida, it is important to recognize that

> in a classical philosophical opposition we are not dealing with the peaceful coexistence of a *vis-à-vis*, but rather with a violent hierarchy. One of the two terms governs the other (axiologically, logically, etc.), or has the upper hand. To deconstruct the opposition, first of all, is to overturn the hierarchy at a given moment. To overlook this phase of overturning is to forget the conflictual and subordinating structure of opposition.[15]

Analysis of the 'violent hierarchy' that exists within the 'binary oppositions' of man/woman or owner/slave formed the basis for the feminist and postcolonialist versions of deconstruction that developed from Derrida's ideas. In one of his *Crow* poems, 'Apple Tragedy', Hughes deconstructs conventional, authoritative oppositions and parallels by rewriting the story of the fall of man in the Garden of Eden. In doing so, he completely inverts established parallels between God and goodness and the serpent with evil. In Hughes's version, it is God who tempts the serpent into persuading Adam and Eve to partake of the apple which leads to the fall of man. Although all of the same structures that we associate with this story are in place – good and evil, God and the Devil, Adam and Eve – in 'Apple Tragedy', Hughes undermines their established relationship to one another to tell a very different story in which it is God who introduces evil into the world.

Around the same time that Derrida was publishing his deconstructionist response to Saussure, Roland Barthes was revising his early structuralism and, in 1968, published his essay 'The Death of the Author'. In line with the structuralist approach, Barthes objected to the tendency of interpreters to explain a text by considering it as a product of its author's intentions or biography, noting that

> The explanation of a work is always sought in the man or woman who produced it, as if it were always in the end, through the more or less transparent allegory of the fiction, the voice of a single person, the *author* 'confiding' in us.[16]

Barthes argued that this approach was misguided because 'to give a text an Author is to impose a limit on that text, to furnish it with a final signified, to close the writing'.[17] He claimed that if the meaning of a text was to be found in its author then interpreting a text would really be no different from looking it up in a dictionary. In order to discover the meaning of the text, all we would have to do would be to 'look up' corresponding details about the author or the author's intentions. However, departing from the structuralist approach, which suggested a closed system and, therefore, a final meaning, Barthes argued that there is no 'ultimate meaning' to a text because 'writing ceaselessly posits meaning'.[18] Finally, Barthes dramatically called for the 'death of the author', that is, an end to the interpretation of texts through the consideration of authorial intent, position and contexts, and suggested instead that meaning was actually created by the *reader*. For Barthes, the 'birth of the reader must be at the cost of the death of the author'.[19] Here, again, Barthes's ideas differed from the structuralist approach which did not consider the effects of social influences on the interpretation (or interpreter) of texts. According to Barthes, the reader was the 'one place where [the] multiplicity' of writing was concentrated and the 'space on which all the quotations that make up a writing are inscribed without any of them being lost'.[20]

As pointed out in the Introduction, in a letter to Keith Sagar, Hughes himself similarly emphasized the importance of the reader in the poetic process, stating that 'poems belong to readers – just as houses belong to those who live in them [and] not to the builders' (*PC* 43). Like Barthes, Hughes acknowledged that poems had a structure (the house) that could be interpreted without reference to their author (the builder), but that the richness and variety of interpretations of the poem depended on the reader (the inhabitant of the house). The deconstructionist approach sought to focus the search for literary meaning on the text itself while suggesting the reader as the place where infinite meanings were made possible. This allowed for a multiplicity of meanings rather than accepting that there could be a definitive authoritative meaning or some 'final signified' for any text.

This approach differed considerably from the structuralist attempt to situate texts definitively within various structures which could then deliver authoritative symbolic meanings.

According to James D. Marshall, 'there is little caught by the term "poststructuralism" other than a widely differing, diverse and multi-faceted group of theses and thinkers'.[21] The term covers the theories of writers such as Jacques Derrida, Jean Baudrillard, Roland Barthes, Jacques Lacan, Michel Foucault, Gilles Deleuze, Luce Irigaray and Julia Kristeva, among others. Each of these theorists used a variant of deconstruction to emphasize a particular approach to interpreting texts. For example, Lacan is associated with psychoanalytical struc-turalism and deconstruction, while Irigaray and Kristeva advocated a feminist deconstructionist approach.[22] Often, deconstruction is subsumed within the category of poststructuralism, as it will be within this chapter. However, the label poststructuralism is also used more specifically to denote the focus on *discourse* in deconstruction emphasized by Foucault and suggested by Derrida in his analysis of the 'violent hierarchies' that exist in 'binary oppositions'.[23]

Terry Eagleton has proposed that the major distinction between structuralism and poststructuralism lies in the notion that structural-ism impersonally considers '"Language" [as] speech or writing viewed "objectively", as a chain of signs without a subject', whereas post-structuralism goes some way to acknowledging subjectivity and the social dimension of textual interpretation by considering '"Discourse" [which] means language grasped as *utterance*, as involving speaking and writing subjects and therefore also, at least potentially, readers or listeners'.[24] Behind the discourse of history, for example, there are complex power structures which can be deconstructed to gain a better understanding of why they exist, how they function and how they affect individuals.[25] Edward Said's poststructuralist demystification of the structures of colonial representation in his important postcolonial text *Orientalism* (1978) has been suggested by Christopher Norris as an excellent example of the significance of discourse to this approach.[26]

Defining each of the structuralisms is complicated by the move-ment of many of these theorists towards more nuanced structuralist or poststructuralist approaches during their careers. Although Barthes, for example, began his critical career as a structuralist, he later came to be classified among the poststructuralists following the publication of 'The Death of the Author'. Lacan was also initially associated with psychoanalytic structuralism but later adopted a more broadly decon-structionist approach. Similarly, Foucault never referred to himself as a poststructuralist but has become synonymous with that movement.

Over the years, structuralists and poststructuralists reacted to one another and developed their ideas accordingly, which has led to some fluidity in the boundaries of each of the structuralisms. This revisionism perhaps best explains the need for the term poststructuralism.

A structuralist reading: 'A Motorbike'

Structuralists consider the oppositions, parallels and equivalences within a work and suggest a system, based on these structures, which explains or interprets the text. Hughes himself undertook a vast structuralist project with his most extensive piece of prose *Shakespeare and the Goddess of Complete Being* (1992). In this book, Hughes suggested that all of Shakespeare's plays after *Hamlet* could be explained by a 'Tragic Equation' (*SGCB* 1). Hughes's 'equation' depended heavily on oppositions that he observed in Shakespeare's long poems *Venus and Adonis* and *The Rape of Lucrece*. Hughes read the characters of Venus, Adonis, Lucrece and Tarquin as representing 'four poles of energy' or 'phases in a narrative cycle' (*ACSV* 190). This cycle, Hughes believed, was apparent in all of Shakespeare's plays after *Hamlet*. It is unsurprising that Hughes's formulaic interpretation of Shakespeare's plays suggested a structuralist system. Although he always avoided conventional literary criticism, Hughes had studied Anthropology at Cambridge University in the mid-1950s and was profoundly interested in the shared structures that could be observed in vastly different societies that Lévi-Strauss had been studying and writing about from the 1940s. From early poems such as 'The Jaguar' and 'The Thought-Fox' to a later work like *Crow*, Hughes's own work frequently depended upon oppositions, equivalences and modes of storytelling that depicted deep societal structures, such as folklore and mythology, to establish narratives.

A poem by Hughes that lends itself well to a structuralist reading is 'A Motorbike' from *Moortown* (1979). Throughout this poem, Hughes uses a series of oppositions and equivalences to suggest that the dull experience of everyday life following participation in a war compares unfavourably to the more exciting experience of wartime uncertainty. This interpretation is suggested by structural aspects of the poem such as the balance between images in particular lines, Hughes's use of equivalent or contrasting words, and opposing invocations of sound and silence.

The image of the motorbike is central to the meaning of this poem and provides its title. Through the opening description of the motorbike several important oppositions and associations, which will be sustained and developed throughout the poem, are set up by Hughes. 'Cramped in rust, under washing' and owned by a family, the motor-bike is associated with domesticity, which is later associated in the poem with an anti-climactic return from the war to everyday life and is contrasted with work outside the home and exciting participation in the war abroad (*CP* 547). Indeed, the motorbike is being stifled by domesticity as it is forgotten beneath a pile of laundry. In its mechan-ical simplicity, the motorbike is compared with the sophisticated tech-nical superiority of the bombs and weapons of the war mentioned in the opening stanza. In these lines, the reader's attention is also drawn to an important, sustained opposition within the poem – that between sound and silence. Although the motorbike sits silent and smothered by domesticity in this first stanza, it was once associated with 'thunder, flight, disruption'. The contrast between sound and silence within this poem is invoked consistently to compare the quiet boredom of everyday life with the noisy excitement of life at war.

The second stanza, which is concerned with the abrupt change in the pace of life for former soldiers following the war, again invokes the opposition between sound and silence when we are told that 'the explosions stopped'. Continuing to develop many of the associations that were established in the opening of the poem, in the second stanza of 'A Motorbike', Hughes also introduces some new oppositions and parallels. The fate of the soldiers who returned home following the end of the war is that 'Peace took them all prisoner'. Hughes creates a parallel between the words 'peace' and 'prisoner', two terms that are normally juxtaposed with one another to describe circumstances at the end of a war that will allow conflict to be resolved. Here, how-ever, he uses this parallel to describe the manner in which the former soldiers are imprisoned by the banality of the peace that ensues as they go back to their ordinary, eventless lives. For them, a new con-flict begins as they resist the return to everyday life following the war. The men are also aligned with animals in this stanza when they are described as being 'herded into their home towns'. This image of passivity continues the parallel with sleepy domesticity that was asso-ciated with the family-owned motorbike in the first stanza.

The third stanza of 'A Motorbike' begins with a list of parallels that explain that the peacetime in which the former soldiers are now living is just as tortuous as their worst wartime experiences. The bus ride to work is compared to a 'labour truck' and the boss is compared to an SS commander. It could be argued that Hughes's use of vocabulary specific to the Second World War here requires some historical contextualization which would go against a structuralist interpretation by moving outside the poem. However, even if we do not know the meaning of 'S. S.' in the second stanza, we can go some way to inferring its meaning through the parallel which is established in the previous line between the bus and the labour truck. If the bus is 'as bad as' the labour truck, we can understand that the 'S. S' represents something bad that is associated with the war. Similarly, in the opening stanza, we don't have to know exactly what 'Brens' and 'Bazookas' are. Through Hughes's use of the word 'Bombs' as a parallel, we can infer that these are weapons without needing a more precise historical context. Hughes continues his list of parallels in this stanza by comparing the 'shallowness' of the shops to that of the beer in his description of the lifelessness of the town. Throughout this stanza, Hughes makes repeated use of sibilant 's' sounds to convey the tortuous quiet of the town in peacetime which is in contrast to the noisy explosions that accompanied the war.

In the next stanza, Hughes introduces the man who buys the family's motorbike and continues the sustained opposition between silence and sound by describing him as a 'quiet young man'. The quiet-ness associated with this man suggests that he is one of the returned soldiers who have been taken captive by peace following the war. Once he gets the motorbike going, 'it erupted'. The word 'erupted' importantly recalls the word 'disruption' that was associated with the motorbike in the first stanza and also suggests an abrupt noise. The young man has jerked the motorbike out of its 'sleep' (another word that suggests silence) and into 'life', which has been associated with noise throughout the poem. Similarly, the young man's own lethargy has been broken. This stanza contains all of the sustained parallels and oppositions within the poem so far.

'A Motorbike' concludes with the description of the young man's apparent suicide as he drives the motorbike 'Into a telegraph pole / On the long straight west of Swinton'. The word 'escaped', used to describe the man's death, recalls the earlier description of the returned soldiers as 'prisoners' and resolves the opposition of prisoner and peace that has been suggested throughout the poem. The poem also ends by describing the victory of masculine virility and activity over the domestic passivity that has been portrayed. On their return to home and domesticity, the soldiers are emasculated and the 'shrunk-back war ached in their testicles'. By contrast, the young man vio-lently recovers his masculinity and virility by crashing into the phallic symbol of the telegraph pole on the 'long straight'.

A historicist reading that considers the context of the war to which 'A Motorbike' refers might seem like the most appropriate way in which to read this poem due to overt references in the poem to items and personnel directly associated with the Second World War. However, a structuralist approach, which does not refer to any social or historical context for the poem, yields a perfectly comprehensive interpretation that raises complex questions about society, history, politics and gender roles. Without using any particular context, an ambiguous narrative of a tragically curtailed redeemed masculinity and a sustained consideration of the psychological effects on soldiers of participation in, and return from, war is suggested by a structuralist reading of 'A Motorbike'.

A poststructuralist reading: 'Her Husband'

In an interview for *The Paris Review* in 1995, Hughes claimed that 'Within the poem [...] is all the evidence you need for explaining how the poem came to be and why it is as it is. [...] [E]very poem that works is like a metaphor of the whole mind writing, the solution of all the oppositions and imbalances going on at that time.'[27] Hughes's submission that it is best to approach a poem as the written record of all the 'oppositions and imbalances' taking place in the mind of the writer at the time of composition suggests Derrida's concept of *différance* and the deconstructionist methods of textual interpretation which concentrate on what is happening *between* words, ideas and oppositions in a text. Like Derrida, Hughes sees more than oppositions that suggest a clear structure or hierarchy. Rather, Hughes acknowledges that imbalances within a poem must also be considered as part of its 'solution'. That Hughes saw the poem itself as yielding the 'solution' to its meaning also corresponds with Derrida's statement that 'there is nothing outside the text'. Despite Hughes's oft-stated reluctance to engage with literary criticism, the similarities suggested here between Hughes's thinking on poetry and Derrida's formalized critical theories seem like a neat coincidence. However, it is important to remember that both Hughes's creative thinking and Derrida's critical thinking had both been profoundly influenced by the work of Lévi-Strauss and other anthropologists. Their corresponding ideas may be considered to be the logical result of their engagement with Lévi-Strauss's writings.

A poem by Hughes which can be read using a deconstructionist approach is 'Her Husband' from *Wodwo* (1967). This poem describes the volatile dynamics of a failing relationship between a husband and wife. In the poem, both partners express their annoyance with one another and their wish to assert their own authority through subversive actions which are presented as being more powerful than words. In the opening stanza, the husband, a miner, returns home covered in coal dust and deliberately soils the sink and towels that he knows his wife will have to clean in order that she will learn the 'stubborn character of money' (*CP* 148). In the third stanza, however, the wife has her revenge when she serves her husband 'fried, woody chips, kept warm two hours in the oven' (*ibid.*). Although Hughes does not polemically debate the problems associated with stereotypical gender roles in this poem, throughout 'Her Husband' he is continually exploring this theme. Both partners are reacting against the roles that they have been assigned through marriage – the husband must provide financial stability, while the wife's obligation is to run a comfortable and efficient household. Just as the couple portrayed in the poem find it easier to express their dissatisfaction through their actions rather than by using words, it is through what it does *not* say that this poem questions the roles conventionally assigned to men and women when they become husband and wife.

Hughes begins to undermine the customary dominance of the male in the male/female binary through his use of the title 'Her Husband'. Although appearing to suggest that it is the husband who is the centre of this poem, the possessive pronoun 'her' in this provocative title demonstrates that wife and husband are inextricably linked throughout the poem. The possessive pronoun could be referring to the domestic burden which the wife associates with her husband, or it could alternatively suggest the wife's possession, or domination, of her husband. The play between the words in this title and between the subversive, undermining actions of the husband and wife throughout this poem allow the reader to infer several meanings which can never certainly assign the power of domination or control to either partner in the marriage. It is the power struggle between husband and wife that motivates everything in this poem. Suggestively titling the poem in this way, Hughes demonstrates that neither party is clearly entitled to be regarded as dominant in this relationship.

'Her Husband' is a poem that depicts binary opposites, for example, husband/wife, man/woman and industrial/domestic. As Derrida suggested, overturning the seemingly clear relationship between binary opposites in a text is an important strategy in deconstructionist readings as it can reveal preconceived assumptions about that relationship that do not always hold true. In 'Her Husband', the husband is associated with manual labour while the wife is associated with the opposite – domestic work. It is clear, however, that both husband and wife believe themselves to have the more difficult job, which leads the reader to consider the differences between manual and domestic work. Because husband and wife both seek to assert dominance within their relationship through the work they perform, the reader must question whether either of these forms of work can be considered more or less worthwhile than the other. As Barthes suggested, the reader must participate in the couple's argument, which is never resolved in Hughes's poem.

At the end of 'Her Husband', Hughes draws attention to his own use of language throughout the poem. The last stanza becomes legalistic in its language and hinges on the word 'brief': 'Their brief / Goes straight up to heaven and nothing more is heard of it' (*CP* 148). The word 'brief' can be read here in the sense of a letter from the Pope sent to a person regarding a matter of discipline rather than in the more usual sense as a set of instructions given about a task. Both husband and wife in this poem have maliciously tried to 'discipline' one another throughout their marriage, and Hughes suggests in the final stanza that they will be judged for this. The word brief also works here in the sense of brevity suggesting that, due to the couple's inability to reconcile their differences or to communicate properly, their marriage may be brief.

'Her Husband' is a poem in which Hughes establishes oppositions and parallels so that meaning can never be arrived at simply. Although at times appearing to suggest easy associations – between the wife and cooking, for instance – Hughes does not describe this as a certain or comfortable connection. It is through her cooking that the wife shows her dissatisfaction at both her husband's boorish behaviour and her own role. Stereotypical gender roles are, in fact, highly fraught and contested throughout the poem. Rather than describing a relationship between husband and wife in which the power is obviously held by either party, in 'Her Husband', Hughes carefully deconstructs several oppositions and parallels to reveal that the establishment of authority in any relationship (linguistic or personal) is not an automatic right, but rather, consists of complex interactions between participants.

'All the evidence': 'The Thought-Fox'

It was in answer to a question about his most famous poem 'The Thought-Fox' that Hughes claimed that a poem itself provides 'the solution of all the oppositions and imbalances going on' at the time of writing.[28] Hughes's comment appeared to suggest that a structuralist or a poststructuralist approach, which considers only the text itself, would be a suitable one to take in reading his poetry. Beginning with the imagination and a 'blank page', in 'The Thought-Fox', Hughes details the process that the poet goes through while writing until finally 'The page is printed' (*CP* 21). The poem both describes this process and embodies it. Without considering anything outside this poem, we have all the information we need to understand the creative process which is inextricably linked to the theme of the poem.

However, in his prose writings and as part of poetry readings and a television programme in the 1980s, Hughes told a contextual story about a dream which inspired 'The Thought-Fox'. In telling this story, Hughes suggested that the reader could look *outside* the poem to gain an explanation for it, contradicting the central structuralist and poststructuralist tenet that the poem itself provided everything that was necessary to interpret it. Significantly, Hughes later stated that the story of his fox-dream was probably a tale he 'should never have told', suggesting that Hughes became uncomfortable with having provided an authoritative reading of the poem that depended on information outside the text provided by the author (*LTH* 423). Like Barthes, Hughes believed in the ability of the text itself to provide everything that might be required to interpret it, but also in 'the birth of the reader',[29] by which the text could be the subject of infinite, and infinitely varied, interpretations.

Hughes is a writer whose biographical details have often been used as a means by which to interpret his poetry. However, Hughes himself encouraged a more text-based approach to interpreting poetry that corresponded in many respects with structuralist and, particularly, poststructuralist strategies. Hughes placed great faith in the imaginative abilities of his readers, both adults and children, to create interesting interpretations of his poems without the need for extra-textual detail. Returning to this strategy through structuralism and poststructuralism can provide each reader with rewarding new readings of Hughes's own poetry.

Notes

1. Ferdinand de Saussure, *Course in General Linguistics*, trans. Roy Harris (London: Duckworth, 1983): 9.
2. *Ibid.*: 66.
3. *Ibid.*: 69.
4. *Ibid.*: 68.
5. *Ibid.*: 9–10.
6. Roland Barthes, *Image-Music-Text*, trans. Stephen Heath (London: Fontana, 1977): 46.

7. Jacques Derrida, *Of Grammatology*, trans. Gayatri Chakravorty Spivak (Baltimore, MD: Johns Hopkins University Press, 1997): 63.
8. *Ibid.*: 158.
9. Jacques Derrida, *Speech and Phenomena: and Other Essays on Husserl's Signs*, trans. David B. Allison (Evanston, IL: Northwestern University Press, 1973): 129.
10. *Ibid.*: 140.
11. *Ibid.*: 134.
12. *Ibid.*: 140.
13. *Ibid.*: 149.
14. Jacques Derrida, *Positions*, trans. Alan Bass [1981] (rev. edn, London: Continuum, 2002): 41.
15. *Ibid.*
16. Barthes, *Image-Music-Text*: 143.
17. *Ibid.*: 147.
18. *Ibid.*
19. *Ibid.*
20. *Ibid.*: 148.
21. James D. Marshall, *Poststructuralism, Philosophy, Pedagogy* (Amsterdam: Kluwer Academic, 2010): xv.
22. See Chapter 10.
23. Derrida, *Positions*: 41.
24. Terry Eagleton, *Literary Theory: An Introduction* (Oxford: Blackwell, 2008; 1996): 10.
25. Michel Foucault, *The Archaeology of Knowledge*, trans. A.M. Sheridan Smith (London: Tavistock, 1972): 7.
26. Christopher Norris, *Deconstruction: Theory and Practice* (London: Routledge, 2002): 84–8.
27. Ted Hughes in interview with Drue Heinz, *The Paris Review Interviews III* (New York: Picador, 2008): 293.
28. *Ibid.*
29. Barthes, *Image-Music-Text*: 147.

8

Psychoanalytic Readings

Joanny Moulin

Ted Hughes (1930–1998) and the French theorist Jacques Lacan (1901–1981) were contemporaries. Lacan belonged to the previous generation, but both men published their major works roughly at the same time. Lacan's texts collected in *Écrits* and the essential book XI of the seminar *The Four Fundamental Concepts of Psychoanalysis* had first been produced in the 1950s and 1960s, although they were not published in their English translations before 1977. These dates correspond to Hughes's poetic career between *The Hawk in the Rain* (1957) and *Gaudete* (1977). Lacan's seminars went on being published piecemeal into the first decade of the twenty-first century. It is most unlikely that they ever read one another, and yet they had much in common in spite of their potential antagonism, which is perhaps only natural between two gurus of sorts. Lacan and Hughes were a Freudian and a Jungian, and a Frenchman and an Englishman into the bargain. Very early on Hughes came under the influence of Carl Gustav Jung (1875–1961), whom he must have started reading around 1951, when he went up to Cambridge, with the result that he endorsed much of the ideological disagreement between Freud and Jung, which represented the difference between philosophical empiricism and romantic idealism. Hughes objected to Freudian psychoanalysis because it is a form of materialist rationalism based upon empirical studies, and he tended to view it as the epitome of the secularization of the Western world that he deplored. Paradoxically, Hughes was at the same time an anti-Christian polemist, but this happens to be a paradox that a Lacanian psychoanalytic reading of his work can explain. It was perhaps not always very clear at the time – whichever side of the Channel one happened to live on – that Lacan was actually a dissident within the materialist camp of so-called 'French theory'. Precisely because he remained unknown to Hughes, Lacan's theory affords a vantage point from which to look at Hughes's poetic discourse from outside his own frames of reference. It would, of course, be preposterous to pretend to make a thorough comparative study of these two authors in a few pages, but it is possible to attempt to sketch out some revealing outlines.

A convenient point of departure would be a trio of key concepts in Lacan's theory – the Real, the Symbolic, and the Imaginary – whose initials give the title of his seminar XXII: *R.S.I.* Lacan described them as three 'fields' whose interrelation defines the condition of the human subject, and he envisioned them as being tied together in such a way that it is impossible to isolate one of these fields without the three of them being set loose from one another. An easy short-cut to grasp what that is all about consists in making a short detour via William Blake, who writes, in plate 14 of *The Marriage of Heaven & Hell*: 'If the doors of perception were cleansed every thing would appear to man as it is, infinite. / For man has closed himself up, till he sees all things thro' narrow chinks of his cavern.'[1] Or again, in 'There is No Natural Religion': 'Man's perceptions are not bounded by organs of perception. He perceives more than sense (tho' ever so acute) can discover.'[2] Here the word 'cavern' seems to be an implicit reference to Plato's Myth of the Cave in which people living in the cave see only the shadows of things passing in front of their fire. The philosopher's role is to reveal reality to these people who have 'closed themselves up', as it were, through his ideas that are perfect forms of an ideal reality. Blake was still a Platonist of sorts, believing in the idea of an ideal of beauty and a higher truth, whereas Hughes and Lacan were not, having a rather different sense of the 'infinite' that might be revealed 'if the doors of perception were cleansed'. This difference represents one of Hughes's great innovations in British poetry, which was perceptible in his very first collection of poems, and it can be understood by reference to what Lacan called 'the Real'.

The Real

The title poem of *The Hawk in the Rain* can be read as a rewriting of Gerard Manley Hopkins's great poem 'The Windhover'. In both poems, the subject matter is the same: the poet watches a hawk hover-ing above ploughland. But Hopkins the Platonist records in his poem what he called 'inscape' – an experience of an idea, a representation of Christ in a perfect form, an ideal beauty: 'Brute beauty and valour and act, oh, air, pride, plume, here / Buckle! AND the fire that breaks from thee then, a billion / Times told lovelier, more dangerous, O my chevalier!'[3] Whereas Hughes's non-Christian poem, on the other hand, dramatizes what Lacan would call an 'encounter with the Real': the revelation of something inhuman, radically Other, impossibly beyond the reach of ideas and ideals, outside the pale of understandable reality: 'and I, // Bloodily grabbed dazed last-moment-counting / Morsel in the earth's mouth, strain towards the master- / Fulcrum of violence where the hawk hangs still' (*CP* 19). In an interview with Ekbert Fass, Hughes said: 'I was all for opening negotiations with whatever happened to be out there.'[4] This is not Plato's world of Ideas, but Lacan's Real, the 'infinite' that Blake speaks of, beyond the 'doors of perception'. In *Poetry in the Making*, Hughes said that words are continually trying to displace our experience, which they can do if they are stronger than 'the raw life of our experience' (*WP* 20). The Lacanian Real is exactly this: 'the raw life of our experience' that is unmediated by language.

This swerve away from Platonism was undoubtedly Hughes's first great poetic achievement. Early critics of Hughes had understood it, and were trying to come to terms with the 'violence', the 'energy' of his poetry, for lack of better conceptual tools. For they recognized in Hughes's poetry the familiar production of collections of poems that were so many 'epiphanies', yet the literary notion of epiphany, with its Neoplatonist and Christian subtext, remained inadequate. The literary epiphany can be characterized by James Joyce's definition: 'The soul of the commonest object, the structure of which is so adjusted, seems to us radiant. The object achieves its epiphany.'[5] By contrast, the Lacanian Real is seamless – '*le réel est sans fissure*'[6] – it is infinite, not finite; ungraspable, not clearly understood in the light of pure reason; it has nothing to do with the perfect essence of a discreet object; it is not the 'soul' of an object as opposed to its body; it is not 'radiant', but obscure. Keith Sagar made this clear when he introduced to Hughes studies the critical concept of 'hierophany': '"Sacred" means nothing more nor less than "real". To see something as real, in all its fullness of being, is to recognise it as a manifestation of the sacred, a hierophany.'[7] Here Sagar is in total agreement with Lacan, who says that 'the gods belong to the field of the real'.[8] The godly presence, located in the field of the Real, and which sometimes manifests itself in some other way, is also what Lacan called the Other, as, for example, the 'otherness' of the hawk in the rain. For Hughes, his sense of the sacred Other is embedded in material nature rather than in human-centred ideas or transcendent ideals.

Nearly all the poems that Hughes wrote, at least up to *Crow*, are 'hierophanies', that is to say, they deal with manifestations of the sacred, or the Real. In Lacan's jargon, a hierophany is an 'encounter with the Real', and is defined by a word that he borrowed from Aristotle: a *tuché*.[9] In Aristotelian philosophy *tuché* stands for a revelatory event, a manifestation of the gods. One archetypal *tuché* poem by Hughes is 'Meeting', where the Real is encountered under the guise of a devilish black goat with 'A square-pupilled yellow-eyed look' (*CP* 36) as elemental and revelatory as Blake's prophetic vision, or the new earth in the Bible's Book of Revelation (21.16). The poem which best dramatizes the tension of this binary opposition of Platonism and the Real is probably 'Egg-Head', whose hero is a rationalist intellectual, impervious to Sagar's sense of hierophany or Lacan's *tuché*: 'Long the eggshell head's / Fragility rounds and resists receiving the flash / Of the sun, the bolt of the earth' (*CP* 34). Much later on, Hughes elaborated on his experience of the hierophany by distinguishing two modes of encounter with the Real, in a short poem from the 'Epilogue' of *Gaudete*. The poem begins 'Sometimes it comes, a gloomy flap of lightning', but goes on to evoke 'the sun / Which is itself cloudless and leafless'. In both the traumatic lightning and the transparent sun the poet senses the presence of the life-force, the goddess of these 'Epilogue' poems, with the final insight that she 'Was always here, is always as she was' (*CP* 369).

Lacan made a similar observation when he talked about 'the place of the Real, which stretches from the trauma to the fantasy – in so far as the fantasy is never anything more than the screen that conceals something quite primary'.[10] The first modality of the hierophany described by Hughes in this poem – 'a gloomy flap of lightning' – is the trauma, the shock, the sudden revelation of a presence that imposes itself. That is the case of the poems mentioned above, like being 'Bloodily grabbed dazed last-moment-counting' in 'The Hawk in the Rain', the encounter with the eye in 'Meeting' or receiving 'the flash of the sun' that 'Egg-Head' resists. The second modality – 'Sometimes it strengthens very slowly / What is already here' – is the fantasy, when the veil of appearances slowly gets thinner and thinner, to the point where the poet's vision can see through them. A good example of this second modality is in the poem 'The Horses', which begins with a narrative description of a rather banal scene: horses standing in the frost, glimpsed at twice by a poet climbing up a hill at dawn, and then retracing his steps just after sunrise. But these horses grow into a unique, revelatory experience under the persistence of poetic attention that changes and charges everything seen with this new cleansed perception: 'The curlew's tear turned its edge on the

silence. // Slowly detail leafed from the darkness' (*CP* 22). An even
better example is the ending of 'The Thought-Fox', where there is no
referent fox in flesh and blood, but only a starless window, a clock that
ticks, the fingers of the writing poet moving on a sheet of paper creating, from his vivid memory of a real fox, a fantasy-fox, a dream-fox,
yet a powerful *tuché*-fox. So, to return to Lacan's trio of key concepts,
we can now go on to observe how Hughes explores encounters with
the Real through either the Symbolic (the trauma), or the Imaginary
(the fantasy).

The Symbolic

At this point, some definition of the Symbolic is needed, and it must
be preceded by a remark intended to avoid a possible misunderstanding from the start. Hughes, like Jung, envisaged the symbol as essentially an almost magical rapprochement, or pairing, of words with
things. Lacan, on the other hand, insists on the 'splitting' (Freud's word
for this is *Spaltung*) that is essential to the symbol. Lacan writes: 'Thus
the symbol manifests itself first of all as the murder of the thing and
this death constitutes in the subject the eternalisation of his desire.'[11]
To translate this in the simplest possible terms, the Symbolic is that
function of human language that alienates man from the Real, yet at
the same time enables him to relate to it through speech (*parole*). The
Symbolic both separates humans from the world and is their mode
of connection to the world; to be human is inevitably to be 'split' in
this way. In Hughes's terms, the Symbolic order of language is the
usurpation by which 'words displace our experience'. It is literally
'interdiction', and therefore, in Lacan's theory, the foundation of what
grounds the humanity of a human being. This is a crucial insight
because what Lacan calls the Symbolic is at the core of Hughes's
attempts to provide a poetic alternative to what he calls 'culture's error'
(*WP* 149), the reason why he considers that maybe 'our Civilisation
is an evolutionary error' (*WP* 129). In *Prometheus on His Crag*, whose
mythological hero is depicted in the process of losing his divinity,
and of becoming human, there is an ironical lizard on his shoulder
who mocks him, saying '"Lucky, you are so lucky to be human!"'
(*CP* 294). Hughes was writing *Prometheus* while working with Peter
Brook on *Orghast*, an experimental play in an a-symbolic language, a
sort of anti-language of sounds, where there would have been no gap
whatsoever between the sounds and their meanings. Hughes had also
made a drawing of Prometheus as a sort of spreadeagled man, with a
bird of prey roosting on his head, driving its talons into his head, thus

splitting him through the middle right down to the crotch – a perfect image of Lacan's 'splitting' (*Spaltung*)!

It may be enlightening to briefly return, once again, to Blake: the bird of prey in Hughes's *Prometheus* is an equivalent of Urizen, or of 'the Covering Cherub', which in plate 89 of *Jerusalem* is an allegory of 'Selfhood, Body put off […] A Human Dragon terrible / And bright'.[12] The Blakean image is derived from the Scriptures – 'So he drove out the man; and he placed at the east of the garden of Eden Cherubims, and a flaming sword which turned every way, to keep the way to the tree of life' (Genesis 3.24) – it symbolizes the symbol: the interdicting Word of the Logos-God, which forbids human beings from fully enjoying the natural world. (The god Logos, from which we derive the word 'logic', obviously depends upon the Word, or language: in Christian theology Christ is *Verbum incarnatum*, the Word made flesh.) Very much the spiritual heir of Blake, Hughes developed a dualistic cosmogony: in *Orghast*, the male Logos-god is called 'Krogon', and his female antagonist 'Moa', the two of them corresponding roughly to Blake's Urizen and Los. The first clear occurrence of Hughes's inarticulate, a-symbolic deity, that he would later call the 'Goddess of complete being', is the eponymous character of the tripartite poem 'Gog'. Keith Sagar has zeroed in on exactly what it is all about, by writing that Gog is 'All that is not logos'.[13] In the Bible, Gog and Magog stand for the arch-enemy of the Lord: 'Thus saith the Lord God; Behold, I *am* against thee, O Gog, the chief prince of Meshech and Tubal' (Ezekiel 38.3). 'What was my error?' Gog asks, 'My skull has sealed it out' (*CP* 162). Gog's error is the same as Prometheus' in Hughes's rewriting of the myth: it is to use symbolic speech, and to say 'I'. This casts a divine light on the question of what Blake called 'Selfhood', and Lacan the 'Subject'. It is important to clearly understand the distinction between the Ego – the 'Me' – and the Subject – the 'I'. The Ego is an object, it is an image, however sophisticated, and as such necessarily false or inadequate. The Subject is pure function: it acts, speaks, desires, but has no substance, no image, just as the voice of God on Mount Sinai is a disembodied voice. Whereas the Ego belongs to the field of the Imaginary, the Subject belongs to the Symbolic, always 'under erasure', actively disappearing, characterized by the splitting, or, as it were, the irremediable inadequacy to its image. Lacan has tried to explain the accession of the human infant to the symbolic function of a Subject by a little fable called 'The Mirror Stage':[14] at an early stage, the human child recognizes what he sees in the mirror as an inadequate image of himself, distinct from the rest of the world, and yet which is not himself. Thus, a human subject is characteristically defined as this active gap, his Ego being only one of the multitude of objects in a world of which he perceives only false appearances, forever unsatisfied, forever desiring, barred while he lives from the plenitude of being by Blake's 'Covering Cherub' of his inexact selfhood.

That is precisely the main problem on which Hughes was working in *Wodwo*, the collection in which the poem 'Gog' was first published. 'What am I?' These are the first words of the title poem, 'Wodwo' (*CP* 183). The persona of the wodwo is derived from *Sir Gawain and the Green Knight*: a green man of the woods, a part-human being, often represented with a very hairy body, but with foliage growing around his mouth instead of a beard. He is a distant relative of the classical satyr who was himself an avatar of the god Pan, being both half man and half goat. The wodwo, who is at one with his natural world, can most aptly be defined as a sort of wild William Wordsworth, utterly encased in the 'presence', the 'sense sublime of something far more deeply interfused' of his poem 'Lines written a few miles above Tintern Abbey'. He would be mad if he were human, for, as Lacan says, 'the captivation of the subject by the situation gives us the most general formula for madness'.[15] Like Prometheus and like Gog, the wodwo is yet another case of a persona in the process of becoming a human subject. In other words, Hughes's poem 'Wodwo' is a poetic equivalent of Lacan's fable 'The Mirror Stage'. That his speech should be deprived of punctuation marks, except for one full stop in line 3 and a few question marks here and there, is appropriate. The wodwo is undertaking what T.S. Eliot called 'a raid on the inarticulate', but in reverse – a raid on the articulate, since his language flows without pause. 'What am I to split / The glassy grain of water looking upward I see the bed / Of the river above me upside down very clear / What am I doing here in mid-air?' (*CP* 183). Clearly the wodwo does not see the difference between himself and his image reflected on the surface of the water, and speaks as if he were his own reflection, seeing himself from below in the air. 'But what shall I be called am I the first / have I an owner what shape am I what / shape am I am I huge if I go / to the end on this way past these trees and past these trees / till I get tired that's touching one wall of me'. The wodwo has no proper name, no conscious history, no consciousness of the limits of his 'Me', and manages to say 'I am' only by inadvertence, by stutteringly repeating his self-questioning about his own existence as a subject. This may not be one of Hughes's very best poems, but it is also a comic piece and a mild forerunner of the devilish humour of *Crow*.

Anti-Christianism and anti-Platonism

The personae of 'Wodwo' and 'Gog' are the prototypes of Crow, but whereas the first two characters, like Prometheus later on, are emerging into the Symbolic field, Crow is characterized by a stubbornly cynical and ironical refusal to do so, as if he knew better than to become a human subject. Remarkably, Crow is not a persona: even 'Crow's Song of Himself' (*CP* 247), a poem of which he is the speaker, is written in the third person. He is not a subject of language, not a subject of the Logos-God. Much has been said about Crow being derived from the trickster of Native American mythologies, and as such he serves Hughes's satirical purpose. For *Crow* is a satire, whose target is Jehovah, envisioned very much like Blake's Urizen, with the crucial difference that Hughes is certainly not a Christian. This hardly needs demonstrating, yet if it did, it would be enough to quote 'A Childish Prank': 'Crow laughed. / He bit the Worm, God's only son, / Into two writhing halves. // He stuffed into man the tail half / With the wounded end hanging out' (*CP* 216). Although Hughes follows in the steps of Blake up to a certain point, the author of *Jerusalem* would most certainly have passed on Hughes a judgement very similar to what he passed on Wordsworth: 'I see in Wordsworth the Natural Man rising up against the Spiritual Man continually, & then he is No Poet but a Heathen Philosopher at Enmity against all true Poetry or Inspiration.'[16] Incidentally, there may be something subversive in Hughes's attitude to Blake, and other Christian poets like Hopkins and Eliot, as if he was referring to them only to surf on the wave of their intellectual authorities, but to convey, in fact, a poetic discourse radically opposite to theirs. What is new in *Crow*, is that while the voice of the polemist could occasionally be heard in the previous poems, it is now pitting all its poetic power against the Christian God, albeit under the mask of the trickster, Crow. True, Hughes would explain this away by saying that he stood against puritan Christianity, but his ideological discourse is rather Nietzschean, that is to say anti-Christian, and he inherited it from Jung, who himself claimed to be a disciple of Nietzsche. But 'Ye cannot serve God and mammon' (Matthew 6.24). Neither can you serve Christ and the Goddess. The stumbling block is the Logos – and to the Christian, Christ *is* the Word – which Hughes kept storming against.

Hughes's second target, the one he aimed at in *Cave Birds*, his next collection after *Crow*, is Platonism. The link between Christianity and Platonism is historically established by the Neoplatonism of St Augustine of Hippo and the Fathers of the Church. To sum it up as simply as possible, Plato's idealist philosophy postulates a world of Ideas which, by being embedded in earthly objects – in the Real – in the human psyche, perpetrates the self-same 'murder of the thing', the self-same splitting, that is inherent in the Symbolic. Here lies the whole difference between poetic epiphanies – manifestations of Platonic essence, of perfect forms or ideas – and hierophanies – manifestation of the infinite, the sacred, and the inarticulate Real. This other aspect of Hughes's fight against 'culture's error' was adumbrated in a little poem in *Lupercal*, entitled precisely 'The Perfect Forms', where he rather venomously described Socrates, Plato's pupil, in these terms: 'Visage of Priapus: the undying tail-swinging / Stupidity of the donkey / That carries Christ. How carefully he nurses // This six-day abortion of the Absolute' (*CP* 82). And he would very clearly make his point in *Shakespeare and the Goddess of Complete Being*:

> In both the Greek world and Shakespeare's the archaic reign of the Great Goddess was being put down, finally and decisively, by a pragmatic, scep- tical, moralizing, desacralizing spirit: in Greece by the spirit of Socrates, and in England by the spirit of the ascendant, Puritan God of the indi- vidual conscience, the Age of Reason cloaked in the Reformation. (*SGCB* 85)

Hughes has explained that the project of *Cave Birds* is to evoke the journey after death of Socrates in the other world, where his Ego is put on trial and, found guilty, he is dismembered and ultimately reborn in the Egypt of Isis to be taught music.[17] The idea derives from Plato's *Phedo*, where he relates that Socrates, as he lay dying, said that he had a dream where he was commanded to 'learn the art'. The structure of Socrates' journey is that of the shamanic flight, described by Mircea Eliade in *Shamanism* as the descent to the underworld and the return with healing songs. The underworld is the unsymbolic, inarticulate part of the human psyche, the 'subconscious' according to Jung or, so to speak, the intersection between the Real and the Imaginary in Lacan's tripartite *R.S.I.* Gog and the wodwo were only just emerging out of this netherworld, and so was the horseman in part III of Gog: 'Out under the blood-dark archway, gallops bowed the horseman of iron' (*CP* 164). Crow refused to get out of it and played havoc on the borderlines: 'And kept on and slept and at last // Crashed on the moon awoke and crawled out // Under his mother's buttocks' (*CP* 219–20).

The hero of *Cave Birds* has been plunged into the underworld by death. Unlike Wodwo and Crow, but in a way that the triptych struc- ture of 'Gog' foreshadowed, the protagonist of *Cave Birds*, who starts

out as an arrogant, complacent cockerel, appears under diverse guises at
different stages of his transformative journey: he is 'The Accused', 'The
Knight' and 'The Risen'. This is interesting because it is precisely his
'Selfhood', his 'Ego', his 'Me', what Jung would call the 'false envelope
of the persona', which is being dissolved. The entities that he meets –
'The Judge', 'The Executioner', 'The Baptist' – are all embodiments
of the life-force goddess, the Earth Mother, that ultimately grip him,
dismember him, drown him and dissolve his Ego. What he is undergo-
ing is the deepest possible regression, by which he is going back to the
uterine state, to be finally born again in 'The Risen'. This last poem is
an evocation of the 'individuation', a concept which Jung derived and
adapted from Nietzsche. The individuation is an ideal psychological
condition in which the psyche – now called the Self – would no
longer be centred on the 'Me', but on a virtual point of equilibrium,
halfway between the conscious and the subconscious, between what
Jung called the female 'anima' and the male 'animus': 'The individuation has no other aim than to liberate the Self, on the one hand from
the false envelops of the persona, and on the other hand from the
subjective force of subconscious images.'[18] Jung goes further to say
that 'the individuation corresponds at the same time with the Christian
ideal of the Kingdom of Heaven "which is within ourselves"'.[19] After
a long study on 'the symbol of the transubstantiation of the mass', he
comes to the conclusion that 'we can designate the mass as a rite of the
process of individuation'.[20] Perhaps Hughes had something like that in
mind when, in 'The Risen', he wrote: 'In the wind-fondled crucible of
his splendour / The dirt becomes God' (CP 440).

Hughes's poetic discourse

After Cave Birds came Gaudete, of which the first part is a sort of
light erotic farce, but this has tended to distract from the fact that
its 'Epilogue' contains some of Hughes's strongest poetry. However,
Gaudete did not break any new ground, as nearly all the previous
collections did. It is a repetition and a variant of the same shamanic
flight in its archetypal narrative, which describes a form of the
'regression' that is essential to the psychoanalytic experience, whether
Jungian or Freudian. Only the interpretations of the value, the aims
and the uses of the archetypal narrative differ, and this is a matter of
ideological difference in that it depends upon the world-view of the
reader. For Lacan – and this is one of the aspects of his work that
attracted most misunderstanding and polemical resistance – ideology
belongs to the field of the Imaginary. Like the Ego, like dreams and

fantasies, ideology is discourse, and as such it is essential binary – it is always a matter of what belongs to 'me' or not, what one believes and what does not believe, appearance and reality, truth and error, good and evil, nature and culture, the demiurge and the good god in dualistic systems like those of Blake and Hughes. Almost unavoidably, any discussion of an author's poetic discourse – of the ideas that he stands for and defends against others – runs a high risk of quickly becoming polemical. It is undeniable that Hughes attracted strong advocacy from some people, and strong distaste from others, and it has always been very difficult to discuss his work without necessarily choosing sides, as it were, and appearing to be either an admirer or a detractor. That is because Hughes was a poet of strongly ideological poetic statements – pagan, anti-Christian, anti-Platonist, anti-rationalist, anti-modernist, a Promethean romantic with a mission to correct 'culture's error' in a postmodernist age.

In the last two decades of his life, that is to say after *Gaudete*, Hughes's poetic discourse had reached its maturity and he was busy consolidating it. He gave it a theoretical basis by gathering his critical texts in *Winter Pollen* and engaging in the almost academic enterprise of *Shakespeare and the Goddess of Complete Being*. At the same time, he developed his poetry and tales for children which expanded what had always been, since 1961, an educative element in his poetic work – a deliberate effort to influence the minds of schoolchildren, and therefore of the coming generation. These productions are pedagogic declensions of his major works, innovative only in terms of publishing strategies. With all due respect, the same thing applies to his later 'adult' poetry, which, from *Season Songs* onwards, became mainly contemplative in *Moortown Diary*, *River*, *Flowers and Insects*, and autobiographical in *Wolfwatching* and *Birthday Letters*. The later Hughes offers a splendid example of what Harold Bloom – a decidedly Freudian critic – has called 'The *apophrades*': 'the dismal or unlucky days upon which the dead return to inhabit their former houses, come to the strongest poets, but with the very strongest there is a grand and final revisionary movement that purifies even this last influx'.[21] Via a tacit return to the influence of the early Wordsworth – whom ideologically he is certainly much closer to than to Blake – Hughes revisited and perfected the 'hierophanies' of his earlier days, so beautifully that the 'fishing poems' of river have become epitomes of the encounter with the Real: 'Join water, wade in underbeing / Let brain mist into moist earth / Ghost loosen away downstream / Gulp river and gravity // Lose words' (*CP* 652). Free at last from the tensions of the mythic narratives, by a form of Romantic irony, Hughes's voice was enriched with touches of humour, as in 'Milesian Encounter on the Sligachan', which is very much a fisherman's tale of 'the one that got away'. A comparable distancing is perceptible in *Wolfwatching*, where poems like 'Two Astrological Conundrums' revisit the notion of the shamanic flight in the quieter mythic mode of the folk tale. *Flowers and Insects* concentrates on blooming flowers and allegorical births of insects, as in 'Mayflies', which is typical a new style of poem, of which 'The Risen' was the prototype, and that could aptly be designated by Hughes's own word borrowed from *Shakespeare and the Goddess*: 'theophanies'. Whereas 'hierophanies' are poems of the encounter with the Real, 'theophanies' are poems of the individuation:

> The Boar and Adonis meet, that is, in the corpus callosum – which is where the Flower springs, to be reborn on into the Tarquin and tragedy of an irrational crisis in the left side, or to be sublimated as if vertically into the transcendent illumination and 'wholeness' of total consciousness, as the reborn flower child of the Goddess. The Theophany which Shakespeare eventually achieves is a mythic form for this inclusive 'aura' of the perfectly (as possible) achieved co-operation of the two hemispheres. (*SGCB* 162)

More than 'nature poetry', Hughes's is 'ecopoetry' *par excellence*, and his commitment to environmental causes testifies to that.[22] More than just militant literature, this is deep ecology poetry. At the heart of Hughes's poetic discourse lies a Promethean rebellion against the logos-God, that is to say, the excessive, totalitarian prevalence given to what Lacan called the Symbolic order of language, which, in the empiricist and scientist extremes of the rational spirit, or in the fanatical or 'puritan' forms of Christianity, resulted in an alienation of Western man both from his earthly habitat and from the spiritual dimension of his own unconscious. On this latter point, both Freudian and Jungian schools of psychoanalysis agree, as is quite clear in Freud's *Civilisation and Its Discontent*. Hughes's analysis of this problem, and his poetic commitment and contribution to solve it, are very much a continuation and a revision of what McGann has called 'the romantic ideology',[23] which itself originated in the Kantian reaction against the pure reason of the philosophy of the Enlightenment, that is to say, what Marx has called the 'French Ideology'. Lacan has come to be seen as a paragon of the period of the dominance of 'French theory', that was a latter-day *baroud d'honneur* of Marx's 'French Ideology', but Lacan was certainly not one of those hardboiled, 'egghead' rationalists, and his psychoanalysis is useful to better understand what is at stake in Hughes's poetic achievement. They would certainly have agreed on the sacred, and the *jouissance* of our best human encounters with the Real, if perhaps not quite on the desirability of bridging the symbolic *Spaltung*. What a pity they never met!

Notes

1. William Blake, *Blake's Poetry and Design*, ed. M.L. Johnson and J.E. Grant (New York: Norton, 1979): 93.
2. *Ibid.*: 15.
3. Gerard Manley Hopkins, *Poems and Prose*, ed. W.H. Gardner (Harmondsworth: Penguin, 1953): 30.
4. Ekbert Faas, *Ted Hughes: The Unaccommodated Universe* (Santa Barbara, CA: Black Sparrow Press, 1980): 201.
5. James Joyce, *Stephen Hero* [1944] (London: Jonathan Cape, 1956): 218.
6. Jacques Lacan, *Le Séminaire livre II: Le moi dans la théorie de Freud et dans la technique de la psychanalyse* (Paris: Seuil, 1978): 122.
7. Keith Sagar, *The Art of Ted Hughes* (2nd edn, Cambridge University Press, 1978): 210.
8. Jacques Lacan, *The Four Fundamental Concepts of Psychoanalysis* [1977] (London: Vintage, 1998): 45.
9. *Ibid.*: 53.
10. Lacan, *Four Fundamental Concepts of Psychoanalysis*: 60.
11. *Ibid.*: 104.
12. Blake, *Blake's Poetry and Design*: 350.
13. Sagar, *Art of Ted Hughes*: 74.
14. Jacques Lacan, *Écrits: A Selection* [1966] (London: Routledge, 1995): 1–7.
15. *Ibid.*: 7.
16. William Blake, *The Complete Poetry and Prose of William Blake*, ed. D.V. Erdman and H. Bloom (Berkeley: University of California Press, 1982): 665.
17. Terry Gifford and Neil Roberts, *Ted Hughes: A Critical Study* (London: Faber & Faber, 1981): 260.
18. Carl Gustav Jung, *Dialectique du Moi et de l'inconscient* [1933] (Paris: Gallimard, 1964): 117 (my translation).
19. *Ibid.*: 232 (my translation).
20. *Ibid.*: 299 (my translation).
21. Harold Bloom, *The Anxiety of Influence: A Theory of Poetry* [1973] (Oxford: Oxford University Press, 1997): 141.
22. See Terry Gifford, 'Hughes's Social Ecology', in Terry Gifford (ed.), *The Cambridge Companion to Ted Hughes* (Cambridge: Cambridge University Press): 81–93.
23. Jerome J. McGann, *The Romantic Ideology* (Chicago: University of Chicago Press, 1983).

9

Trauma Theory Readings

Daniel O'Connor

Trauma theory

In a letter to his son, justifying his decision to publish his account of his relationship with Sylvia Plath in *Birthday Letters*, Ted Hughes wrote of his need to resolve his feelings about his first marriage:

> That was the big unmanageable event in my life, that had to be somehow managed – internally – by me. Somehow through my writing – because that's the method I've developed to deal with myself. (*LTH* 711)

Plath's suicide, this 'big unmanageable event', is a trauma that haunts Hughes's work. He goes on to state that he had begun to 'deal' with this trauma in Ireland in the mid-1960s when he was working on his translation of Seneca's *Oedipus* and, more significantly, *Crow: From the Life and Songs of the Crow*. *Crow* and *Birthday Letters* form two very different responses to this trauma. The ostensibly direct tone of *Birthday Letters* contrasts with the more symbolic method of *Crow*. Hughes felt that the symbolic method was traditionally the most success-ful, but that this had been foreclosed by the scrutiny he considered applied to his work for signs of him discussing his relationship with Plath. *Crow*, which is in part a deeply concealed effort at discussing Plath's death symbolically, is dedicated to the memory of Assia Wevill (Hughes's partner) and her child Shura. The deaths of Assia and Shura in 1969 saw Hughes abandon his work on *Crow*. As we shall see, what is a personal trauma in *Birthday Letters* had already been explored as a global trauma in the symbolic shadow play of *Crow*; it was, how-ever, an exploration that remained unfinished in *Crow*. Yet, even the foundational myth of Hughes's career, the much-repeated 'Burnt Fox' dream, demonstrates signs of an underlying traumatic sensibility. Its formation of femininity shapes the way Hughes responds to traumatic female figures in his later work, particularly in the guise of the Goddess. The traumas of the 'Burnt Fox' dream and of *Crow* – war, the atomic bomb, the Holocaust and its whole horror show of the twentieth century – lead us towards trauma theory more generally, in particular the inability of language to express its subject.

In relation to literature, trauma theory revolves around the capacity of language to contain and resolve the traumatic event. At the heart of much work on trauma theory is the work of Sigmund Freud, especially in relation to his understanding of the repression of traumatic events and their unconscious return. The unconscious itself, in this regard, is traumatic. Freudian theorist Jacques Lacan specifically highlighted this relationship between trauma, the unconscious and language. As explained in the previous chapter, central to Lacan's theories is the idea that our entry into language (the symbolic order) is itself traumatic, separating us from what he calls the Real. This is present in Hughes's work as the divide between culture and nature, where culture has been traumatically separated from nature. Hughes, in a curious opposition of spirituality and science, repeatedly argues for man as having suffered a Fall from nature to the rational ego. His poetry (culture) attempts to bridge the gap and express nature. For Lacan, however, the unconscious is not simply 'natural' man – man as animal – but 'is structured like a language'.[1] Lacanian theorist Slavoj Žižek elucidates what Lacan meant by this notorious maxim, arguing that it is not the job of the ego to tame the 'wild drives' of the id, but to approach the unconscious as an 'unbearable truth I have to live with'.[2] Nonetheless, what trauma theory returns to repeatedly is the difficulty language has in expressing this 'unbearable truth'.

Equally, representations of trauma in Hughes's work return to this same problem. He labelled the years of his lifetime as 'Decades of calamity', though it was his father's experience in the First World War, before Hughes was born, that would come to typify his understanding of the relationship between trauma and language. Indeed, he even compared himself to veterans of the war, observing that his own struggle to write about Plath's suicide 'gagged my whole life, arrested me, essentially, right back there at that point. Like those first [*sic*] World War survivors who never climbed entirely out of the trench' (*LTH* 731). Unlike his uncles, Hughes's father was notably reticent in speaking about his experiences in the war. In the poem 'Dust As We Are', a young Hughes learns about the war not from his father's words but from tender physical contact, combing his father's hair to 'divine [...] / The fragility of skull', finding himself 'filled / With his knowledge' (*CP* 753–4). During research for a planned work on the war, Hughes's various interviews with veterans led him to conclude that it was those who said the least that expressed the most, through 'hesitating vague words' and 'half movements' that 'released a world of shocking force and vividness' (*WP* 123). His reading of contemporary poets, who were attempting to cope with trauma of the Second World War and its aftermath in Eastern Europe in their work, confirmed his understanding of the First World War. The work of the Eastern European poets that he admired and promoted seemingly counters Theodor Adorno's much-quoted assertion that there can be no poetry after Auschwitz.[3] Hughes writes that the 'silence of artistic integrity "after Auschwitz" is a real thing', the consequence of which is to raise 'the price of "truth" and "reality" and "understanding" beyond what common words seem to be able to pay' – on the one hand making poetry more difficult, but on the other demanding its use as language refined beyond 'common words' (*WP* 232). In his introduction to Vasko Popa's *Collected Poems* he wrote of this group of Eastern European poets (Popa, Miroslav Holub, Zbigniew Herbert and Yehuda Amichai) that 'Their poetry is a strategy of making audible meanings without disturbing the silence' (*WP* 223).

Julia Kristeva argues that poetry is an appropriate language for trauma in that it is a form of language that plays with the boundaries of the 'symbolic order', in particular the want or lack at its heart: that it is 'a language of want, of the fear that edges up to it and runs along its edges'.[4] Indeed, the foundational myth of Ted Hughes's poetic career is fundamentally traumatic. In his dream of 'The Burnt Fox' (*WP* 8–9), which Hughes felt was a kind of poetic initiation, we encounter an instance of what Kristeva terms the 'abject'. The disfigured state of the fox is particularly important; 'A wound with blood and pus', Kristeva writes, 'does not *signify* death', but 'shows' death:

> These body fluids, this defilement, this shit are what life withstands, hardly and with difficulty, on the part of death. There, I am at the border of my condition as a living being.[5]

This burnt fox is what culture has cast off in order to become culture: not only the primordial, but also 'what life withstands': death. Accordingly, the burnt fox is 'abject' in that it belongs prior to the 'symbolic order' – it is a reminder of primordial nature.

However, it is also serving another, similar purpose. Through a careful reading of this account of the dream alongside two others (in a letter and a television appearance), we can see how the trauma of this dream sets the tone for Hughes's later traumatic representations of woman. In a brief but cogent appraisal of Freud's *The Interpretation of Dreams*, Žižek argues that the tendency to read the surface of the dream as inherently sexual is a misunderstanding of Freud. He insists that what Freud proposes in having the patient recount the dream a number of times places greater emphasis on the discrepancies between each version. This, he argues, is where we encounter 'the difference between reality and the Real', where 'the "insignificant" omissions, or added details, allude to the Real of the dream'; it is not in the latent thought of the dream that we ought to find the unconscious desire, but in 'the very distortion of the latent thought into the dream's explicit texture'.[6] In the case of Hughes's dream of the burnt fox, the latent thought of the dream is, as he writes to Keith Sagar, the status of his poetic ability under the pressure of Cambridge English and its 'social rancour on creative spirit' (*LTH* 423). Hughes, in short, interprets his dream as a warning of the dangers of rational intelligence to the 'creative spirit', and this interpretation frames his telling of the dream.

In the letter to Sagar, Hughes mentions a crucial detail excluded from two other versions of the dream (one given during a television appearance and the other, as we have seen, included in *Winter Pollen*).[7] He was struggling with his weekly essay, which in all three accounts he indicates was a familiar experience during this period of his undergraduate years; only in the letter to Sagar does he reveal that he was writing about Samuel Johnson, 'a personality I greatly liked' (*LTH* 422). This significantly changes the complex of the dream. When reading these versions alongside each other, as the burnt fox walks in on its 'hind legs' (as he says in both the television appearance and in the *Winter Pollen* text, but crucially not in the letter), are we not reminded of Dr Johnson's infamous misogynistic quip that a woman preaching is like a dog walking on its hind legs? The letter to Sagar 'protects' itself from this reading by omitting the phrase 'hind legs', whilst the public versions omit the reference to Samuel Johnson. The Real of Hughes's dream, then, is the woman occupying the place of 'traumatic Thing', witnessing the primordial flesh 'roasted, smouldering, black-charred, split and bleeding' (*WP* 9). It is a representation of 'abject' femininity. The Lacanian 'Thing', which is the lack or hole at the heart of the Real, acts as an obstruction to pleasure – what Lacan would know as *jouissance* – in its traumatic guise. This trauma distinguishes Hughes's representation of the female throughout his career – though, as we shall see, *Birthday Letters* finds an alternative.

The 'big unmanageable event'

In *Crow*, Hughes begins to deal with the 'big unmanageable event' of Plath's suicide through transference. The narrative frame for the collection pieced together from readings by Keith Sagar in his book *The Laughter of Foxes* opens with suicidal impetus: Man comes to God in a dream – God's nightmare – asking him to take life back.[8] Just as Freud's 'discovery' of the unconscious proved traumatic, Hughes traumatizes his God with an unconscious. The voice of God's dream, mocking his prize creation Man as a failure, creates Crow as an attempt to 'do better'. Accordingly, Crow is not only a product of the unconscious (God's nightmare), but is also a response to the suicidal desires of Man. In other words, Crow is a symbolic response to the trauma of the 'big unmanageable event'. In this regard, we can also see how Hughes's whole effort to produce the 'super-ugly' language of *Crow*, and indeed Crow himself, is a 'discourse of the unrepresentable'.[9] Moreover, mourning instigates this requirement for a style of language that can cope with the demands of its subject. As Lacan argues in his seminar on *Hamlet*, the rites of mourning account for a hole created by the inadequacy of 'signifying elements' to cope with loss.[10] As such, mourning requires a new symbolic register to deal with the loss – this is what Hughes is searching for through *Crow*.

Throughout *Crow* there are instances of previously successful poetic modes being cast off in favour of a new language to cope where the 'old' poetic language has failed. 'Crow and the Birds' moves from the erstwhile Hughesian idiom of 'the eagle soared clear through a dawn distilling of emerald' to a new Hughes: 'Crow spraddled head-down in the beach-garbage, guzzling a dropped ice-cream' (*CP* 210). Likewise, 'Crow Goes Hunting' (*CP* 236) mockingly subverts Hughes's earlier technique of hunting animals with words. 'Crow Tries the Media' (*CP* 231–2), the most poignant of these linguistic failures, provides the template for Hughes's attempts to deal with the 'big unmanageable event'. Crow wants 'to sing about her' – an unspecified female figure – but finds the means insufficient, as all of the cultural accretions of what poetry is and how it can grasp its subject act as an obstruction to the subject itself. Crow rejects the modes of love poetry, denouncing 'comparisons with the earth' and later even words. Crow wants 'to sing to her soul simply', but in doing so finds that 'her shaped dimmed'. There is, of course, no overt reference to Plath in this poem (nor in the *Crow* volume); we could successfully read this poem (and in many ways ought to) without drawing any attention to

Hughes's biographical circumstances. The traumatic impetus behind the poem has driven Hughes to symbolism rather than direct address.

In Hughes's attempt to deal with the 'big unmanageable event', *Crow* is ultimately a failure, an incomplete masterpiece. This is due in no small part to the deaths of his partner Assia Wevill, her child Shura, and his mother, Edith, in 1969 (the year in which Hughes abandoned *Crow*). It was after this second loss that Hughes began work on *Orghast*, inventing a language in response to his feeling that it is almost impossible to express human suffering 'by any deliberate means'(*WP* 123). Hughes, of course, returns to English after *Orghast*, and 'Crow Tries the Media' sets the tone for what follows. In his later attempts at dealing with the 'big unmanageable event' symbolically, Hughes undertakes what Neil Roberts describes as the 'sublimation' of women he had known into the Goddess of the poems, usually referred to as 'her' and more often than not represented as unrepresentable: 'She reveals herself, and is veiled' (*CP* 364).[11]

However, there is a notable difference between the 'her' of *Crow* and the Goddess figures of Hughes's poetry from the 1970s: where *Crow* is largely mournful the Goddess poems are melancholic. Freud's theory of melancholia, as taken up by Lacan, asserts that the melancholic subject does not accept the loss of the loved object, allowing for the liberation and transference of desire, but incorporates it into his or her ego, accusing his- or her-self from the lost object's point of view. Freud writes that 'In mourning it is the world that has become empty; in melancholia it is the ego itself.'[12] The melancholic subject 'reproaches himself, vilifies himself, and expects to be cast out and punished', which is exactly the position of Hughes's male protagonists in the mythical poetic sequences (*Prometheus on His Crag, Gaudete, Cave Birds*).[13] Interestingly, we can see how this melancholia found an early, symbolic cure in *Crow* with Crow's eating: Freud notes that the melancholia is recognizable in a 'refusal to take nourishment'. In this regard, Crow's search for 'something to eat' is a significant epiphany in 'That Moment', as it is a return, rather than a melancholic objection to, 'the instinct which compels every living thing to cling to life'.[14] Where the Goddess is involved the poetry reverts to this melancholic role, admonishing the masculine ego. Heather Clark even argues that some of the more accusatory poems of *Cave Birds* are 'deliberately written in Plath's voice to suggest that she is the plaintiff and he is the defendant in the ongoing public trial of their marriage'.[15] Similarly, the way in which Hughes adapts the myth of Actaeon in *Gaudete*, for instance, recalls Plath's speaker in the last line of 'Lady Lazarus' – 'I eat men like air' (*SPCP* 244–7) – with its frequent references to devouring, such as: 'She fell into the earth / And I was devoured' (*CP* 361), 'the maneater / On your leash' (*CP* 362), 'Where one who would have devoured me is driven off' (*CP* 366); and most clearly in relation to the myth of Diana and Acteaon where we find the speaker hunting himself, 'The one / I shall rend to pieces' (*CP* 363).

Birthday Letters

Whilst Hughes's published work was becoming increasingly mystical during the 1970s, ever more occupied with union with (and chastisement from) the Goddess, he was intermittently working on the direct poems that would eventually appear towards the end of his life in *Birthday Letters*. It seems safe to presume that insufficiencies of the method of his published work demanded the private, personal address of *Birthday Letters*. However, it remains surprising that Hughes should abandon the symbolic method altogether and attempt to deal with this trauma directly (contravening near enough everything that trauma theory tells us about how trauma is dealt with, let alone his own thoughts about poetry). Yet, at the core of *Birthday Letters* remains a kind of silence, or a quietness at least, that sets about doing the real work of dealing with the trauma.

Although we ought to be cautious about directly equating the Plath of *Birthday Letters* with the Goddess of his prior work, there is a significant change of tone in Hughes's relationship with the female protagonist of his poems. Where the Goddess poems of the 1970s are distinguished by melancholia, *Birthday Letters* is less marked by this melancholic self-reproach. Indeed, in this respect, the collection is less 'confessional'. The Ted Hughes of *Birthday Letters* resembles Crow in that he tends towards bemusement at the circumstances in which he locates himself. Just as Crow finds himself as 'what his brain could make nothing of' (*CP* 240), Ted Hughes in *Birthday Letters* is similarly placed: 'the gnat in the ear of the wounded / Elephant of my own / Incomprehension' (*CP* 1070). Much of the collection finds him trying to locate a place for himself in Plath's story. He tries on numerous costumes, from being another of Plath's false gods and the wrong 'witchdoctor' (*CP* 1052–3), through his role as the 'stone man' husband of 'Fever' (1073), to the 'husband / Performing the part of your father' of 'Suttee' (*CP* 1140) – the latter a role he performs in many of these poems. Plath's life is mythologized as an ill-fated attempt at finding and destroying the 'Minotaur' of her relationship with her father; but the Hughes of *Birthday Letters* lacks this defined role: 'I woke up on the empty stage with the props, / The paltry painted masks. And the script / Ripped up and scattered, its code scrambled' (*CP* 1133). 'Sebetos' likewise plays upon this trope of incoherence, mixing up ripped scripts, where their restaging of *The Tempest* in the roles of Miranda (Plath) and Ferdinand (Hughes) finds Otto not as Prospero but King Minos, with the Minotaur interrupting the scene. Bewildered, Hughes asks: 'Which play / were we in?'; and as the whole scene crumbles in the antithesis of the denouement of *The Tempest*, Hughes's Ferdinand crawls back 'Under a gabardine', redolent of Caliban but now in the shape of Actaeon (again), 'hearing the cry / Now of hounds' (*CP* 1129).

What is perhaps most surprising about *Birthday Letters* is that, unlike his prior prose on Plath and her work, which repeatedly stresses how her poetry was leading to a sense of rebirth rather than death, her death is heavily fated in these poems. *Birthday Letters* offers a somewhat ambiguous representation of Plath, obsessed with her own 'abject' self. 'The Rabbit Catcher' ends with the suggestion that in the snares she hated she actually found 'Your doomed self, your tortured, crying, / Suffocating self', with her poems like the 'smoking entrails' of dead rabbits (*CP* 1138). Not only had Hughes regarded her suicide as avoidable prior to *Birthday Letters*, but also that it had distorted readings of her later work, which, had she not died, 'could only be read as the scenes of a victorious battle for so-called "self-integration"' (*LTH* 446). Yet, in *Birthday Letters* we find a 'Fate' that is almost the complete opposite to that of *Crow*. Where Crow faces death as his fate, 'Slowly rending the vital fibres' (*CP* 222), by virtue of his very existence he is also found to be 'stronger than death' in 'Examination at the Womb-Door' (*CP* 219). Where *Birthday Letters* echoes the structure of 'Examination at the Womb-Door' ('Who owns these unspeakable guts? *Death*.'), it is not so defiant (*CP* 218). '9 Willow Street' takes an ominous incident of Hughes being bitten by a potentially rabid bat whilst trying save it and responds to the earlier *Crow* poem: 'It confirmed / The myth we had sleepwalked into: death. / This was the bat-light we were living in: death' (*CP* 1090). We could argue reasonably that Hughes had no choice – he could hardly alter the story so that Plath survives – but the change in tone (and tense) between these two collections, which are to some extent dealing with the same material, is significant. The overriding sentiment of *Birthday Letters* is of a fated resignation that contrasts unfavourably against the verve of *Crow*.

Such an ineluctable end, cemented by the passage of over thirty years between Plath's death and the publication of *Birthday Letters*, changes the way in which the poems come to terms with the trauma of this 'big unmanageable event'. The 'free energy' and 'release' that Hughes felt in finalizing *Birthday Letters* extends to the language employed in the collection.[16] The untroubled language of the poems seems to deny any hint of what Lacan refers to as the 'inadequacy of signifying elements' engendered as a consequence of mourning.[17] However, the way in which the *Birthday Letters* poems relate to his prior poetry through the establishment of 'Ted Hughes' as a character works to destabilize the *Birthday Letters* poems to the benefit of his earlier work.[18] This doubling is evident almost immediately in the collection. The opening poem, 'Fulbright Scholars' (*CP* 1045), finds the 'Ted Hughes' of the poems (that of his fallible memory) behaving without knowledge of the wider significance of his actions, a significance afforded by the Ted Hughes who writes the poems. What is just the new experience of a peach in austerity Britain for the 'Ted Hughes' of the poem represents the arrival of glamorous American Sylvia Plath and everything that follows. Hughes holds his historical self at a distance, keeps him ignorant, and yet arrives at him in the poems with the wonder of a discovery. Where Plath intervenes there is a doubling of the lens: here we find Hughes observing Plath observing Hughes. In other words, he sees himself through his idea of Plath. 'Ted Hughes' in 'The Shot', for instance, is portrayed as the unwitting target of Plath's retributive anger towards her father (as he is in most of the collection), recalling Plath's lines in 'Daddy': 'If I've killed one man, I've killed two – / The vampire who said he was you' (*SPCP* 222–4). This represents a significant shift from the Goddess poems. Whereas the self-criticism in the Goddess poems is measured through a fantasy ideal of the female (an ideal that the poems do not appear to realize is of their own creation), in *Birthday Letters* Hughes looks back at himself knowingly through his own idea of Plath. We can see this in two poems in particular: 'Black Coat', which leans back on his earlier work, and 'Red' (with a little help from 'St Botolph's'), which demonstrates that silence remains effective in *Birthday Letters* as a work of mourning.

'Black Coat' recounts an occasion when Hughes visits the sea for a sense of isolation, only to find that he is being observed by Plath. Her gaze is possessed with an 'inbuilt double exposure' that sees her father's ghost behind a 'blurred see-through' Hughes; the poems ends, 'I did not feel / How, as your lenses tightened, / He slid into me' (*CP* 1109). Accordingly, the Hughes as speaker of 'Black Coat' observes Plath observing Hughes as protagonist. Much has been made of the intertextuality between Plath's poems and *Birthday Letters*; less so of the collection's concern with Hughes's own work.[19] Two poems are most obviously present in 'Black Coat': 'Ghost Crabs' from *Wodwo* and 'Crow on the Beach', but I will restrict this discussion to 'Ghost Crabs'. In 'Black Coat' Otto, Plath's father, emerges like the 'Ghost Crabs' of the earlier poem, having crawled from a freezing sea. The poet of 'Ghost Crabs' receives with interest his image of these crabs: 'An invisible disgorging of the sea's cold / Over the man who strolls along the sands' (*CP* 149). 'Black Coat', in this sense, translates the symbolism of 'Ghost Crabs' back into the 'realism' of *Birthday Letters*. Just as Otto slides into the Hughes of the poem, the 'Ghost Crabs' slide into the empty minds of those asleep. Their symbolism, where 'We are their bacteria, / Dying their lives and living their deaths', is likewise contained in the figure of Otto: Hughes sees himself in 'Black Coat' as the living manifestation of Plath's dead father, suffering her figurative attempt to kill him. 'Black Coat' is conscious of how Hughes had already dictated his own mythology in prior poems; he is remembering this incident through the lens of 'Ghost Crabs'. The first line-break on the awkward phrasing of 'I did not feel / How, as your lenses tightened, / He slid into me' creates enough of a pause (with that lumbering, necessary stress on 'How') to nudge out the implication that though he 'did not feel', he does now (*CP* 1109).

'Black Coat' works to confirm the earlier symbolic and indirect rendering of the experience in 'Ghost Crabs'. In doing so, it resolves the work of mourning by confirming that the prior symbolic language is equitable to the loss. This comes about where Hughes occupies Plath's absence: her gaze is actually his. Hughes reconsiders his own poem through Plath's viewpoint, watching 'Ted Hughes' becoming Otto, but also 'Ted Hughes' becoming Ted Hughes: 'He slid into me'. This 'He' stands for both 'Ted Hughes' and Otto in that Hughes willingly adopts the Plath mythology of himself as Otto; he therefore occupies Plath's position in witnessing both 'Ted Hughes' and Otto Plath. As a result, the biography of 'Black Coat' seeks to confirm the symbolic accuracy of 'Ghost Crabs' by validating it through Plath's disembodied, perhaps even metaphysical, viewpoint: her 'tightened' lenses. It is almost as if Hughes is confirming the efficacy of his poetry with the supernatural agency of Plath's afterlife. This 'afterlife', however, occurs only where Hughes occupies the place left by her absence.

Just as he 'did not feel', the 'Ted Hughes' of 'Black Coat' had 'No idea / How that double image, / Your eye's inbuilt double exposure / [...] Came into single focus'; the Hughes who writes 'Black Coat' seemingly knows. This transition is prefigured in the phrase 'potato crisps' (in a reference to a photograph that intrudes upon the poem for no obvious reason): a peculiar Anglo-American compound of 'potato chips' and 'crisps', a kind of coming together of Plath's American nationality and Hughes's Englishness. As with all the *Birthday Letters* poems, Hughes performs the roles of both himself and Plath. The 'double exposure' is not Plath's, but Hughes's, coming into 'single focus' where Hughes sees through his poems to himself. As such, Hughes does not just simply occupy Plath's absence, but sees himself occupying Plath's absence: it is not Plath but Ted Hughes that is 'Looking towards me. Watching me' (*CP* 1109). And he is looking at 'Ted Hughes'. As Hughes finds himself occupying the absent position of Plath, *Birthday Letters* finds a method of mourning that is not fraught with the melancholia of the mythical sequences. However, we could still argue that this is a traumatic representation of Plath, whose role in the poem includes chastising Hughes even as he adopts her voice and suggests its fallibility.

However, in a sleight of hand between 'St Botolph's' and 'Red' there lies a more positive representation of Plath and femininity, suggesting an alternative to Hughes's norm of the traumatic woman. 'Red' provides the enigmatic final line of the collection: 'But the jewel you lost was blue' (*CP* 1170). This indirectly recalls an incident early on in the collection, in 'St Botolph's', which recounts the launch party of the magazine, *St Botolph's Review*, that Hughes started with his university friends. It was at this party that Hughes and Plath first met, and the poem tells from his side the now famous encounter whereby he stole her headscarf and earrings whilst she bit his face. Plath's account of this meeting is published in her journals and was heavily edited on its first publication. The earrings are tellingly absent from the poem, leaving all emphasis on the headscarf. After Plath has left his company, the poem states that he remembers nothing else, other than his girl-friend's 'hissing rage':

> And my stupefied interrogation
> Of your blue headscarf from my pocket
> And the swelling ring-moat of tooth-marks
> That was to brand my face for the next month.
> The me beneath it for good. (*CP* 1052)

The 'blue headscarf' appears to have been something of an after-thought, showing up as a marginal insertion into a draft of the poem, changing the syntax of these final lines in order that the 'stupefied interrogation' does not simply pertain to the bite on his cheek.[20] There are many such occasions where Hughes is left with a physical remainder of Plath's absence. In the next poem in the sequence, 'The Shot', he manages to catch of her 'flight' just 'A wisp of your hair, your ring, your watch, your nightgown' (*CP* 1053). Such things are always insufficient, unable to atone for her absence; they are symbolic reminders of her absence. The 'blue headscarf' of the poem undergoes that symbolic transformation before our eyes: to the 'Ted Hughes' of 'St Botolph's' it is a kind of stain under his 'stupefied interrogation'. It cannot be assimilated in much the same way that Crow is unable to understand the sea, for instance. Except, it is already serving a symbolic purpose in the poem, symbolizing Plath's absence and all that Hughes would be able to retain of her. (The positioning of this poem next to 'The Shot', where he saves those sundry items, is surely no accident.) This takes on an added significance in the final line of 'Red'.

The poem opens with the suggestion that 'Red was your colour', as well as white, before recounting various reds and whites associated with Plath: her choice of bedroom decoration, a red skirt, poppies. This 'red' Plath is a condensed portrait of the 'abject', suicidal Plath we have encountered throughout *Birthday Letters*: traumatic, with roses not symbolizing love but 'the heart's last gouts'. However, amongst her blood-red and bone-white painting, she would occasionally add a 'bluebird'; 'Blue was better' for her, as a 'kindly spirit'. Even though the final line is prefigured a little by blue being 'better', representing wings, enfolding pregnancy, being a 'kindly spirit', this ending remains somewhat enigmatic. If we are to take 'the jewel' as life, then surely red and white, though figured corporeally as both life and death in 'Red', represent an equal loss; they are, after all, supposed to be 'her' colours and are therefore tokens of her life. This blue jewel, in that it exists independent of the body as a 'kindly spirit', poses a problem: it is a remainder, and has survived Plath, who has 'lost' it in committing suicide.

The 'blue headscarf' of 'St Botolph's' returns here as the blue jewel, and it is not Plath's at all, but Hughes's: the subject of his 'stupefied interrogation'. In her journals, Plath recorded that the headscarf she was wearing on the evening of her first meeting with Hughes was actually her treasured red headscarf (red, after all, being her favourite colour).[21] Hughes's misremembering, whether deliberate or otherwise, takes on a quiet significance.[22] 'St Botolph's' lays the seeds of the 'blue' Plath of 'Red', not the 'abject', traumatic Plath of the remainder of the collection, but a tender version of her. Accordingly, the 'blue jewel' at the end of 'Red' is not her loss but his. If Plath's 'abject' red is what life withstands, then her blue is life itself: it 'folded your pregnancy' (*CP* 1170). It is in having survived Plath's death that it becomes a manifestation of Hughes's loss. Just like his 'stupefied interrogation' of the blue headscarf, this blue jewel remains somewhat enigmatic: nonetheless, it represents a symbolic closure, healing the traumatic, 'abject' representation of woman that haunted Hughes's career.

Notes

1. See Jacques Lacan, 'The Agency of the Letter in the Unconscious or Reason since Freud', in *Écrits: A Selection* (London: Routledge, 1995): 161–97.
2. Slavoj Žižek, *How to Read Lacan* (New York: W.W. Norton, 2006): 3.
3. This is, in fact, a widely used misquotation; Adorno actually writes: 'to write poetry after Auschwitz is barbaric'. Theodor Adorno, *Prisms*, trans. Samuel and Shierry Weber (Cambridge, MA: MIT Press, 1983): 34.
4. Julia Kristeva, *Powers of Horror: An Essay on Abjection*, trans. Leon S. Roudiez (New York: Columbia University Press, 1982): 38.
5. *Ibid.*: 3.
6. Slavoj Žižek, *Did Somebody Say Totalitarianism? Five Interventions in the (Mis)use of a Notion* (London: Verso, 2011): 192, 191.
7. The television appearance was 'Poets International: Ted Hughes', ITV Schools (Thames Television), 15 February 1988.
8. See Keith Sagar, *The Laughter of Foxes* (Liverpool: Liverpool University Press, 2006).
9. James Berger, 'Trauma and Literary Theory', *Contemporary Literature*, 38(3) (Autumn 1997): 573.
10. Jacques Lacan, Jacques-Alain Miller and James Hulbert, 'Desire and the Interpretation of Desire in *Hamlet*', *Yale French Studies*, 55/56, *Literature and Psychoanalysis: The Question of Reading: Otherwise* (New Haven, CT: Yale University Press, 1977): 38, at http://www.jstor.org/stable/2930434, accessed 22 August 2014.
11. Neil Roberts, *Ted Hughes: A Literary Life* (Basingstoke: Palgrave Macmillan, 2006): 202.
12. Sigmund Freud, 'Mourning and Melancholia' [1917], in *The Standard Edition of the Complete Psychological Works of Sigmund Freud, Volume XIV (1914–1916): On the History of the Psycho-Analytic Movement, Papers on Metapsychology and Other Works*, ed. James Strachey (London: Vintage, 2001): 237–58, 245.
13. *Ibid.*: 245.
14. *Ibid.*
15. Heather Clark, *The Grief of Influence* (Oxford: Oxford University Press, 2011): 209.
16. Following the publication of *Birthday Letters*, Hughes wrote that his 'feeling of release is marvellous' (*LTH* 731). This release extended to his poetry: 'Once I'd determined to [publish *Birthday Letters*] [...] & started repairing them wherever I could, & writing the last few ones, I suddenly had free energy I hadn't known since Crow' (*LTH* 720).

17. Lacan, Miller and Hulbert, 'Desire and the Interpretation': 38.
18. Janet Malcolm makes a similar observation (prior to the publication of *Birthday Letters*) in relation to Hughes's introductions to Plath's work: 'Hughes can no longer sustain the fiction – on which all autobiographical writing is poised – that the person writing and the person being written about are a single seamless entity. In his second foreword Hughes needs to spell out his awareness of the discontinuity between the observing and observed self.' Janet Malcolm, *The Silent Woman* (2nd edn, London: Picador, 1994): 5.
19. See, e.g. Clark, *Grief of Influence* and Diane Middlebrook, *Her Husband: Hughes and Plath – A Marriage* (London: Little, Brown, 2004).
20. An early version of 'St Botolph's' already forms part of a sequence that would become *Birthday Letters* under the numerical title 'V' (by which we can reasonably infer this is not the first draft of the poem). This version appears to contain the first mention of the 'blue headscarf', given that the marginal insertion changes the syntax rather than just adding a forgotten line from a prior version. See BL Add 88918/1/6.
21. Hughes redacted his 'theft' of Plath's headscarf and earrings from the original publication of Plath's *Journals* – an omission that Jacqueline Rose makes a great deal out of in *The Haunting of Sylvia Plath* (London: Virago, 1991): 121. In the version published after Hughes's death and edited by Karen V. Kukil, we can read Plath's full note, where she writes of her 'lovely red hairband scarf which has weathered the sun and much love, and whose like I shall never again find': *The Journals of Sylvia Plath: 1950–1962*, ed. Karen V. Kukil (London: Faber & Faber, 2000): 212.
22. In no extant version of the poem I could find in the British Library archives is the headscarf described as red, nor do any versions of 'Red' make reference to Plath's favourite red headscarf.

10

Postcolonial Indian Readings

Usha VT and Murali Sivaramakrishnan

Reading Hughes in India

This chapter is a modest attempt to reread Ted Hughes's poetry from an eclectic perspective offered by postcolonial theory and by some aesthetic concepts from Indian traditions.[1] Postcolonial theory is mostly concerned with issues and ideas arising from those countries and peoples who were once colonized by imperial European powers and who have eventually gained political independence. However, this term has also evolved into an umbrella term for problematizing and challenging power, and sites of resistance to any form of dominance, authority and privilege. Postcolonial theory also includes reading and writing from a non-Eurocentric perspective. Because it is concerned with human relations with the natural world, this chapter inevitably also draws from ecocriticism.[2] There is also here an Indian feminist reading[3] which endeavours to seek out the contemporary relevance of Hughes's poetry in a posthumanist context.[4] In all, this chapter argues for a multidimensional holistic perspective on the poet's concerns while attempting to explicate some selected poems from a non-Eurocentric perspective.

Seamus Heaney has pointed out that Ted Hughes, like Geoffrey Hill and Philip Larkin, was 'afflicted with a sense of history that was once the peculiar affliction of the poets of other nations who were not themselves natives of England but who spoke the English language'.[5] We would take this as a starting point towards a reading of the poetry of Ted Hughes from a non-Eurocentric perspective since Hughes could and did find significant readership, not only in his own country, but overseas. In the poem 'Pibroch' Hughes wrote that 'A pebble is imprisoned / Like nothing in the universe' (*CP* 179) and we might say that his poetic vision veers between that of a 'pebble' as a small natural phenomenon in a geographic locale and the deep sea as a sort of limitless and borderless 'universe' of infinite variations. Seamus Heaney goes on to write of Ted Hughes: 'Hughes attempts to make vocal the inner life, the simple being-thereness, "the substance, nature and consequence in life" of sea, stone, wind and tree.'[6] Perhaps we might expand Heaney's notion to suggest that Hughes's work also speaks to those with a sense of non-Eurocentric history, and it is from this context that we begin to read Ted Hughes.

Ted Hughes holds a special appeal to the Indian mind on account of his near-mythic status as a major poet from Britain whose work is sensitive to the mystical and the miraculous. His poems find their significant place in the Indian academic syllabus alongside the work of Shakespeare, W.B. Yeats and T.S. Eliot as canonical writers of English literature whose work can also be approached through Indian cultural concepts. Often, he has been hailed as a poet deeply drawn into the world of power and its portentous politics. This aspect of his poetry has specific postcolonial relevance.

Having said all this, we would like to examine briefly the contexts under which poetry in English from overseas has been academically discussed in Indian universities, because any explication of Hughes's work requires a placing of the British poetic canon in its present postcolonial situation as well, despite his own singular stance as a poet revealing little explicit inclination towards Euro-American Modernism or postmodernism.[7] Postcolonial critics have, for the most part, paid less generous critical attention to poetry from Britain on account of their position as obviously on the other side of the colonial spectrum and therefore seeming quite alien to the demands of the postcolonial Indian reader as issuing from different conditions. Nevertheless, we contend that Hughes demands a greater recognition, not only as a last considerable link with the Romantic tradition (which in its Germanic roots extolled a subversive stance), but as a poet in the fundamental sense as of *vates*, or seer, who struggled to reinspire and reconnect the neglected aspects of human sensibilities with those dormant sources of energy in non-human nature, rather than merely being seen as a British national poet. Hughes's professed position as a poet distinct and disconnected from any Modernist Eurocentric mould invites such a reading and invests him with an *a-historical* position as poet, or *Kavi*, whose work speaks beyond his historical context.

Seen in the light of the theories inspired by the great Sanskrit aestheticians such as Bharata, Bhamaha, Anandavardhana and Abhinavagupta, Ted Hughes occupies a significant position in being part of that long line of poets who uphold the role of 'poetry in life' – *kavi* in the Indian context. In the vision of Sanskrit aestheticians the threefold endowments of a good poet are *pratibha* (inborn genius), *vyutpatti* (extensive and exact learning) and *abhyasa* (constant practice). Hughes exemplifies these three in abundance, especially in his practice of producing volumes of poetry quite different from the previous ones; he was always on the lookout for new sources of inspirational directions to rekindle his own inner *pratibha*.[8] In Hughes's world, poetic vision and poetic voice are integrated, and the poet comes to occupy the sacred role ascribed from ancient times as being endowed with the *srotasya strotram* – the ear within the ear – able to hear and speak of elusive connections and unities in nature. Hughes has written a great deal that explores the possibilities for human reconnection with the elemental sources of creative energy at the heart of all being. By an integration of inspiration and revelation his poetry is able to move between nature – outer, visible, tangible – and inner nature – those silent spaces of the spirit that constitute its *bhava* (emotional state) and *vibhava* (emotional setting or context). Further, in the light of theories inspired by the Dravidian culture of South India (different from those offered by the dominant Sanskritic culture), Hughes's exploration of the human–nature nexus achieves singular significance, especially in the light of *Tinai poetic* – a formalistic concept of linking the environment with poetic situations and seeking correspondences in the human–nature nexus. His nature poetry would be recognized by Dravidian culture as having reached new dimensions in reaching after an aesthetic expression of the elemental and holistic.

In what follows we would also highlight Hughes as a poet who is open to pre-modern and pre-Christian mythologies. Like Yeats, he moves easily between the rational and the irrational, and critiques the simplistic binaries assumed by the still largely patriarchal global culture. His yearning for the sacred and leaning towards the powers of the 'Goddess of complete being' can be seen as clear indications of this arc of poetic energies. This demands a reciprocal openness on the part of his readers to his challenging critical perspectives on patriarchal materialist culture. Together with the many avatars of feminist thinking, postcolonialism has ushered in several critical concepts, applications, strategies and subversive practices for challenging patriarchal value-systems.[9] And a theoretically sophisticated reading need not be either reductive or essentialist, as we hope to show by beginning with an examination of the status of power relations in two popular poems.

The politics of power and the poetic voice

Among the poems which have repeatedly appeared in anthologies, two pieces stand out as resonant for the non-native English speaker: 'The Thought-Fox' and 'Hawk Roosting'. Both are simple narratives with one central or key image: an animal or a bird. However, the hawk in the poem is a little more forcefully physical and corporeal than the fox. Perhaps this could be because there is an attempt to veer between the planes of the real and the symbolic in 'Hawk Roosting'. The hawk is ensconced on a high tree half-asleep and dreaming in his haughty egotistical complacency. The image of a patriarchal dictator pompously slouching behind the self-styled comforts of political power may be familiar to anyone from any of the erstwhile colonial countries. The bird muses on his uniqueness that allows no space for sophistry:

> The sun is behind me.
> Nothing has changed since I began.
> My eye has permitted no change.
> I am going to keep things like this. (*CP* 69)

Such self-deceptive hubris is internationally recognizable in the hawk as allegorical for the human.

On the other hand the fox, albeit depicted in all its animal wholeness as a living creature foraging in the dark, is slowly transformed into the dimension of a symbol. 'The Thought-Fox' epitomizes the struggles of poetic creation. The poem veers between black and white – the process of setting neat prints on white sheets of the human imagination: 'this blank page where my fingers move' (*CP* 21). The presence of the clock and the open window that is starless until the very end juxtaposes absence and presence, the duality of creativity and materiality. The fox, of course, is quite real with its wide green eyes – alive, vibrant, and with its distinct stink. Thus the encounter between the living world and the human imagination is enacted by the poem. A vital reality recharges or engenders the creative.

It is the fusion of nature and the human imagination that sets neat footprints in the white snow that prints out the poem on the blank page. The poet sits in the dark completely drained of the sophistry of the intellect, with the obsessive sound of the ticking clock that works as a reminder of human mortality, while through the window that is starless, the dark presses in. And all this activity occurs in the loneliness of 'this midnight moment's forest' – that is, in the language of the symbolic in the human unconscious.

Ted Hughes was among the generation of English poets who had experienced not only the aftermath of the tremendous upheavals of two world wars, but a post-Second World War opening-up to cross-cultural encounters with America, international folklore and Eastern European poetry. As the twentieth century drew to a close there were also innumerable intellectual and theoretical movements which contested and defied privileged positions and previously held conventional prerogatives. Large-scale immigration and cultural infiltrations into Britain – historically, politically and economically – necessitated, and also ushered in the need for incorporating newer peripherals into the erstwhile canonical positions. Nothing was sacrosanct any more; God was proclaimed dead, and the author eclipsed from the text. The postmodern poet's role was at once restrained and expanded. New and ever newer aesthetic sensibilities came to be incorporated into literatures in English so that the idea of 'commonwealth literature' came to be replaced by 'postcolonialism' and postcolonial literatures. Poetic language in English also consequently underwent multiple revisions, variations and modifications. The journey of imagination that passed from the early works of *The Hawk in the Rain* and *Lupercal* – reworking the early Romantic strains through intimate explorations into the vital world of animals and birds – found sardonic satisfaction in the irreligious evocations of the *Crow* poems. If a poet's silence could also be considered as their means of aesthetic expression, then Hughes also incorporated the dark periods of silence and withdrawal from the public eye into his poetic corpus. (There were seven years of silence between *Lupercal* and *Wodwo*.) The later feminist movement ushered in the idea of the personal as the public and formulated it as an aesthetic. Hughes's personal tribute to his first wife and one-time poetic collaborator, Sylvia Plath, was collected in the volume *Birthday Letters*. A feature of that collaboration was famously Hughes's interest in the paranormal and the occult, especially through their joint use of the Ouija board. This interest in super-consciousness could be linked with the idea of the poet as the visionary. This is where Indian Sanskritic theorizing would come to our aid.

There are innumerable theories and positions to choose from in the Indian context. But whatever might be the school of poetics that one chooses to side with, and whatever the concepts one wishes to apply to any given poetic work, the major idea would be to trace the process of the aesthetic route towards the poem's final culmination or *rasa*. In the final analysis the aesthetic object would be reckoned as the creation of a heightened awareness, or of a sensibility that is fine-tuned. The *Kavi,* or poet, fulfils his/her vision as the seer or *vates*.

Vision is beheld as the characteristic power of the poet. To this extent Ted Hughes fulfils the Sanskrit aesthetic criteria as a visionary poet endowed with a heightened sensibility.

But an Indian reader will not forget that Hughes could also be seen to epitomize the visionary eye of the unified spirit of European poetry. There is a powerful line of visionary insight that could be traced from Shakespeare (the supreme British bard), through W.B. Yeats (the characteristic Celtic visionary), down to Ted Hughes (specifically, for instance, in *Remains of Elmet*). In him the two separate streams merge and blend together. His openness to the non-insular posthumanistic and emergent ecological sensitivity mark his work out as an undying orphic strain – an integration of the Apollonian and the Dionysian spirits of classical European tradition.

Early in his career Hughes was dubbed the 'voyeur of violence'.[10] His poems describe in detail a great deal of the violence in nature – and in the everyday repressions of post-war England – in its stark rawness. The violent quality of the pike or the hawk, or even the magical speed of horses in 'A Dream of Horses', is highlighted through his early poems. Hughes seems to revel in violence, but only an awareness of his theories of energy would enable a serious insight into his poetic world. As Hughes states in his interview with Egbert Faas, 'Any form of violence – any form of vehement activity – invokes the bigger energy, the elemental power circuit of the universe. Once the contact has been made – it becomes difficult to control. Something from beyond ordinary human activity enters.'[11] His early nature poems in particular attempt to invoke this elemental energy, whose force is quite overpowering and never mundane. Hughes explains the impact of these energies further when he says, 'If you refuse the energy, you are living a kind of death. If you accept the energy, it destroys you.'[12] His poems are peopled with personae relating to both extremes, in keeping with his theory that the only solution to the problems of the modern wasteland would be to 'accept the energy, and find methods of turning it to good, of keeping it under control – rituals, the machinery of religion'.[13] To this end Hughes explores through his poetry the religious rituals of several religions. He travels from the practices of Christianity through pre-Christian Dionysian rituals and moves beyond conventional European myths to the practices of Tibetan Buddhism or Egyptian Manichaeanism. The shamanistic practices of Native Americans and the mystery of the Cabbala impressed Hughes equally. He experimented poetically with rituals and practices that enabled him to invoke the elemental energies.

He believed that the role of the poet was a very important one, a link between the human and those universal energies. The shaman in many primitive religions took on the form of animals and sometimes of women. So Hughes placed animals and female figures on a higher pedestal and looked up to them for deliverance from the ailments of the modern age. He also revered the insights provided by a goddess-centred religion such as the European Dionysian, or the various world folk traditions wherein the goddess was all-powerful. He believed that it was the banishing of the influence of the 'goddess of complete being' from the contemporary world that led to the current situation of decadence. This is evidenced in his portrayal of postwar complacency through the human personae of his early poetic world. His notions of barrenness and spiritual deprivation could also be interpreted in the context of several mainstream Indian religious notions.

Indian traditions speak of *Ardhanareswara*, where both the male and female principles are fused together as one unit. Thus, neither the male nor the female god is complete without the spouse, and the female is usually seen as the source of power, the vital energy, as in the relationships between Siva and Shakti, Lakshmi and Vishnu, Brahma and Saraswati. Each of these godheads are worshipped both individually and jointly, each representing a unique form of goodness, or universal energy, such as prosperity or learning, the emphasis being on acceptance and acquiescence rather than denial or abstinence. The goddess in these traditions is revered and feared due to her immense elemental power. Her calm presence as virgin and spouse and mother (*Devi* and *Durga/Amma*) is respected, and her violent form as *Kali* or avenger is treated with awe. This is true in the case of the high Sanskritic traditions (*marga*) as well as the small (*desi*) local traditions. Folk tales and rituals also link the goddess to the earth and nature in its many avatars, whether violent or peaceful. Indeed, worship of the goddess pre-dates the emergence of organized religions, just as it pre-dated, but provided ready roots for, Indian feminism.

The goddess takes multiple forms in Hughes's poetic corpus. She is, at once, the source of his creative inspiration and his characters' despair – their failures to find her being linked to his own despair, as is most clear from the 'Epilogue' poems of *Gaudete*. She is, indeed, the White Goddess as described by Robert Graves, who is linked to the Catholic figure of Mary by Ted Hughes,[14] or with the ancient and suppressed tradition of witchcraft. That is to say, Hughes recognizes

that she can be *Devi*, 'A Green Mother' of *Cave Birds* (*CP* 431), or
Kali as in 'Witches':

> Bitches still sulk, rosebuds blow,
> And we are devilled. And though these weep
> Over our harms, who's to know
> Where their feet dance while their heads sleep? (*CP* 80)

Retrospectively, it can be seen that Hughes's early attempts to evoke
the universal powers of energy and vitality were an expression of his
passion for the goddess as represented by animals and birds. Hughes's
Crow, for instance, seems to represent the vital energies from the
animal world that does not recognize notions of universal order and
harmony, as sanctioned by religious beliefs. In the poem 'A Horrible
Religious Error', for instance, the emergence of the serpent reduces
man and woman to a stage where 'knees melted, they collapsed [...]
and whispered "Your will is our peace"'. Only Crow remains unper-
turbed, acts within his nature, dealing with it as a predator from the
animal world would have. He stepped forward, 'Grabbed this creature
by the slackskin nape, // Beat the hell out of it, and ate it' (*CP* 231).
The action of the crow, though apparently irreligious and lacking in
guile or sophistication, is very effective in dealing with the situation
through an instinctive animal response.

The human personae of Hughes's early poems reflect his disillusion
with the post-war mood of despondency and desolation. Many of them
are represented as dull and frustrated, leading mediocre and repressed
lives. But the presence of universal energy is revealed in some of them
in rare glimpses through surges of repressed power, as well as in the natural world of animals, birds, fishes and the wind and the moon, making
the reader aware of the presence of the goddess. 'The Secretary' in his
poem of this title in the first collection *The Hawk in the Rain*, is very
much like the typist of T.S. Eliot's *The Waste Land*, leading a routine life,
without hope, without feeling, and satisfied to be 'safe home at last' set-
tling down to unproductive domesticity. By denying her sexuality and
hiding her beauty, Hughes suggests that she represents a society denying
itself rejuvenation and vitality. At other times the divine power of the
goddess is misused and distorted by commercialization and exploitation, as seen in the poem 'The Hag'.

The uncompromising old woman, in the folkloric figure of 'The
Hag', not only denying herself, but forcing a life of austerity upon
her young daughter for fear that 'the world shall make a jam of it /
To spread on every palate', is a typical representative of the post-
war world, for she would prefer to reveal 'nine bolts of spite' than

'one leash of love', even to the girl she loves passionately (*CP* 40). The dread of the force and power of love, and its ability to turn the incumbents astray through lack of trust and fear of betrayal, is reflected in every line of the poem. Unlike Christabel in Coleridge's poem of that name, Hughes's poetic persona, the lovely girl, finds it easier to ignore the true love repressed within her mother, the hag's heart, and prefers to accept a corrupted loveless world. The situation approximates to what Hughes has described in his Introduction to *A Choice of Shakespeare's Verse*:

> When the physical presence of love has been degraded to lust, and forbidden lust has combined with every other forbidden thing to become a murderous devil, life itself becomes a horror, the maiden has become a whore and a witch, and [the] miraculous source of creation has become the empty hole through into Nothing.[15]

To Hughes this represents the decadence of the present age with its lack of faith in any God or goddess. The mood of despair and gloom is reiterated in many of his poems. The 'Famous Poet' has become a misnomer in that poem, for he has lost his creativity, and is presented as a monstrosity, a blot on the civilization, for he had traded verbal pyrotechnics for genuine creativity. His 'heady ambition' had led him to his current state of humiliation, denying him his creative inspiration, making him pursue false gods and leaving him ultimately a mere wreck.

Hughes draws the reader's attention to the power of primal energy even in these early poems where he contrasts the lack of vitality with the hidden powers implicit in the natural world. This energy is seen in such early poems as 'Macaw and Little Miss', where both the macaw and the girl display short fits of passion, but are not able to sustain it to connect with the elemental. The 'staring combustion' and the 'stroking devils' in the macaw's eyes provide insights into the hidden energies still within the caged bird. The girl's dreams of the warrior and his sexual assault are a reflection of the possible connection with the universal power source which cannot be sustained. In 'Full Moon and Little Frieda' from *Wodwo*, the routine and the mundane reality develops a magical quality when the connection with elemental energy is established briefly. Even the moon is overawed at the wonder that is evoked by the words of the child, the little goddess. The simplicity of the words and the directness of tone weave a magic of immense poetic beauty.

> 'Moon!' you cry suddenly, 'Moon! Moon!'
> The moon has stepped back like an artist gazing amazed at a work
> That points at him amazed. (*CP* 183)

Another short early lyric, 'To Paint a Waterlily', reveals the innate poetic vision of the seer in Hughes by an integration of boundless revelation and poetic inspiration. The perceptual part of the poem veers between nature (outer, visible, tangible) and inner nature (silent spaces of the spirit that constitute its *bhava* and *vibhava*).[16] The sort of advisory voice that the poem poses appears to whisper to the painter how to capture the elemental essence of the water lily that is apparently both in water and out of the water. But the poet's eye reaches between the real and the imagined, and explores the space–time of the infinite: there is a Zen-like quality in this short lyric that reaches for a synthesis of the elemental and the holistic.

Hughes's discovery of the South Indian (specifically Kannada) vacana form of poetry through the translations of A.K. Ramanujan[17] brought an immense linguistic freedom to the poems that constitute the 'Epilogue' to *Gaudete*. Hughes wrote 'about a hundred of them',[18] mostly preserved in his unpublished 'Vacana Notebook', from which only eighteen were published as the 'Epilogue' poems. Vacanas within the Kannada Virarasaiva tradition were popular in the twelfth to sixteenth centuries in South India. Like the poets Basavanna and Mahadeviyakka, who addressed their individual/personal gods through vacana songs, Hughes's character Lumb addressed his poems to his goddess. What inspired Hughes was both the stance and the language of these poems, which were simple, direct and honest. In the Indian *bhakti* traditions, where the poems were sung, both men and women poets assumed the role of a female lover pining for her male beloved in his absence whilst awaiting his arrival. The speaker of Hughes's vacana poems takes on the form of a male lover speaking to his goddess. The Indian poems belong to the *dasa* tradition, closely allied to the folk practices and often located within the *desi,* the little conventions, which are often placed in opposition to the then mainstream Sanskritic or *marga* discourses. The Indian poets spoke directly to their specific and personal god and placed complete faith in Him. Hughes, on the other hand, explores doubts and confusions through these poems addressed to the goddess, bringing the modern predicament to the fore. While the identity of the goddess of Lumb's vacana poems is not directly revealed, Ann Skea suggests that Hughes identifies the goddess of the Vacana Notebook as largely 'the Lady of the Hill', but also in some poems as his mother and in some as Sylvia Plath.[19] In *Birthday Letters* Hughes manages to break his silence following Plath's death and speak out about his personal relationship with her and their intensely creative partnership. With these poems he was finally able to make the personal into the poetical.

Decades ago, in his book *The Turning Point*, Fritjof Capra deciphered the interrelationship of the evolving history of ideas and pointed out that 'rational thinking is linear, whereas the ecological awareness rises from an intuition of nonlinear systems'.[20] He went on to argue:

> Ecological awareness, then, will arise only when we combine our rational knowledge with an intuition for the nonlinear nature of our environment. Such intuitive wisdom is characteristic of traditional, non-literate cultures, especially of American Indian cultures, in which life was organized around a highly refined awareness of the environment.[21]

Ted Hughes reveals the clear strains of an emerging ecological awareness in the human species. Indeed, it might not be out of place to mention that a true mixture of social conscience and eco-consciousness is evidenced especially in his later volumes like *River*. These poems, with their centralizing image of the river, bring together the ecological and the aesthetic. In the light of Heaney's claim, cited at the beginning of this chapter, that Hughes was 'afflicted with a sense of history' which was mythic and ancestral, could it be this which drove him to create these poems?

> The whole river
> Listened to me, and, blind,
> Invisibly watched me. And held me deeper
> With its blind, invisible hands.
> 'We've got him,' it whispered, 'We've got him.' (*CP* 660)

What is remarkable about these poems is Hughes's being able to identify with the river and its environment wholly as a living thing and seeing with a sense of being both in it and outside it at the same time. Wading through the *River* poems are both a British angler and an ancient ahistorical human native in quest of food, totems, guiding spirits in the form of fish or, perhaps, otters and foxes.

In Dravidian aesthetic terms (as drawn from the ur-text of medieval Tamil grammar, *Tolkappiam*[22]), the notion of *Tinai*, or environmental thinking, runs parallel to creative and emotional expression. An eco-poetic reading of Ted Hughes's poems with the aid of this Tamil aesthetic could certainly offer very interesting results for future scholars. However, the spiritual essence of the ecological vision seems to find its ideal expression in the feminist spirituality advocated by the modern women's movement, but long practised in India by the goddess cults, in their counterbalancing relationship with their paired masculine gods, as described above. Feminist spirituality is based on awareness of the oneness of all living forms and of their cyclical rhythms of birth and death, thus reflecting an attitude towards life that is profoundly ecological.

Ted Hughes: 'english' poet

When we read poetry at any level it would, of course, be worthwhile to inquire into its origins and background. Poetry from the West read by a culturally and linguistically alienated reader in another code of reception in, say, the Indian subcontinent, calls for an additional level of understanding as well. In due recognition of diverse cultural contexts and historical differences, poetry from England would make a little more sense and could appeal to a wider audience when understood in the light of the reader's indigenous poetics.

The Indian critic Sri Aurobindo pointed out as early as 1917 that there were characteristic streams that served to differentiate and identify each geographic locale and each cultural milieu in poetry worldwide. In *The Future Poetry* [23] he argued that poetry is an indicator of the evolving human soul, and in history it is also an instrument of the evolutionary upsurge. This general evolution of the aesthetic consciousness within cultures and nations, as he sees it, has its own natural periods or ages, but it is necessarily not linear or sequential. Each nation develops a spirit in its inner being that is a special soul-form and a law of its nature which determines the course of its evolution. All cultural self-expression would be conditioned by this soul-form. And it is the English poetic spirit, at the meeting place of the Teuton and the Celt, which reveals itself as an excellent instance of a national creative spirit describing with remarkable fidelity the natural curve and stages of the psychological evolution of poetry. Thus, in the Aurobindian scheme of things, the history of world poetry traces an arc of evolving human consciousness. Ted Hughes's poetry occurs at that point in world poetry where the vital powers evolve into unity with the higher spiritual. With his integral visionary eye the poet is endowed with a unified sensibility: of being and becoming. His poetry also reveals the deeper powers of the human psyche that perceives the spiritual unity of the human–nature nexus.

In the final analysis, Ted Hughes's work, albeit in his own region-specific voice, remains an open text allowing multiple possibilities of interpretation and approach. The readings offered here do not seek any qualitative analysis or attempt to pass any value judgements on his merits and demerits. It is not our intention to 'punish him under a foreign code', as Auden put it when he wrote about reading Yeats's work.[24] The intention has been primarily to inquire into the possibilities of unravelling Hughes's vision in the light of an Indian postcolonial context and re-examine him with some conceptual ideas having their origin in a set different cultural codes. Ted Hughes remains interesting as a visionary poet whose themes are indeed wide-ranging despite their being rooted in Englishness. His profound love for his own Yorkshire Pennines and Devon rivers have not limited his range of cultural reference, or his most profound meanings to just those of Yorkshire outcrop stone or Devon river spirits, for example. Like a pebble that is trapped in its own nothingness in the universe of difference, Hughes's work reaches that universal sea of poetic expression in what postcolonial scholars call an 'english' that is in use beyond England. He may not be a postcolonial poet in some political senses of the term. Neither was he genuinely aware of the vagaries of cultural differences couched in the 'english' language in the true postcolonial sense. But his visionary eye that roves between the pebble and the deep blue sea is a clear indication of his value as a poet for our own times, not tied only to his geography, not tied only to the island's insularity and not tied only to his national history.

Perhaps as a poet of our times Hughes inherits the traumas and travails of a generation that speaks multiple languages, engages with a host of cultural influences, and yet stands its own ground resisting the dominance of power and its self-important games. Hughes speaks a lot about power, and his work affords innumerable signs of the complexity of vitality and the desire to learn from the energies of non-human nature. On that level his poems offer hope and faith for postcolonial times of turmoil and opportunity like ours. He allows the element of wonder to grow like the full moon; his male ego is diminished in the face of the posthuman energies and mysteries of nature; and yet he does not let go of the humanity that reaches beyond his rooted condition as a white Anglo-Saxon poet. It is his deeper involvement with the elemental forces of nature that leads him to see beyond the rock and the star, the pebble and the universe. In this sense he is a *Kavi* – the seer who sees with the inner eye and hears with the inner ear.

Notes

1. There is no pan-Indian aesthetic theory that one can refer to, for all times, in equal measure – postcolonial or otherwise. Sanskrit aesthetics is one among the many dominant theories and has evolved alongside the regional in India. However, Sanskrit poetics has a continuous history

over a millennium, with concepts, texts, interpretations, theory and counter-theory that are invariably non-Eurocentric. Of course, many of the specialized conceptual categories and terms have undergone historical change through use and overuse in different cultural and regional situations, and even merged indistinguishably over the years into a sort of generalized *Indic* perspective. While resorting to Sanskrit aesthetics in the light of postcolonial theory in reading Ted Hughes here, we are not equating the two; on the other hand, our attempt is to link poetic theories with comparative perspectives. For a detailed discussion of Sanskritic views of poetry and poetics see Krishna Chaitanya, *Sanskrit Poetics: A Critical and Comparative Study* (Delhi: Asia Publishing House, 1965) and P.V. Kane, *History of Sanskrit Poetics* (4th edn, Delhi: Motilal Banarsidass, 1971). As for Dravidian theories, we have used the *Tinai poetic* as gathered from the earliest Tamil grammatical text of *Tolkappiam* (*c.* first century BC). For an introductory reading see S. Murali, 'Environmental Aesthetics: Interpretation of Nature in Akam and Puram Poetry', *Indian Literature*, 185 (May–June 1998): 155–62. (See also note 23 below.)

2. See also Chapter 12.
3. See also Chapter 6.
4. See also Chapter 11.
5. Seamus Heaney, 'Hughes and England', in Keith Sagar (ed.), *The Achievement of Ted Hughes* (Manchester: Manchester University Press): 15.
6. *Ibid.*: 21.
7. See Chapter 2.
8. A poet is one who is a seer, a prophet, who sees visions and possesses the additional gift of conveying to others less fortunate through the medium of language, the visions he has or the dreams he dreams (Kane, *History of Sanskrit Poetics*: 348).
9. For the history and evolution of the term 'postcolonialism' see Kirsten Holst Peterson and Anna Rutherford (eds), *From Commonwealth to Postcolonial: Critical Essays* (Sydney: Dangaroo Press, 1992). For further clarifications of the term and related concepts see Stephen Slemon and Helen Tiffin, *After Europe* (Aarhus: Dangaroo Press, 1989) and Vijay Mishra and Bob Hodge, 'What is Postcolonialism?', in Patrick Williams and Laura Chrisman (eds), *Colonial Disourse and Postcolonial Theory: A Reader* (New York: Harvester Wheatsheaf, 1993): 276–90.
10. Calvin Bedient, *Eight Contemporary Poets* (London: Oxford University Press, 1974): 108.
11. Egbert Faas, *Ted Hughes: The Unaccommodated Universe* (Santa Barbara, CA: Black Sparrow Press, 1980): 200.
12. *Ibid.*
13. *Ibid.*
14. *Ibid.*: 197–8.
15. Ted Hughes, *A Choice of Shakespeare's Verse* (London: Faber & Faber, 1971): 199.

16. See p. 147 above for an explanation.
17. A.K. Ramanujan, *Speaking of Siva* (London: Penguin, 1973).
18. Faas, *Ted Hughes*: 138.
19. See Ann Skea, 'Ted Hughes' Vacanas: The Difficulties of a Bridegroom', in Mark Wormald, Neil Roberts and Terry Gifford (eds), *Ted Hughes: From Cambridge to Collected* (Basingstoke: Palgrave Macmillan, 2013): 81–95.
20. Fritjof Capra, *The Turning Point: Science, Society and the Rising Culture* (London: Flamingo, 1983): 25.
21. *Ibid.*
22. *Tolkappiyam*, the oldest available work on poetics in Tamil, is an essential treatise on poetry, grammar and meaning. The text, which was composed over many centuries, spans the Tamil Sangam period roughly between the third century BC to the third century AD. In many ways, the Sangam Age in South India is a unique instance of an ecological wisdom in collective practice.
23. Sri Aurobindo, *The Future Poetry* (2nd edn, Pondicherry: Sri Aurobindo Ashram, 1983).
24. W.H. Auden, 'In Memory of W.B. Yeats', in *W.H. Auden: A Selection by the Author* (Harmondsworth: Penguin, 1958): 66.

11

Posthumanist Readings

Iris Ralph

What are the dimensions of posthumanism?

Since the publication of Hughes's first poetry collection *The Hawk in the Rain*, scholars writing on his animal poems have done so in terms – philosophical, ethical, moral and aesthetic – that betray a trenchant, albeit laudable, *humanist* mode of intellectual inquiry. In this same period of time another kind of thinking has emerged out of a number of disciplines straddling the arts and sciences that in many instances has challenged this mode. The second kind of thinking – a *posthumanist* mode of intellectual inquiry, mentioned at the end of the last chapter – forms the basis of the following discussion of Hughes's work which is aimed at broadening critical approaches to Hughes. Drawing mainly on the work of posthumanist animal scholar Cary Wolfe, it examines Hughes's poetry according to what Wolfe distinguishes as two trajectories of posthumanism – 'posthumanist posthumanism' and 'humanist posthumanism'[1] – and according to two areas of posthumanism – animal studies and systems theory.

Humanism, broadly speaking, refers to a mode of thinking that emerged in the early modern period in Western Europe around the time of the Renaissance, when older beliefs about the essential baseness and corruption of humans began to be overturned. The human body, the earth's body and other bodies in what was known of the solar system then began to be appreciated as indeed marvellous mechanisms, systems and machineries. In the time of the Enlightenment and with the establishment of the natural sciences, this mode of thinking gained further ground. Although one of the enduring legacies of the latter period in Western history is the focus on the physical and material properties of being and existence, the privileged position given to the human subject in humans' new-found, object world was not seriously questioned. Carolus Linnaeus, the 'founder of modern scientific taxonomy',[2] unintentionally helped to promote this under-standing of the human when he placed the human species above all the other species in his famous *Systema naturae*.[3]

In later centuries, many humans, or those who most prominently spoke for the human species, did not fundamentally question either the belief that the human species was superior to other species, or the belief that in order for humans to realise their full potential they must overcome their baser, animal, object natures. Between the nineteenth century and first half of the twentieth century humans were less sure about their species, particularly under the influence of Charles Darwin's theory of the evolution of the species, Sigmund Freud's theory of the unconscious (which put into doubt that the human subject is fully self-conscious or constituted by what it claims constitutes its self) and Karl Marx and Friedrich Engels's historical materialism (which holds that thought, or consciousness, does not determine, but rather is determined by an individual's social and material existence). At the same time, in both the sciences and the humanities, distinctions made between humans and other animal species continued to give pre-eminence to the human species. One of these distinctions, a fundamental one, claims that whilst humans possess both an external objective identity and an internal subjective identity, nonhumans possess only an exterior objective identity. Critically tied to this distinction is the assumption that the interior subjective realm, that is exclusive to humans, is far more complex, capacious and multi-dimensional than any anterior objective realm or environment.

Beginning in the 1940s and 1950s, gaining momentum in the next two decades, and making an appearance in the expansion of literary theory in the 1980s, a different kind of thinking, posthumanism, emerged. This can be described in some instances as the reaction against humanism and in many other instances, the continuation of it. Wolfe distinguishes the first kind rather inelegantly as 'posthumanist posthumanism' and the second kind as 'humanist posthumanism'. The latter is focused on how, in the wake of leaps in science and technology, the human mind and body are being extended or altered in such ways as to make it difficult to determine where actually the human parts of humans end (our minds, brains, consciousnesses, sensitivities, subjectivities, and so on) and where the nonhuman parts of us begin. The extensions and enhancements of humans according to the invention of, and then dependence upon, a vast array of prosthetics – computers and other digital devices, implants such as pacemakers, pharmaceuticals, organ transplants, artificial limbs, contact lenses, hearing aids, and so on – suggest that we have been, all along, already 'cyborgs', that is, part human and part nonhuman. Here, however, humanist posthumanist thinking diverges according to two different sets of interests and ethical positions. The most popular humanist posthumanist arguments are those that defend humans' management or exploitation of nonhuman animals and other nonhuman species according to the interests of humans. This approach is based upon the humanist belief that human interests are separable from, but have priority over, nonhuman interests. Under these kinds of arguments, there is also an enthusiastic support for scientific and technological experiments that promise one day to liberate humans from their nonhuman biological bodies, to allow humans to discard their bodies altogether in a kind of post-cyborg existence.

Notwithstanding the humanist posthumanist arguments that give priority to transcendent human agendas, a different set of humanist posthumanist arguments – one that is more pertinent to studying the poetry of Hughes – characterizes many of the debates about distinctions between humans and nonhumans.[4] Here the focus is on where (and when) the human stops (if it actually ever stops) being a nonhuman animal and (in face of the mounting evidence that there is no single defining human trait) on the ethical implications of treating animals as if they are *not animals*. Donna Haraway's famous essay, titled (in its shorter form) 'A Cyborg Manifesto' (1985), might be used here to represent this second kind of humanist posthumanism. Whilst her writing may not have been known to Hughes and whilst the study of cybernetics might not have interested Hughes especially, both deserve a brief mention, for they fall into the category of posthumanist inquiries and they have been used to support rights for nonhuman animals, which do relate to Hughes and to the prodigious number of poems he devotes to the other-than-human animal species.

Cybernetics received attention from scholars in the humanities almost immediately in the wake of Haraway's essay. Haraway makes the case for the cyborg – the creature that is simultaneously 'animal and machine' which she variously describes as 'fiction', 'natural' and 'crafted'.[5] Although she mostly focuses on the female human as a cyborg creature, she also represents and defends the nonhuman animal as such a creature. She argues that animal rights movements are not 'irrational denials of human uniqueness'; rather they are 'a clear-sighted recognition of connections across the discredited breach of nature and culture'.[6]

The mainstream animal rights movements that Haraway refers to typically operate according to a humanist posthumanist logic.

Peter Singer[7] and Tom Regan[8] are the two most important Western animal rights philosophers of the twentieth century in this regard. Although there are significant differences between Singer and Regan – the former calls for a practical, so-called utilitarian defence of animals and the latter for a radical defence of animals – both implicitly rely on the human subject as the standard or norm for defining and categorizing the other-than-human animal species. Analogous to classic human rights arguments, which advocate for an oppressed human minority (for example, women, non-whites or people who are mentally or physically disabled), the animal rights arguments of Singer and Regan are defences of animals on the basis of shared traits, in particular the shared traits of subjectivity and capacity for suffering.

Whilst the most popular (and powerfully successful) humanist post-humanist arguments in defence of nonhuman animal species focus on similarities between humans and animals, and thus garner rights and respect for the latter, 'posthumanist posthumanist' arguments, also in defence of nonhuman animal species, dispute using the human species as a measuring stick for defining and categorizing other species. The main premise under these arguments is that the human, in any shape or form, ought not be used as a 'norm' for appraising other species. As Wolfe points out, popular humanist posthumanist animal rights arguments might be faulted for their speciesism: if an animal cannot be shown to be *like* the human, it stands less chance of being given the rights that humans have as a species, let alone the rights that a human has as both a 'subject' and an 'individual'.[9] Posthumanist posthuman-ist scholars thus look elsewhere for an approach that recognizes the other-than-human animal. Wolfe finds this approach in systems theory, an area of study which emerged in the cognitive sciences at the same time as cybernetics.

Systems theory puts emphasis on the differences between species. It does not 'occlude, deny, or otherwise devalue difference';[10] rather, it '*begins* with difference'.[11] This emphasis upon difference is based on the premise that the autonomy of a species, and differentiation or complexity within a species, are the key to a species' ability to 'progress'. At the same time, however, a species' survival or autonomy critically depends on the kinds of pressure exerted on it by other species and their systems. In response to external pressure, a species will adapt by differentiating internally, or by becoming more, not less, complex. However, it will do so as long as it is relatively *free* to do so. It will adapt as long as *its* response to the pressure exerted on it by other species and systems is generated as much on its *own* terms as on the terms that the other species and systems are imposing upon it. On the one hand, with too little pressured *interaction* with other species and systems, it will reduce and stagnate; on the other hand, with too much interference from other species and systems, it will be compromised and suffer loss.

According to systems theory, therefore, animal species and their systems are not inferior to the human species and its systems. By the same token, the human species and its systems are potentially as unique and complex as other species and systems. To recapitulate, this uniqueness and complexity do not depend on the ability of the species to overrule the terms of existence of other species and systems; rather these features depend upon the capacity of the species to interact with other species and systems. When one species dictates in too stentorian terms the existence of another species and its systems it will ultimately face extinction.

Hughes's early animal poems

Hughes's interest in the figure of the animal in almost all of the poetry he produced has been commented on by many critics, including foremost Hong Chen, Terry Gifford, Keith Sagar and Leonard M. Scigaj. These scholars have not addressed this interest by engaging in posthumanism scholarly inquiries, but their work presses other scholars to do so according to one or more of posthumanism's trajectories. Hughes's interest in nonhuman animals that he acknowledges as entities who are as curious, sensitive, vulnerable, rapacious, terrifying and capacious as humans are – that is to say, as complex as humans – supports the posthumanist argument that humans are not essentially more noteworthy, distinct, sophisticated or knowledgeable than other species. With regard to the belief that human intelligence can be clearly distinguished or separated out from nonhuman intelligence, Hughes uses sight, which has a long history in Western philosophy as a metaphor for pure, objective or unbiased perspective, in a way that questions this belief.

In the early poem 'Meeting' (*CP* 35–6) the poet-speaker is surprised by a goat that suddenly appears in front of him on the mountain precipice. The animal runs 'Towards him' before stopping still and looking down at him from 'above'. As the human confronts the animal's 'square-pupilled yellow-eyed look' and 'black devil head against the blue air', he becomes an object of inspection. 'Gigantic fingers' seem to take him up on a 'bare / Palm […] close under an eye / That was like a living hanging hemisphere'. It watches him with a stare 'Slow and cold and ferocious as a star' until the moment the goat leaps away. There is a sense that, in the encounter with a fellow animal being as an Other, the human's sight is dislocated and his complacent foothold or perspective on the world might subtly need to shift to accommodate this other that faces him.

The poem 'The Casualty' (*CP* 42–3) and the poem that follows it, 'Bayonet Charge' (*CP* 43–4), both from the first collection *The Hawk in the Rain,* confront interhuman violence, specifically two interhuman conflicts which had a tremendous impact on Hughes and his generation, the two world wars. A posthumanist reading offers the insight that such poems are also about the recognition and registering of the human by the nonhuman world as well as about the question of where and when one stops being nonhuman. 'The Casualty' describes the death of a human aviator from an imagined nonhuman as well as from a normative human perspective. One of the ways the poem achieves this is through the many nouns that refer to nonhuman figures (to animals in particular) and the many pronouns that refer and give secondary notice to human figures. Two other ways the poem achieves this are the abrupt shifts from stanza to stanza between human and nonhuman perspectives, and, again, the displacement (literally) of human sight.

In the first stanza, in which an ostensibly human perspective is offered, the poem's third-person speaker tells us that a plane has been shot down over the English countryside. 'Farmers in the fields, housewives behind steamed windows, / Watch the burning aircraft across the blue sky float, / As if a firefly and a spider fought'. Afterwards, they 'wait with interest for the evening news'. In the second stanza we read:

> But already, in a brambled ditch, suddenly-smashed
> Stems twitch. In the stubble a pheasant
> Is craning every way in astonishment.
> The hare that hops up, quizzical, hesitant,
> Flattens ears and tears madly away and the wren warns. (*CP* 42)

On first reading these lines and before reading the remaining five stanzas, 'suddenly-smashed stems' appears to be a reference to grass or other vegetation in the fields that have been flattened, perhaps by the aircraft that has been shot down, or by the movements of one of the small animals alluded to in this second stanza. However, after reading the poem through to its end, 'suddenly-smashed stems' also appears to refer to the torn, mangled limbs of the man who has fallen from the burning aircraft.

The swinging back and forth between human and nonhuman perspectives in the remaining five stanzas and the continuation of references to the animals in the field who see, feel, hear and *sense* the man who has fallen 'out of the air alive' intensify the referential ambiguity begun in the second stanza. The use of pronouns in reference to human figures, which occurs in all but the first stanza, also creates ambiguity about who, or what, is being referenced. In the third stanza, the appearance of the words 'some' and 'they' might be taken to be references to human spectators who are drawn to the site of the fallen burning aircraft and man. 'They jostle above, / They peer down' upon the human–nonhuman wreckage, as if expecting to see 'there / A snake in the gloom of the brambles or a rare flower'. By the time we reach the fourth stanza, we are being asked or persuaded not to presume who or what is doing the looking, hearing, seeing or feeling in response to the man who has fallen out of the sky. Propped up against some 'heaped sheaves', the casualty's body gives a sudden heave of its heart which 'shakes his body'. The abrupt and violent movement causes one of his eyeballs to fall from its socket on to the ground and come to rest on his handkerchief. It 'Widens childishly' and 'they look down / On the handkerchief at which his eye stares up'. Human yet not human, the eye stares back and up at its witnesses from its resting place on its diminutive burial shroud and from a level that aligns with the sight of the animals in the field – a hare, a pheasant and a wren in the vicinity.

One can consider as gratuitous gore the description of the burned pilot who 'has / No spine', whose body must be propped up against 'heaped sheaves', who is barely recognizable as a human and whose eyeball has been ejected by the death-throes of his heart. One can also view this language, including the description of the dislocated eyeball that stares back up and out at the human from and out of a nonhuman place, from a humanist posthumanist perspective according to the claim that the boundary between the human and the nonhuman, and the human animal and the nonhuman animal, is not a fixed division.

The many poems by Hughes about caged, hunted and discarded animals relate in particular to posthumanist engagements with the ethical issue of the exploitation of the nonhuman animal by the human animal. Many scholars have commented on the poet's 'violent bestiary' of animals,[12] or on the ways in which Hughes's animals function as symbols of primal nature, the elemental, or base motivation. Not only do we find in this scholarship an underlying or unacknowledged assumption that animals are, in fact, more primitive, or more *natural*, than humans, we also find a lack of recognition of the idea that Hughes might be considering the animals as having histories, narratives, lives and deaths that lie outside the identities that humans thrust upon them. The ways in which animals are discarded by humans, or not given the kind of respect that humans give to their own dead, once the animals have lived out their 'usefulness' as defined by humans, is a powerful theme of Hughes's writing. Many of the poems suggest that animals and animal identities are stymied or reduced by the human species. 'February' (*CP* 61), from the second collection *Lupercal*, implicitly comments on the loss of the world's large vertebrate animal species (also called 'mega fauna') as a consequence of human depredation. It describes in stark language what is left of the wolf species – a photograph of 'the hairless, knuckled feet / Of the last wolf killed in Britain', engravings of 'gibbet-hung wolves', a cage that had once housed a malnourished 'scraggy Spanish wolf' begging for a ball to be thrown by human spectators. The poem also comments on the attrition of animal identity as a result of the domestication of animals by humans: the wolf species has been reduced to 'so much mere Alsatian'. 'An Otter' (*CP* 79–80) focuses on the suffering of animals used for sport by humans and the ways in which humans divest animals of their identities when they are so debased. Chased by human hunters and their 'hounds and vermin-poles', caught at last and 'yanked above' the hounds by the hunters, an otter 'reverts to nothing at all, / To this long pelt over the back of a chair'.[13]

Another posthumanist concern – one that relates in particular to the humanist posthumanist interest in the hybrid nature of human/ nonhuman being – surfaces in Hughes's interest in classical Greek and Roman myth. This long-time interest, well documented by scholars,[14] culminated late in Hughes's career in his translations of the ancient Greek tragedians Euripides and Aeschylus, and the Latin poet Ovid. We see early instances of this interest in such poems as, for example, 'The Perfect Forms' (*CP* 82) in *Lupercal*, which is a defence of the single most important nature deity in Greek and Roman pagan animistic myth. It alludes to Pan's long-suffering nature, as well as to Pan as scapegoat figure for nature.

In Greek and Roman myth, Pan typically is represented as a grotesque, deformed or misshapen figure, as a hybrid, pre-cyborg human/ animal and god–nature identity, as half-man and half-goat, and as a figure of gross sensual appetite and limited intelligence. He is the deity, or semi-deity, most picked upon and ridiculed by the other gods. He appears in Hughes's poem 'The Perfect Forms' in the theriomorphic figure of the apparently stupid donkey carrying Christ. He has been 'fostered' by fish and reptile from the ages before human gods (Buddha and Christ), before human thought (represented by

Socrates) and its complacent assumption of superiority. Hughes ironically comments on the human invention of monotheistic religions and anthropocentric philosophies that have replaced, or rather repressed, animism and pagan belief: Buddha actually has the 'visage of Priapus'; Socrates is 'complacent as a phallus'. The 'perfect forms' of these gods are distorted by the suppression of the Pan in themselves, their followers and their culture that denies the animal in the human: 'This monstrous-headed difficult child! / Of such is the kingdom of heaven'.

Systems theory

In turning to the first of two areas of posthumanism that are deeply relevant to Hughes, we might begin by referring to a powerful essay, 'Can Thought Go On Without a Body?', by the poststructuralist thinker Jean-François Lyotard, who suggests that

> what makes thought and the body inseparable isn't just that the latter is the indispensable hardware for the former, a material prerequisite of its existence. It's that each of them is analogous to the other in its relationship with its respective [...] environment.[15]

Lyotard is arguing against 'the hypothesis [...] of a principle of the "separability" of intelligence' in humans,[16] or the belief that (human) thought or (human) intelligence can be isolated from the (nonhuman) world. Systems theory pushes Lyotard's humanist posthumanist argument further. It holds that intelligence, thought, subjectivity or consciousness is not locatable *inside* a particular body, system or environment, let alone inside the human body or brain. As Wolfe summarizes part of this claim by systems theory, the human does not occupy 'any particularly privileged position in relation to matters of meaning, information, and cognition'.[17] As commented on earlier, the other part of this claim by systems theory is that a species' intelligence, embedded in its system, has less to do with the ability to outdo another species, and more to do with the ability to negotiate with another species and its system – that is, more to do with the ability to 'structurally' couple with, not dominate, another species and its system.[18]

Elmet, one of Hughes's finest collections, speaks for the kind of posthumanist posthumanist thinking found under systems theory. It is a moving tribute to the 'part of West Yorkshire that includes the deep valley of the upper Calder [river] and its watershed of Pennine moorland' (*CP* 1200). Referencing the Industrial Revolution's legacy of mills, memories of the First World War and the region's geophysical exposure and precipitousness, *Elmet* gives us a sense of a world of many interlocking human and nonhuman elements, often expressed as cogs and wheels. Each system fits into the other, yet each is of 'fermenting independence', if also 'pressurized stagnation' (*CP* 1201): dynamic systems of weather, stone, steepness and human history. Had he written about systems theory, Hughes would have objected to its dry, secular, scientific and rational Enlightenment inheritances and legacies. Yet, as with Hughes's poetry in *Elmet*, systems theory reflects an immense inclusive thinking. For systems theory, as well as for Hughes, it is argued here, meaning might be thought of as *external* as opposed to *internal*, and a *function* not a *matter* of being. Referring again to Wolfe's characterization of systems theory, one might argue further that Hughes's poetry actually represents the view that 'human and other-than-human species and systems are both open *and* closed'.[19] As Wolfe puts it, in order 'to exist and reproduce themselves', they must 'maintain their boundaries and integrity' through a process of 'self-referential closure' since it is only on the basis of such closure that species and systems can 'then engage in "structural coupling" with their environment'. The 'fundamental logic' of this existence is 'recursive'. Species and systems 'use their own outputs as inputs in an ongoing process of "self-making" or "self-production"', and 'constantly (re)produce the elements that in turn produce *them*'.[20]

Elmet, and the collection that preceded it by fifteen years, *Remains of Elmet*, illuminate the marvellous complexities, resiliencies, porousness, impassivity, defeats and victories of a nonhuman region that was pressed into hard service by the human and in turn partly shaped by the human. Analogous to systems theory, poems such as 'Hill-Stone was Content' (*CP* 463), 'Wild Rock' (*CP* 464–5) and 'When Men Got to the Summit' (*CP* 470) forward the argument that when a particular species and its systems aggressively encroach upon the systems and species around it, they are threatened as much with decline as the species and system(s) that it seems bent upon outwitting or outmanoeuvring. 'Hill-Stone was Content' refers to the cutting of stone by humans to build the mills of the Industrial Revolution. Up to a point the nonhuman environment of gritstone accommodates or yields itself to the humanist agenda. It was 'content' to be 'carted' and 'fixed' in its 'new place'. It 'let itself be conscripted'; it 'forgot its wild roots / Its earth-song / In cement and the drum-song of looms' (*CP* 463). However, the excessive exploitation of it by the human species and the systems associated with this species (the mills) is so self-destructive that the human species and its systems in turn suffer decline, attenuation and stagnation. Eventually, 'inside the mills' the bodies of 'mankind' also become 'stony' and diminish in an ultimately futile 'long, darkening, dwindling stand' against the 'guerrilla patience' of the environmental non-human systems like 'soft hill-water'.

A similar posthumanist perspective is offered by the poem 'When Men Got to the Summit'. The human relentlessly presses its own interests on the region and thus brings about the loss of its own species and systems – social, cultural and material. It brings houses, builds streets on the vertiginous hills and erects mills. Its lack of recognition of the interests and agencies of the nonhuman world and its exhausting of the nonhuman world under the monolithic humanist industrial enterprise cause the collapse of its own systems and supports – the backbones of the bodies of its workers, streets and mills. The human holds sway only for some brief 'giddy moments'. Its streets, once 'bent to the task / Of holding it all up', eventually lost strength, their 'vertebrae slipped' and the hills 'went on gently / Shaking their sieve' (*CP* 470). Depopulation left, for a time, a literally posthuman landscape.

In Keith Sagar's introduction to *The Challenge of Ted Hughes*, Sagar notes the absence of metaphysical language, or language of 'transcendence', in Hughes' poetry. He observes: '[Hughes's] god is to be looked for under our boot-soles.'[21] Terry Gifford makes a similar claim in his essay 'Gods of Mud: Hughes and the Post-Pastoral'. Gifford traces engagements with pastoral through Hughes's poetry as the poet responded to and challenged pastoral conventions by producing pronouncedly if not always successful 'anti-pastoral' poems as well as more balanced and controlled, or less angry, 'post-pastoral' poems.[22] Of the six characteristics of post-pastoral that Gifford identifies, four are germane to *Elmet*, which Gifford singles out. Three of the four also resonate with systems theory. Gifford characterizes post-pastoral as the recognition of non-static processes in nature (and the tensions in these processes), 'direct responsibility for the management' of nature, inseparability between 'inner processes' and 'outer processes', and human and nonhuman processes that collectively constitute 'the workings of weather and landscape' in *Elmet*.[23]

Leonard M. Scigaj also points to the importance of the volumes *Remains of Elmet* and *Elmet*. In his essay 'Ted Hughes and Ecology: A Biocentric Vision', he states that 'the ecology of the Pennines, not the human observer, is the protagonist' of the two collections.[24] Scigaj's pre-humanist and posthumanist recognition of 'the subject' (or entity that is given moral and ethical consideration) is central to the strain of environmental thinking known as biocentrism. The biocentric perspective rejects dominant Western 'I-it' dualist attitudes towards animals and the environment, and holds that ethical rights extend beyond the human to 'animals, plants, rocks, and the entire planetary environment'.[25] Discussing *Elmet*, Scigaj characterizes it as the description of a 'live ecological system that imprinted its landscape and weather upon all inhabitants' and, through natural processes of composition and decomposition, reclaimed 'the spent labour of the Industrial Revolution' and the 'anthropocentric utilitarianism' of industrialization.[26]

Animal studies

Hughes's sustained and profound interest in the subject of the animal invites an approach informed not only by systems theory, but also by animal studies. Similar to systems theory, animal studies is treated as a discipline which overlaps with posthumanist inquiries. Initially a 'smattering of work in various fields on human–animal relations and their representation' within both the arts and sciences, animal studies is now a disciplinary area in its own right.[27] In its 'full force', Wolfe argues, animal studies fundamentally 'unsettles and reconfigures the question of the knowing subject'.[28] Animal studies scholar and sociologist Richard Twine writes that it is causing us to re-evaluate 'the role and presence of nonhuman animals' in a wide range of disciplines where nonhuman animals were 'for the most part ignored'.[29] In the sciences, where it is referred to by the name of Critical Animal Studies (CAS), in order to distinguish it from the older term and area of study known simply as 'animal studies', it is deeply politicizing human practices involving animals. These practices are endemic. The use of animals for sport and entertainment, the trading in exotic species of animals (a highly lucrative industry) and the keeping of animals as pets are several areas that have incited scrutiny and criticism. Another area, one with which Hughes engages in the collection *Moortown Diary*, is the traditional farming of animals.

Whilst 'the question of the animal' was first being confronted in the newly emergent field of animal studies in the early 1990s, Hughes had been engaging with it a quarter of a century earlier in the collections he was working on in the 1970s, and again, almost half a century earlier, in the collections he was working on in the 1950s. Animal studies is thus extraordinarily useful and perhaps required reading for understanding Hughes's *Moortown Diary*, a collection inspired by Hughes's first-hand experience in the 1970s of raising, nurturing, feeding, caring for, and slaughtering farm animals on Moortown Farm, a 95-acre property not far from his village of North Tawton in Devon.[30] *Moortown Diary* is neither an apology for, nor an animal rights attack upon, animal farming. Nonetheless, the frank and unsentimental descriptions of traditional animal farming bring the lives of farmed animals before us in ways that are being denied in our post-industrial world. 'Dehorning' (*CP* 504–5) is about the controversial practice of painfully cutting out the horns of farmed animals. 'Struggle' (*CP* 508–10) describes a newborn calf that Hughes strenuously tried to save:

> But his eye just lay suffering the monstrous weight of his head,
> The impossible job of his marvellous huge limbs.
> He could not make it. He died called Struggle.
> Son of Patience. (*CP* 510)

'Ravens' (*CP* 517–18) describes the body of a stillborn lamb torn apart by birds in a field not supervised at the time by humans. 'February 17th' (*CP* 518–19) describes when, in order to save the life of a ewe, Hughes 'hacked off' the head of her lamb while its body was still in its mother's womb unable to be birthed and pulled the lamb's torso out after it. 'Orf' (*CP* 522–3) describes a sick lamb that Hughes 'shot between the ears' and the enormous emotional and physical shock this has on him.

For the majority of us who live in cities, our contact with farmed animals is mostly in the form of the meat we purchase from supermarkets. We benefit from the standard 'animal testing' that hundreds of thousands of products undergo before being released for human use. These products range from food colouring, to eyeliner, to Alka-Seltzer, to toilet cleaner, and are first tested on live animals (on their eyes, ears, noses, skin and intestines) to determine the extent of their harmful effects. The traditional animal farming methods that *Moortown Diary* describes may seem disturbingly benign to many readers who are familiar with the treatment of animals in research and in modern animal farming, including the brutal confined animal-feeding operations (CAFOs). Nonetheless, the collection confronts the reader from the farmer's perspective with difficult questions about raising animals merely for human consumption and choosing to inflict pain upon animals in order to make it easier to farm them.

Conclusion

Many Hughes scholars, including Hong Chen and Terry Gifford, have argued that Hughes's animals are metaphors for the human.[31] Their focus is on the human implications of Hughes's observation and allegorizing of animals. From a posthumanist perspective, it can be argued, conversely, that Hughes's animals also are representations of the animals in their own right, as intriguing and complex, and as seemingly unfathomable, as human animals. Perhaps no poem conjures Hughes's interest in animals for their own sakes so well as the famous early poem titled 'Jaguar' (*CP* 19–20). As with the poem that follows it, 'Macaw and Little Miss' (*CP* 20–1), which also describes an exotic animal species import, Hughes implicitly comments on one of the worst kinds of speciesism – humans' imprisonment of nonhuman animals for use as diversion or entertainment and human's 'reduction' of nonhuman animals. It suggests that the nonhuman animal is not as limited as we have taken it to be in so far as it is 'more-than-human'.

One might argue that 'Jaguar' does not make an animal rights poem on the basis of the implied claim it makes that no cage can curb the jaguar's life, strength or 'stride': 'He spins from the bars, but there's no cage to him // More than to the visionary his cell: / His stride is wildernesses of freedom: / The world rolls under the long thrust of his heel. / Over the cage floor the horizons come' (CP 20). However, in describing the tremendously constrained and suppressed conditions of an animal who is particularly physically powerful, large-bodied and agile, Hughes also questions the humanist presumption that an animal hardly 'suffers' or otherwise is hardly compromised when its existence – it confinement, imprisonment, exile, its existence as an object of inquiry, and even its existence as an object of worship – is almost entirely on some other animal's terms. As a young man Hughes had worked as a dishwasher in London Zoo. 'The Jaguar' questions the humanism of zoos and articulates what Hughes scholar Roger Elkin has identified in Hughes's writings as 'the rejected ordure of a religious order' exiled and driven 'almost to extinction and zooimprisonment' under orthodox humanism.[32]

Animal studies scholars, cognitive scientists, ecologists, environmentalists, ethologists (animal behaviour scientists), zoologists and many other human thinkers are finding tremendous knowledge and technicities in animals and other nonhuman species. Ted Hughes leads us to this immense, capacious and other-than-human world through the most human yet most other-than-human realm of poetry.

Notes

1. Cary Wolfe, *What is Posthumanism?* (Minneapolis: University of Minnesota Press, 2010): xiii–xvii; 124–5.
2. Giorgio Agamben, *The Open: Man and Animal*, trans. Kevin Attell (Stanford, CA: Stanford University Press, 2004): 23.

3. Carolus Linnaeus, *Systema naturae* (Lugduni Batavorum: Haak, 1735).
4. Neil Roberts enters this debate when he writes about 'A Childish Prank' in Chapter 5 above: 'The poem's determination to identify the spiritual with the animal is not necessarily nihilistic.'
5. Donna Haraway, 'A Cyborg Manifesto: Science, Technology, and Social Feminism in the Late Twentieth Century' [1985], in Neil Badmington (ed.), *Posthumanism* (Basingstoke: Palgrave Macmillan, 2000): 70.
6. *Ibid.*: 72.
7. See Peter Singer, *Animal Liberation: Towards an End to Man's Inhumanity to Animals* [1975] (London: Pimlico, 1995).
8. See Tom Regan, *The Case for Animal Rights* (London: Routledge, 1998).
9. Wolfe is critical of the mainstream animal rights arguments that in effect look for human traits in nonhuman animals, but he also acknowledges the immeasurable contribution that these arguments have made to defences of nonhuman animals. As he emphasizes, study after study has shown that 'possession of a soul, then "reason", then tool use, then tool *making*, then altruism, then language [and a host of other traits once believed to be exclusive to humans] flourish quite reliably beyond the species barrier' (Cary Wolfe, *Animal Rites: American Culture, the Discourse of Species and Posthumanism* (Chicago: University of Chicago Press, 2003): 2). For an extended discussion of the studies that Wolfe points to here, see also page 40 and all of Chapter 2, 'In the Shadow of Wittgenstein's Lion: Language, Ethics and the Question of the Animal': 44–94.
10. Wolfe, *What is Posthumanism?*: 14.
11. *Ibid.*
12. Paul Bentley, 'The Debates about Hughes', in Terry Gifford (ed.), *The Cambridge Companion to Ted Hughes* (Cambridge: Cambridge University Press, 2011): 27. By contrast, see Alice Oswald's Introduction to her selection *A Ted Hughes Bestiary* (London: Faber & Faber, 2014): xiii–xvi.
13. The 1970 edition of *Lupercal* pays homage to both the poems 'February' and 'An Otter' in the cover illustration (by Chris Riddell). It depicts the head and pelt of a wolf carcass draped over the back of a chair.
14. See, for example, the critical collection edited by Roger Rees, *Ted Hughes and the Classics* (Oxford: Oxford University Press: 2009).
15. Jean-François Lyotard, 'Can Thought Go on Without a Body?' [1987], in Badmington (ed.), *Posthumanism*: 135.
16. *Ibid.*
17. Wolfe, *What is Posthumanism?*: xii.
18. *Ibid.*: 111.
19. *Ibid.*
20. *Ibid.*
21. Keith Sagar, 'Introduction', in Keith Sagar (ed.), *The Challenge of Ted Hughes* (London: Macmillan, 1994): xiv.
22. Terry Gifford, 'Gods of Mud: Hughes and the Post-Pastoral', in Keith Sagar (ed.), *The Challenge of Ted Hughes* (London: Macmillan, 1994): 130.

23. *Ibid.*: 134–6.
24. Leonard M. Scigaj, 'Ted Hughes and Ecology: A Biocentric Vision', in Sagar (ed.), *Challenge of Ted Hughes*: 171.
25. *Ibid.*: 162, 160.
26. *Ibid.*: 171–2.
27. Wolfe, *What is Posthumanism?*: 99.
28. *Ibid.*: xxix.
29. Richard Twine, *Animals as Biotechnology: Ethics, Sustainability and Critical Animal Studies* (London: Earthscan, 2010): 1.
30. *Moortown Diary* was first published in *Moortown* in 1979.
31. See Hong Chen, 'Hughes and Animals', in Gifford (ed.), *Cambridge Companion to Ted Hughes*: 40–52; Terry Gifford, *Ted Hughes* (Abingdon and New York: Routledge, 2009): 35.
32. Roger Elkin, 'Neglected Auguries in *Recklings*', in Sagar (ed.), *Challenge of Ted Hughes*: 34.

12

Ecocritical Readings

Richard Kerridge

Ecocriticism and nature poetry

Ecocriticism is literary and cultural criticism from the viewpoint of environmental concern. Does a literary work help us think scrupulously about environmental threats such as catastrophic climate change and biodiversity loss? Is it helpful or harmful to our social and individual efforts to prevent disaster? Does it confront us with the ecological implications of the stories it presents, including implications reaching far across space and time? These questions form the criteria by which ecocritics evaluate texts. The basic hope is that environmental criteria will become an expected part of debate about all kinds of new artistic work, and that this will be a sign of a general shift in cultural values and, most importantly, in everyday behaviour.

Ted Hughes, the most influential British nature poet of the last fifty years, is an obvious candidate for ecocritical exploration and gratitude. In the late 1950s and early 1960s, Hughes restored the subject of wild nature to literary topicality. He gave passionate attention to the natural world in a renewed form, a modern form – or was it just a modern *feel*, a vivid redramatization of an old cultural politics? For ecocritics, that is one of the fundamental questions about the work of Ted Hughes. Did he genuinely wrest nature writing away from the impulse to search for a sheltered evasion of modernity? As environmentalism was emerging, did Hughes produce a new nature writing with environmentalist potential, or a re-enlivened version of the conservative mode? Or a mixture of the two?

A common charge against nature writing is that it turns away from social life and from modernity. Often the suggestion is that evasion is the principal motive: the fascination with wild nature is a way of creating a space emptied of human challenges. Nature lovers are said to be seeking refuge from the urban industrial spaces in which most people must live and work, and from domestic spaces and responsibilities. To show that nature writing need not serve such purposes only, Kathleen Jamie writes about watching peregrine falcons from her window 'between the laundry and the fetching kids from school'.[1] Her essay is a response to the way the domestic and social worlds are excluded from J.A. Baker's *The Peregrine* (1967), an extraordinary example, much admired among nature writers now, of the solitary-obsessive tragic mode of nature writing.[2]

It is not that the need for such refuges is not sometimes powerfully valid. But ecocritics must always examine the political and cultural implications. Does the love of the solitary encounter with nature collude with a selfish politics? Environmental problems call for a new sensitivity to ecological relations. A new cultural centrality for the love of wild nature could have an important part to play, which is why ecocritics must take care to distinguish the new version from the old, especially when the two are intertwined in the same work – and especially since a stock accusation against environmentalists is that they are nostalgic for an idealized pre-industrial rural life. As many ecocritics have pointed out, environmentalism is a definitively modern movement, which has emerged in response to a distinctly new set of problems. The scale of those problems is perceptible only by means of new scientific methods and instruments. Environmentalists hope for a new phase of modernity, adapted technologically, scientifically and culturally to new forms of understanding, not a reversion to the pre-industrial past (although a new synthesis of recovered traditional practices and recently invented ones is sometimes involved). We have new reasons to familiarize ourselves culturally with natural ecosystems, distinct from the old familiarity that went with pre-industrial farm work. This is the context that makes the love of wild nature a form of social responsibility, not an evasion or purely personal interest.

Nature poetry was often approached with the suspicion that it must be in the tradition of the *Georgian Poetry* anthologies of 1912–1922, famous for their unwillingness to face the realities of industrial modernity and the First World War. To contrast these anthologies unfavourably with the work of the 'war poets' was a standard classroom routine. Scarcely less suspect was the prose nature writing of the 1920s and 1930s, a period in which the genre was popular, as were books about traditional rural life. These two linked genres had often expressed – or been embraced, or scorned, as expressing – a desire for escape from modern urban life. In the aftershock of the war came intensified forms of this desire. The search was for surviving enclaves of the life that existed before the industrial society that was held to have produced the war, enclaves that could shelter the traumatized observer, and be imagined not merely as isolated pockets but as portals to an underlying reality or hinterland.

One such imaginary hinterland was a mythical old England still to be found beneath the surface of modern culture. Another was wild nature, representing a purity of unalienated, honest, instinctive life, from which modernity was felt to have alienated human beings, leaving them as wistful, obscurely excited spectators. In the 1920s and 1930s, nature writing motivated by this idea was an adaptation of the Romantic sublime to the particular anguished moment of the post-war period. Wild nature offered spectacles of contingent mortality that, innocent of association with the war, could be cathartic without being directly threatening. These are strong themes in the work of Henry Williamson, the most famous nature writer of this period, a war survivor who became a fascist. Williamson's fascism seems to have been at least in part a product of his regret for the war and horror at the thought of fighting Germany again, but he did not recant, and his case demonstrates how this desperate shunning of urban cosmo-politan modernity, and search for rural rootedness, could turn into an extremely dangerous politics. Ecocriticism has to acknowledge this, and insist that a cosmopolitan culture, not an inward-turning one, is the necessary consequence of recognizing global ecological inter-dependencies. The Second World War and following years produced a popular natural history with quite different underlying ideologies, expressing a democratic enthusiasm for British wildlife as heritage and homecoming. But the tragic, anti-modern themes did not disap-pear. They were present at times in Hughes's own work (he admired Williamson's writing, though not his politics), and are sometimes to be encountered in new nature writing now. Ecocritics must make distinctions between the various traditions and desires to be found in the nature-writing genre, and ask how those traditions and desires bear now upon environmental priorities. Such critics will be especially keen to differentiate the environmentalist elements in nature writing from those that are anti-modern. Sometimes these are hard to disentangle. A good starting point is that Hughes made the love of nature feel mod-ern, energetic and dangerous rather than nostalgic and comfortable.

Hughes's realignment of nature poetry

Take the famous description of thrushes in the poem of that name: 'Terrifying are the attent sleek thrushes on the lawn, / More coiled steel than living' (*CP* 82). This view of a common garden bird (less common now) as uncanny, mechanical and threatening would not have been out of place in Jean-Paul Sartre's *La Nausée* (1938), one of the existentialist and absurdist novels that were highly fashionable in the early 1960s. Young intellectuals devoured these books excitedly. The books seemed to have a modern, unillusioned fearlessness, a willingness to face the collapse of traditional consolatory meaning in a secular, post-Holocaust age of nuclear weapons. Although Hughes's work is undoubtedly influenced by the conservative nature-writing traditions I have discussed, it emerges from this context also. The relationship between continuity and radical newness is usually complicated, and it can be argued that mid-twentieth-century absurdist writing renewed many features of the Romantic egotistical sublime, showing us lone figures heroically confronting the abyss of the absurd.[3]

Hughes later drew a fundamental distinction between his own vision and Absurdism. Reviewing the Yugoslav poet Vasko Popa, he declared that Popa, and several other Eastern European poets, were able to express in their work a vision of elemental life, death and contingency 'which for artists elsewhere is a prevailing shape of things but only brokenly glimpsed, through the clutter of our civilized liberal confusion' (*WP* 221). These were poets 'caught in mid-adolescence by the war' (*WP* 220). Popa was a concentration-camp survivor. For Hughes, they were 'among the purest and most wide awake of living poets' (*WP* 221), and their vision reminded him of Samuel Beckett's. Yet Hughes found in them something decisively different. Hughes wants a writing as intent as Beckett's on taking a large and unillusioned view of life's contingency, temporality, materiality and mortality, and on finding modern symbolic and dramatic forms capable of being archetypal yet intensely personal. But he wants a vision less minimalist and terminal, and more open to enthusiasm unguarded by irony, than he is able to find in Beckett's sardonic sympathy (*WP* 221–2).

Keith Sagar argues that Hughes was rejecting a vision 'traditional from the Greeks to Eliot and Beckett' – the idea 'that death owns everything', 'that nothing which does not last forever is of real value, that the achievements of man are mocked by time and cancelled by death'.[4] Environmentalism brings a new reason why we should strive to be reconciled to our mortality, and not see time as mocking our endeavours. If the planet's carrying capacity is limited, then we must make way, if the ecosystem is to last. The decay of our bodies is the renewal of the system. Sagar finds the beginning of this perspective in Hughes's poems in *Moortown Diary* about lambs dying in the process of birth.[5] Relatively non-industrialized farming provides, as wild nature does, a theatre in which mortality can be seen in the context of ecological relations.

One of these poems, 'February 17th', describes a harrowing death-in-birth. In order to save the ewe, the poem's speaker has to cut the throat and sever the head of a lamb that is irretrievably stuck because it began to emerge head first rather than hooves first. Discarded on the ground, the head stares back at the mother, 'its pipes sitting in the mud / With all earth for a body' (*CP* 519). Because the lamb's remains will be absorbed back into the continuing ecosystem, the earth can be seen momentarily as the body beneath that head, restoring the creature to life. It is a grotesque image, awkward and puppet-like – perhaps necessarily so, since the idea could easily be sentimental, if it came without the bloody dismemberment. In an act of momentary collage, that lamb's face is put on to the shoulders of an abstract, allegorical character representing the world as ecosystem. This shift of scale occurs in the midst of a particularly visceral local realism. We never leave the bloody doings in the field, but we glimpse the working of the universe. Abruptly, this obscure real individual creature, for whom the light only gleamed for an instant (as Beckett himself put it in *Waiting for Godot*), is a figure on an epic stage. There is consolation in this thought, for the farmer-poet and the reader, and by implication – though the thought has to be handled carefully – the possibility of a larger sense of ecocritical consolation.

For Neil Roberts, Hughes is drawing a contrast between the stances of an alienated, ironic observer of an absurd world, and a willing participant in that world, a struggler for life. The former stance is identified with Beckett, the latter with Popa and Hughes himself.[6] Roberts also points to Hughes's insistence that *Crow* should not be seen as belonging to the modern genre of Absurdist Black Comedy, but rather as an attempt to produce a new form of the ancient folkloric tradition of the Trickster tale.[7] Hughes described Black Comedy as 'the end of a cultural process', and Trickster tales as 'the beginning' (*WP* 239). Black Comedy expressed 'the animal despair and suicidal nihilism that afflict a society [...] when the supportive metaphysical beliefs disintegrate', whereas the Trickster genre expressed an 'unkillable, biological optimism' (*WP* 239), 'the spirit of the sperm', the driving spirit of 'every stage of psychological recovery or growth' (*WP* 241). Trickster literature is thus associated with the impulse for survival and adaptation.

It may not be fair to attribute such a degree of nihilism to Beckett and other Absurdists. There has been much debate about this. Fair or not, the contrast was useful to Hughes as a clarification of his own purpose, a stimulus. For ecocritics, it is first of all encouraging that the implications of some of the age's most defiantly modern literature could be interrogated through the medium of nature writing. The genre's capacity to be forward-looking was demonstrated here. Also encouraging is Hughes's insistence on the Trickster impulses, with their mixture of instinct and conscious cleverness, as designed by the whole universe – as opposed to an Absurdist view in which an alienated human consciousness views that universe from a position of wry or appalled detachment. The emphasis on Trickster impulses as products of the whole universe opens up the ecological dimension, though Hughes's frame of reference in the poems is rarely scientific.

Other realignments, too, are taking place in those early nature poems. 'Pike', also from *Lupercal*, is perhaps the poem that became most widely known: 'Pike, three inches long, perfect / Pike in all parts, green tigering the gold' (*CP* 84). 'Tigering' has simple aptness as description, yet is also resonant in the way it transfers the colonial romance of exotic wild nature to the British domestic landscape: the one scaled down, the other scaled up. For the British imagination of the exotic wild as a theatre of fantasy, this was a transitional period. Empire had abruptly ceased to be available as a horizon of personal fantasy, but the animals and landscapes of Africa and Asia were now entering the popular imagination through television wildlife documentaries. Encounters with formidable predators had long been a staple feature of the colonial adventure story. Hughes relocates these encounters to the homely British countryside, discovering in local wildness the world's archetypal wildness. The local world expands, becoming a portal to the open world. A major influence was D.H. Lawrence, whose poems of dramatic encounters with animals – 'Snake', 'Mountain Lion', 'Man and Bat' – had combined intensely precise naturalistic description with a readiness to attribute archetypal meaning to those animals. Lawrence too had sought to establish, through his poems, a modern cultural centrality for animals: a renewed intensity of symbolic meaning equivalent to their ancient meanings. The animals of Lawrence's poems, however, were mostly Mediterranean or from New Mexico. It was Hughes who brought this project to the familiar wildlife of the British countryside. Schools quickly recognized these early collections as poetry that could excite children and make them excited about their local, available world.

As well as colonial tigers, the 'tigering' line may recall Blake's 'tyger', at once real animal and symbol of the ruthless energy of creation. Both senses of creation are involved: the created world itself, and the act or process of making and changing that world. 'In what furnace was thy brain?', asks Blake's speaker. God's creation of the tiger is imagined as an industrial process involving what the poet J.H. Prynne identifies as 'blast-furnace-smelting', the 'standard metal technology of the industrial revolution'.[8] The aligning of the fearsome 'burning' of the tiger and the actual controlled burning of the blast-furnace suggests that the creative violence of industrial production is an extension of primal, generative natural energy, not different in kind from natural processes. Natural life and the industrial manipulation of that life are not contrasted, but seen as different manifestations of the same creative power, though a power in which the divine and the demonic are hard to separate.

Hughes, too, aligns natural and technological processes. It is a recurrent move in his descriptions of animals, a move that insists on the modernity of these primal encounters. The thrushes are like coiled steel. In 'Pike', five lines after 'tigering', there is 'silhouette / of submarine delicacy and horror', and then 'A hundred feet long in their world'. Fifteen years after the war, U-boats still lurked in the popular imagination, and in the late 1950s the USA and USSR had launched the first nuclear submarines. The pike's shape, movement and predatory ferocity give it a resemblance to these machines, and by making the association, almost subliminally, the poem gives the fish a sinister glamour. Less threateningly, a badger's feet in *What is the Truth?* are 'power-tools' (*CPC* 136). *Wolfwatching* brings back the military technology, with a sparrowhawk whose eyes 'in their helmet' are 'wired direct / To the nuclear core', and who targets the lark like a laser beam (*CP* 747).

Ecocritics have reason to be troubled by these analogies, since it is possible to read in them a fatalistic perception that technological warfare and ruthless industrial exploitation are primarily determined by evolved natural instinct, and therefore not susceptible to conscience. 'Thrushes' allows for two polarized states of being only: the 'efficiency [...] too streamlined for any doubt to pluck at it' (*CP* 82) of birds, sharks and Mozart, and an enfeebled fantasizing way of life that the poem attributes to the generality of modern humanity. 'Hawk Roosting' presents the hawk – in more openly anthropomorphic terms – as possessing and soliloquizing an amoral ruthlessness unencumbered by 'sophistry' or 'falsifying dream' (*CP* 68). There has long been controversy about whether the hawk's soliloquy, with its Nietzschean triumphalism, is distanced and presented ironically, but from the ecocritical point of view the concern is that the fatalistic attitude leaves little room for the idea that environmentalist scruples might make a difference. These poems celebrate the amorality of these 'streamlined' and efficient predators, whose behaviour is unalterably set (the pike's jaw is 'not to be changed at this date') and impervious to questioning. Predatory ruthlessness is contrasted only to fantasizing lack of will. For ecocritics, the question is whether, as Hughes's work developed, he was able to move beyond this stark opposition. If not, then his reinvigoration of nature writing was a matter of style only, and did not move the genre on from a Nietszchean–Romantic yearning for unselfconscious being, safely contained because that being was found only in the theatre of wild nature.

Generally, Hughes is careful to naturalize the comparisons he makes in his nature poems, leaving the option of reading the lines as innocent description: 'tigering' as no more than apt for the stripe patterns on a pike, 'submarine' as merely meaning 'underwater', and 'wired direct to the nuclear core' as referring only to the nerve fibres connecting eye and brain. It is almost as if the poet were only seeking the most exact image. The verb 'tigering' does not quite confront us with a tiger. 'Submarine' is partly muted by being turned into an adjective. Hughes threw off this cover when, in *Crow*, he began using a wild creature as a fully allegorical character, a mythic personage rather than a real observed creature with suggestive power.

He was relinquishing the platform for his larger suggestions that a clearly understood, empirical and relatively modest task of observation had provided. The turn from realism to mythical-allegorical writing enabled him to offer a large-scale diagnosis of the human condition across time and space, in the form of a figurative drama. Any of his readers – his British readers, anyway – might have seen a pike, fox or thrush, or could easily do so. But turning them into part-realistic, part-mythical figures was a big step. To a degree, Hughes was sacrificing the ability of his poetry to connect directly with those readers' experience. It was unlikely that the mythic poetry would gain the sort of communal recognition that would enable it to become myth in the larger sense – myth as the foundation of a public culture of ritual. Also, a realist and secular nature poetry, dramatizing the immediacy of personal observation, leads easily, without any great clash of styles, into ecological understanding and the beginnings of scientific perspectives. Mythic poetry would have to produce a collage-like effect of rapid changes of style in order to do this, a project Hughes did not take very far, though he did use a technique of rapid switching between myth and realism, which I shall explore below. Ecocritics need to assess whether the price was worth paying, which means considering the ecocritical value of both kinds of writing.

Photographic flashes of real crows occur throughout *Crow*. The poem 'Lineage' consists mainly of ironical biblical pronouncements of a highly abstract kind, but ends abruptly with the newborn Crow represented by an image of 'Trembling featherless elbows in the nest's filth' (*CP* 218). Neil Roberts observes that this is 'a beautifully concise evocation of an actual nestling'.[9] A similarly exact naturalistic observation, full of dramatic movement, concludes 'A Horrible Religious Error'. After God and the first man and woman have been reduced to powerlessness by the emergence of the serpent, which seems here to represent the tempting idea that the life-urge is inseparable from sin, Crow, representing that life-urge in its no-nonsense directness, notices the snake – suddenly a real snake – and moves in, grabbing the snake by 'the slackskin nape' and flailing it to death before eating it (*CP* 231), as real birds do. In this example, an abrupt return to naturalistic observation of wild nature – to 'nature writing', in other words – is an intervention breaking a paralysis caused by abstraction. But these flashes are clearly in the service of the allegorical scheme. They do not mark a return to naturalistic description focused on a particular object in a particular place and time.

Crow is a departure, then, from the nature-writing genre, even though clearly inspired by landscapes in Yorkshire and Devon where the black shapes of crows are everywhere, strutting in the fields and watching for creatures in difficulty.[10] In the poems, Crow is a trickster figure personifying natural appetite in its innocent ruthlessness; sometimes brutal, sometimes foolishly ingenuous. Hughes gave an informal glossary to his allegory in a letter to Robin Skelton, explaining that

> The whole poem is a definition of Crow – (1) as the ultimate elemental value, & as the femaleness of things, & as the salvation of things. (2) as the most precious thing arrived at only through the most extreme punishment (3) as the intoxication deriving from suffering & encounter with reality (4) as what is destroyed by abstraction and exploitation (5) as the energy of the sun (6) as eros (7) as the pre-adamite spirit (8) as the inventive & creative spirit, which thrives on the pressure of death (9) as the unconquerable thing (10) as the inextinguishable tenacity of the unconquerable thing. (*LTH* 370)

One imagines Hughes lining these entities up almost mischievously: here is everything he wants to champion. Against what? The implied antagonist would seem to be:

1. Reductive, positivist scientism, and the definition of human needs in restrictively consumerist terms.
2. A modern consumerist society that provides material comfort and a high degree of protection from the elemental dangers of life, at the cost of alienating the self from the directly instinctive

behaviour that a way of life more exposed to the natural elements would involve.

3. The alienation from understanding of the natural environment that this first alienation entails.

4. The alienation from mythic, folkloric and symbolic traditions that is also entailed (many of those traditions were stores of what we now call 'ecological' knowledge).

5. The insatiable and ruinous demands made upon natural ecosystems as a result of these alienations.

6. The estrangement from death, and thus from an understanding of death's ecological necessity, that is also entailed.

7. The general loss of creativity, individual and social, that Hughes believes has occurred in consequence of all these alienations.

8. Cartesian dualism: the tradition of distinguishing mind from body and regarding mind – conscious rational thought, distinguished from emotion and bodily sensation – as a faculty that only humans possess and that defines us as human. Many ecocritics regard this Enlightenment tradition as heavily responsible for the environmental crisis. They see Cartesian dualism as associated with the industrial rationality that values the natural world only for its short-term disposable financial worth. Hughes's linking of abstraction to exploitation in the list above suggests that he takes the same view.

Ecocritics will recognize much of this. Most of the things Crow represents are attributes of Nature, in the conventional system of binary oppositions that makes Nature the opposite of Culture. The same system aligns Nature with instinct, intuition, emotion, immediacy and body, against rationality, self-consciousness, abstraction, artifice and mind. It is the Cartesian tradition, and it also separates humanity from the nonhuman Other, and, notoriously, aligns Woman with Nature's attributes and Man with their opposites. When Hughes interprets Crow as representing 'the femaleness of things', is he opposing this tradition or reproducing it, or both? He saw the industrial mindset responsible for ecological crisis as resulting from a historical process of alienation from ancient attitudes of reverence for nature, including the identification of nature with a feminine principle: the mother or the goddess. This view is consistent with some of the historical analysis offered by ecofeminism – with Carolyn Merchant's tracking, in *The Death of Nature*, for example, of a turn, at the beginnings of modernity, from metaphors of nature as (often female) organism to metaphors of nature as mechanism.[11]

Ecofeminists have revealed the oppressiveness of this idea of women's greater naturalness: its cultural legitimation of the subordination of women, ancient and modern. More tentatively, they have also looked for ways in which that same tradition can be used positively, its meaning transformed in the new context of environmental crisis. Continuing debates in ecofeminism and ecocritical Queer Theory[12] are concerned with whether the identification of woman with nature is always restrictive and oppressive. In the new synthesis brought by environmentalism, does the new value that must be given to protective concern for the delicacy of natural processes mean that these traditional views of sex and gender can be reconstituted as positive rather than oppressive? Again, ecocritics must be open to this new synthesis, but always wary lest the old ideology be lurking inside it.

Hughes's Deep Ecology and the prospect of consilience

I have outlined here a number of the questions about Hughes's work that ecocritics must explore. They are important questions, since there is no doubt that his work holds out great ecocritical promise, and the answers will at the very least illustrate the complexities of the cultural transition that ecocritics hope is taking place: the evolution of new environmentally oriented forms and genres from previous traditions. When Hughes started out, environmentalist ideas were only beginning to enter the wider culture. They developed as Hughes's writing developed. Tracy Brain has traced the influence on Sylvia Plath's poetry of Rachel Carson's *Silent Spring* (1962), the book often credited with inaugurating the environmental movement.[13] *Silent Spring* influenced Hughes as well (Brain suggests that he and Plath must have discussed it together in their continual creative dialogue), and by the 1970s he was expressing a growing environmental awareness and concern.

Terry Gifford has revealed Hughes's extensive involvement in campaigning against river pollution, at first locally, in North Devon, and then nationally.[14] In 1976, in *Season Songs*, Hughes published 'Swifts', a poem sometimes quoted in conservation literature. It asks us to see the global in the local:

They've made it again,
Which means the globe's still working, the Creation's
Still waking refreshed, our summer's
Still all to come – (*CP* 315)

We are asked to see the connection between our familiar local wild nature, which marks our seasons, and the global ecosystems on which that local wildlife depends. Or, rather, the poem asserts that people already, tacitly, make this connection: one reason why they feel delight at the return of the swifts is the reassurance the birds provide that the larger systems are still there. We don't only look to 'pit canary' indicator species for warnings that systems are failing;[15] we also find pleasure in the healthy presence of these species as evidence of the system's well-being. In moving, in the same line, from 'globe' to 'Creation', Hughes suggests that a continuity is possible between present-day awareness of ecosystems and traditional communal celebrations, sometimes mediated by Christianity, of the returning seasons. Some of his collections, such as *Season Songs* and *Rain-Charm for the Duchy*, are attempting to establish public ritual as a communal form of ecological awareness. More mythical works, such as *Crow* and *Gaudete*, seem to enact the frustrated convulsions of myth deprived of connection to public ritual.[16]

For Hughes, the campaign to recover a sense of reverence for natural ecological relationships was inseparable from the campaign to recover a cultural centrality for poetry. Environmental values – as he interpreted them, identifying a renewed mythic representation of the natural world as essential to environmental consciousness – were closely related to poetic values as he understood them; each led to the other. In 1970, Hughes wrote that the origin of the present crisis is to be discovered in the founding myths and ideas of Western culture – in 'Reformed Christianity' and 'Old Testament Puritanism' (*WP* 129), and the Enlightenment rationality that followed, including the Cartesian tradition. He calls this line of cultural beliefs an abandonment of Nature and 'an evolutionary dead-end' (*WP* 129). His view is that deep cultural change is required, to rescue Westernized humanity from terminal ecological catastrophe and also from that insatiable exiled quest. Technological and managerial solutions are necessary, but will not be sufficient – and anyway will not be possible without a change to 'the soul-state of our civilization' (*WP* 130). We currently have the scientific and technological understanding to save ourselves, but cannot find the collective political will.

Hughes's environmentalism is clearly a variant of the kind known as Deep Ecology. Soon after these words, that term was introduced to environmental debate by the Norwegian philosopher Arne Naess, who defined Deep Ecology against what he saw as the 'shallow' environmentalism concerned only with pollution, damage and depletion as specific problems.[17] 'Shallow' environmentalism sought particular solutions without making a general challenge to industrialization and consumerism. Naess saw this as inadequate. Environmental problems had to be seen as symptoms of a fundamental failure of values. Without changing those, in ways that would transform every part of life, we would not escape the environmental crisis. The environmental movement had to be concerned with philosophy, morality, psychology and spirituality, as well as ecological science and tactical politics. It had to envision a transformed culture. Hughes comes at environmentalism from a particular set of literary and anthropological preoccupations, but his vision is of the same radical kind.

Leonard M. Scigaj, one of the first Hughes scholars to explore the ecocritical implications of Hughes's poetry, identifying the specific kind of environmentalism to be found there, wrote that 'Hughes is most often concerned with evoking a sense of astonishment and aesthetic delight in the powers and vitality of nature – something akin to the animism of tribal cultures – in order to promote self-renewal in humans and a reverence for nature.'[18] For Hughes, according to Scigaj, this 'ecological animism', as Scigaj calls it, is the cultural development that must accompany the emergence of Deep Ecological ethics, politics and daily life. The vital cultural instrument is poetry, a form of art that yet retains fundamental continuities with myth and ritual, and that 'ideally produces an almost hypnotic, trancelike excitement' that rescues the reader, momentarily at least, from the modern alienation from nature and from self.[19]

A final question, then, for ecocritics concerned with the *usefulness* of texts in the face of environmental crisis, is whether we should see such a deep cultural and behavioural transformation as our only hope of averting catastrophe. Or, in holding out for such revolution, would we lose the chance of practical ways of mitigating the crisis? This is the classical dilemma of political movements, which generally have a radical faction and one more prepared to accept compromise. In practice, the two sometimes have complementary roles, defining and stimulating each other. How should ecocritics apply this model to Hughes's version of Deep Ecology?

Hughes calls for a revival of a communally mythic relation to Nature, and in his poetry attempts to further this aim, or explore the tragedy of its frustration. But does he reject scientific investigation and technological responses to the crisis? What Hughes has to say in his vision of 'consilience' suggests not (*WP* 132–3). Science and industrial technology, having exiled humanity from one kind of accepting intimacy with natural ecosystems, are in the process of giving us a new kind, through the power of computers to store and analyse data. The new intimacy will be greater in spread and depth, since computers have the capacity to process immense quantities of minute information, enabling them to model the global ecosystem and penetrate its smallest recesses. Here is a kind of justification for that troubling alignment of wild nature and machines. With only slight irony, Hughes imagines these computers as new gods restoring our reverence for the old goddess.

But does he further this consilience in his poetic practice? Hughes's mythic poetry may be informed, to some extent, by scientific understanding, but for the most part it does not engage with that understanding directly, by bringing scientific vocabulary into the poem. Whilst scientific writing has the capacity to make direct challenges to the industrial commodification of the natural world, mythic writing stays at a remove from such vocabularies. Hughes merged mythic writing with extraordinarily intense naturalistic observation of wild nature, and of the behaviour of the farm animals on which we rely. His eye for evocative dramatic detail is superb. Few other writers approach it. His project is to restore to us this power of attention, implicit in which, for Hughes, there is a reverence that should be incompatible with the most brutal and heedless forms of industrial exploitation. Taking that project further would mean merging the poetic language with a wider range of scientific and technical vocabularies – perhaps something Hughes's inheritors will attempt.

Notes

1. Kathleen Jamie, *Findings* (London: Sort of Books, 2005): 39.
2. J.A. Baker, *The Peregrine* (London: Collins, 1967).
3. See Chapter 4.
4. Keith Sagar, *Literature and the Crime Against Nature* (London: Chaucer Press, 2005): 236.
5. *Ibid.*: 254.
6. Neil Roberts, *Ted Hughes: A Literary Life* (Basingstoke: Palgrave Macmillan, 2006): 63–4.
7. *Ibid.*: 83–4.
8. J.H. Prynne, *Stars, Tigers and the Shape of Words: The William Matthews Lectures 1992* (London: Birkbeck College, 1993): 26.
9. Roberts, *Ted Hughes*: 74.
10. See 'Ravens', *CP* 517.
11. Carolyn Merchant, *The Death of Nature: Women, Ecology and the Scientific Revolution* (San Francisco, CA: HarperCollins, 1980).
12. See for example Catriona Mortimer-Sandilands and Bruce Erickson, *Queer Ecologies: Sex, Nature, Politics, Desire* (Bloomington: Indiana University Press, 2010).

13. Tracy Brain, *The Other Sylvia Plath* (Harlow: Pearson Education, 2001): 84–91, 105–11.
14. Terry Gifford, *Ted Hughes* (Abingdon: Routledge, 2009): 22–6.
15. Coal miners carried a caged canary down the pit to warn them, by its death, of impure air.
16. See Chapter 1.
17. Arne Naess, 'The Shallow and the Deep, Long-range Ecology Movement: A Summary', *Inquiry*, 16(1) (1973), 95–100.
18. Leonard M. Scigaj, *Ted Hughes* (Boston, MA: Twayne, 1991): 135.
19. *Ibid.*: 1.

Further Reading

Primary works by Ted Hughes

Books

The Hawk in the Rain (London: Faber & Faber, 1957).
Lupercal (London: Faber & Faber, 1960).
Meet My Folks (London: Faber & Faber, 1961).
The Earth-Owl and Other Moon People (London: Faber & Faber, 1963).
How the Whale Became (London: Faber & Faber, 1963).
Nessie the Mannerless Monster (London: Faber & Faber, 1964).
Recklings (London: Turret Books, 1966).
Poetry in the Making (London: Faber & Faber, 1967).
Wodwo (London: Faber & Faber, 1967).
The Iron Man (London: Faber & Faber, 1968).
Seneca's Oedipus (London: Faber & Faber, 1969).
The Coming of the Kings (London: Faber & Faber, 1970).
Crow (London: Faber & Faber, 1970).
A Choice of Shakespeare's Verse (London: Faber & Faber, 1971; 2nd edn 1991).
Earth-Moon (London: Rainbow Press, 1976).
Season Songs (London: Faber & Faber, 1976).
Gaudete (London: Faber & Faber, 1977).
Cave Birds (London: Faber & Faber, 1978).
Moon-Bells and Other Poems (London: Chatto & Windus, 1978).
Orts (London: Rainbow Press, 1978).
Moortown (London: Faber & Faber, 1979).
Remains of Elmet (London: Faber & Faber, 1979).
A Primer of Birds (Devon: Gehenna Press, 1981).
Under the North Star (London: Faber & Faber, 1981).
Selected Poems 1957–1981 (London: Faber & Faber, 1982).
River (London: Faber & Faber, 1983).
What is the Truth? (London: Faber & Faber, 1984).
Ffangs the Vampire Bat and the Kiss of Truth (London: Faber & Faber, 1986).
Flowers and Insects (London: Faber & Faber, 1986).
The Cat and the Cuckoo (Devon: Sunstone Press, 1987).
Moon-Whales and Other Moon Poems (New York: Viking, 1988).
Tales of the Early World (London: Faber & Faber, 1988).
Moortown Diary (London: Faber & Faber, 1989).
Wolfwatching (London: Faber & Faber, 1989).
Capriccio (Devon: Gehenna Press, 1990).
A Dancer to God (London: Faber & Faber, 1992).
Rain-Charm for the Duchy (London: Faber & Faber, 1992).

Shakespeare and the Goddess of Complete Being (London: Faber & Faber, 1992).
The Iron Woman (London: Faber & Faber, 1993).
The Mermaid's Purse (Devon: Sunstone Press, 1993).
Three Books (*Cave Birds, Remains of Elmet, River*) (London: Faber & Faber, 1993).
Elmet (London: Faber & Faber, 1994).
Winter Pollen (London: Faber & Faber, 1994).
Collected Animal Poems: 4 Vols (London: Faber & Faber, 1995).
Difficulties of a Bridegroom (London: Faber & Faber, 1995).
The Dreamfighter and Other Creation Tales (London: Faber & Faber, 1995).
New Selected Poems 1957–1994 (London: Faber & Faber, 1995).
Spring Awakening (London: Faber & Faber, 1995).
Blood Wedding (London: Faber & Faber, 1996).
By Heart (London: Faber & Faber, 1997).
Tales from Ovid (London: Faber & Faber, 1997).
Birthday Letters (London: Faber & Faber, 1998).
Howls and Whispers (Devon: Gehenna Press, 1998).
Phèdre (London: Faber & Faber, 1998).
Alcestis (London: Faber & Faber, 1999).
The Oresteia (London: Faber & Faber, 1999).
Collected Plays for Children (London: Faber & Faber, 2001).
Collected Poems (London: Faber & Faber, 2003).
Collected Poems for Children (London: Faber & Faber, 2005).
Selected Translations (London: Faber & Faber, 2006).
Letters of Ted Hughes (London: Faber & Faber, 2007).
Timmy the Tug (London: Thames and Hudson, 2009).

Recordings

The Thought-Fox and Other Poems, read by Ted Hughes, Faber & Faber, 1994.
The Dreamfighter and Other Creation Tales, read by Ted Hughes, Faber/ Penguin, 1996.
Ffangs the Vampire Bat and the Kiss of Truth, read by Ted Hughes, Faber/ Penguin, 1996.
The Iron Woman, read by Ted Hughes, Faber/Penguin, 1996.
Nessie The Mannerless Monster and *The Iron Wolf*, read by Ted Hughes, Faber/ Penguin, 1996.
Tales of the Early World, read by Ted Hughes, Faber/Penguin, 1996.
Ted Hughes Reading his Poetry, HarperCollins Audio Books, 1996.
By Heart: 101 Poems to Remember, read by Ted Hughes, Faber/Penguin, 1997.
Crow, read by Ted Hughes, Faber/Penguin, 1997.
How the Whale Became and Other Stories, read by Ted Hughes, Faber/Penguin, 1997.
The Iron Man, read by Ted Hughes, Faber/Penguin, 1997.
Tales from Ovid, read by Ted Hughes, Faber/Penguin, 1998.
Poetry in the Making, British Library Sound Archive, 2008.
The Spoken Word – Ted Hughes. Poems and short stories (a two-CD set drawn from BBC radio broadcasts), British Library Sound Archive, 2008.

The Spoken Word – Ted Hughes. Poetry in the Making *and* Season Songs (a two-CD set of five BBC radio broadcasts for schools, plus two programmes reading *Season Songs*), British Library Sound Archive, 2008.

The Artist and the Poet: Leonard Baskin & Ted Hughes in conversation 1983 (a documentary DVD by Noel Chanan), 2009.

The Spoken Word – Sylvia Plath ('Two of a Kind' interview), British Library Sound Archive, 2010.

Secondary works by Ted Hughes

Biographical

Boyanowsky, Ehor, *Savage Gods: In the Wild with Ted Hughes* (Vancouver: Douglas & McIntyre, 2009).

Ely, Steve, *Ted Hughes's South Yorkshire: Made in Mexborough* (Basingstoke: Palgrave Macmillan, 2015).

Feinstein, Elaine, *Ted Hughes: The Life of a Poet* (London: Weidenfeld & Nicolson, 2001).

Gammage, Nick (ed.), *The Epic Poise: A Celebration of Ted Hughes* (London: Faber & Faber, 1999).

Hughes, Gerald, *Ted and I* (London: Robson Press, 2012).

Hughes, Ted, *Letters of Ted Hughes* (London: Faber & Faber, 2007).

Huws, Daniel, *Memories of Ted Hughes 1952–1963* (Nottingham: Five Leaves Publications, 2010).

Koren, Yehuda and Eilat Negev, *A Lover of Unreason: The Life and Tragic Death of Assia Wevill* (London: Robson Books, 2006).

Middlebrook, Diane, *Her Husband* (London: Little, Brown, 2004).

Moulin, Joanny, *Ted Hughes. La terre hantée: biographie* (Paris: Editions Aden, 2007).

Moulin, Joanny, *Ted Hughes: The Haunted Earth* (London: Editions Aden, 2014).

Myers, Lucas, *Crow Steered, Bergs Appeared* (Sewanee: Proctor Press, 2001).

Sagar, Keith, *The Art of Ted Hughes* (Cambridge: Cambridge University Press, 1975, 2nd edn 1978).

Sagar, Keith, *Poet and Critic: The Letters of Ted Hughes and Keith Sagar* (London: British Library, 2012).

Sagar, Keith and Stephen Tabor, *Ted Hughes: A Bibliography 1946–1995* (London: Mansell, 1998). For an updated Supplement see http://www.keithsagar.co.uk/tedhughes.html.

Stephenson, Anne, *Bitter Fame: A Life of Sylvia Plath* (London: Viking, 1989).

Tennant, Emma, *Burnt Diaries* (Edinburgh: Canongate, 1999).

Weissbort, Daniel, *Letters to Ted* (London: Anvil, 2002).

Websites

http://www.thetedhughessociety.org (edited by Gillian Groszewski).

www.earth-moon.org (managed by Claas Kazzer).

www.theelmettrust (The Elmet Trust).
http://ann.skea.com/THHome.htm (managed by Ann Skea).

Reviews of criticism

Byrne, Sandie, *The Poetry of Ted Hughes: A Reader's Guide to Essential Criticism* (Cambridge: Icon Books, 2000).
Byrne, Sandie, *The Poetry of Ted Hughes: A Reader's Guide to Essential Criticism* (Basingstoke: Palgrave Macmillan, 2014).
Gifford, Terry, *Ted Hughes* (London: Routledge, 2009).
Scigaj, Leonard M., *Critical Essays on Ted Hughes* (New York: G.K. Hall, 1992).

Critical studies

Bassnett, Susan, *Ted Hughes* (Tavistock: Northcote House, 2009).
Bentley, Paul, *The Poetry of Ted Hughes: Language, Illusion and Beyond* (London: Longman, 1998).
Bishop, Nick, *Re-Making Poetry* (London: Harvester, 1991).
Gifford, Terry, *Ted Hughes* (London: Routledge, 2009).
Gifford, Terry and Neil Roberts, *Ted Hughes: A Critical Study* (London: Faber & Faber, 1981).
Groszewski, Gillian, *Hughes and America* (Basingstoke: Palgrave Macmillan, 2016).
Hadley, Edward, *The Elegies of Ted Hughes* (Basingstoke: Palgrave Macmillan, 2010).
Hirshberg, Stuart, *Myth in the Poetry of Ted Hughes* (Dublin: Wolfhound Press, 1981).
Lidström, Susanna, *Nature, Environment and Poetry: Ecocriticism and the Poetics of Seamus Heaney and Ted Hughes* (Abingdon: Routledge, 2015).
Roberts, Neil, *Ted Hughes: A Literary Life* (Basingstoke: Palgrave Macmillan, 2006).
Robinson, Craig, *Ted Hughes as Shepherd of Being* (Basingstoke: Macmillan, 1989).
Sagar, Keith, *The Art of Ted Hughes* (Cambridge: Cambridge University Press, 1975, 2nd edn 1978).
Sagar, Keith, *The Laughter of Foxes* (Liverpool: Liverpool University Press, 2000; 2nd edn 2006).
Sagar, Keith, *Nature and Ted Hughes: 'Terror and Exultation'* (Clitheroe: Fastprint Publishing, 2009).
Scigaj, Leonard M., *Ted Hughes: Form and Imagination* (Iowa City: University of Iowa Press, 1986).
Scigaj, Leonard M., *Ted Hughes* (Boston: Twayne, 1991).
Skea, Ann, *The Poetic Quest* (Armidale, NSW: University of New England Press, 1994).
Usha VT, *The Real and the Imagined: The Poetic World of Ted Hughes* (Jaipur: Mangal Deep, 1998).

Xerri, Daniel, *Ted Hughes's Art of Healing: Into Time and Other People* (Palo Alto, CA: Academia Press, 2009).

Collections of critical essays

Dyson, A.E. (ed.), *Three Contemporary Poets: Thom Gunn, Ted Hughes & R.S. Thomas* (Basingstoke: Macmillan, 1990).
Gifford, Terry (ed.), *The Cambridge Companion to Ted Hughes* (Cambridge: Cambridge University Press, 2011).
Moulin, Joanny (ed.), *Lire Ted Hughes* (Paris: Éditions du Temps, 1999).
Moulin, Joanny (ed.), *Ted Hughes: Alternative Horizons* (London: Routledge, 2004).
Rees, R.D. (ed.), *Ted Hughes and the Classics* (Oxford: Oxford University Press, 2008).
Sagar, Keith (ed.), *The Achievement of Ted Hughes* (Manchester: Manchester University Press, 1983).
Sagar, Keith (ed.), *The Challenge of Ted Hughes* (London: Macmillan, 1994).
Schuchard, Ronald (ed.), *Fixed Stars Govern a Life* (Atlanta, GA: Academic Exchange, Emory University, 2006).
Scigaj, Leonard M. (ed.), *Critical Essays on Ted Hughes* (New York: G.K. Hall, 1992).
Wormald, Mark, Neil Roberts and Terry Gifford (eds), *Ted Hughes: From Cambridge to Collected* (Basingstoke: Palgrave Macmillan, 2013).

Selected articles, essays and chapters in books

The Ted Hughes Society Journal (online) publishes essays on the work of Ted Hughes which have not been listed separately here. See http://www.thetedhughessociety.org.

Beer, John, 'Sylvia Plath and Ted Hughes: The Hazards of Incompleteness', in John Beer, *Post-Romantic Consciousness: Dickens to Plath* (Basingstoke: Palgrave Macmillan, 2003).
Bedient, Calvin, *Eight Contemporary Poets* (Oxford: Oxford University Press, 1974).
Bedient, Calvin, 'Ted Hughes's Fearful Greening', *Parnassus* 14(1) (1987): 150–163.
Corcoran, Neil, *English Poetry since 1940* (London: Longman, 1993).
Corcoran, Neil, *Shakespeare and the Modern Poet* (Cambridge: Cambridge University Press, 2010).
Cox, Brian, 'Ted Hughes (1930–1998): A Personal Retrospect', *Hudson Review* 52(1) (1999): 29–43.
Csokits, János, 'János Pilinszky's "Desert of Love": A Note', in Daniel Weissbort (ed.), *Translating Poetry: The Double Labyrinth* (Basingstoke: Palgrave Macmillan, 1989): 9–15.

Eagleton, Terry, 'Myth and History in Recent Poetry', in Michael Schmidt and Grevel Lindop (eds), *British Poetry Since 1960* (Chatham: W. & J. Mackay, 1972).

Faas, Ekbert, 'Ted Hughes and Crow', an interview, *London Magazine* 10 (10 Jan. 1971): 5–20.

Faas, Ekbert, *The Unaccommodated Universe* (Santa Barbara, CA: Black Sparrow Press, 1980).

Gifford, Terry, *Green Voices: Understanding Contemporary Nature Poetry* (Manchester: Manchester University Press, 1995; 2nd edn Nottingham: Critical, Cultural and Communications Press, 2010).

Gifford, Terry, 'Interview with Fay Godwin', *Thumbscrew* 18 (2001): 114–17.

Golden, Amanda, *Annotating Modernism: Marginalia and Pedagogy from Virginia Woolf to the Confessional Poets* (Aldershot: Ashgate, 2014).

Greening, John, *Focus on Ted Hughes* (London: Greenwich Exchange, 2007).

Heinz, Drue, 'Ted Hughes: The Art of Poetry LXXI', *Paris Review* 134 (1995): 55–94.

Holbrook, David, 'The Cult of Hughes and Gunn', *Poetry Review* 54 (1963): 167–83.

Holbrook, David, 'Ted Hughes's *Crow* and the Longing for Non-Being', in Peter Abbs (ed.), *The Black Rainbow: Essays on the Present Breakdown of Culture* (London: Heinemann, 1975).

Hong, Chen, *Bestiality, Animality, and Humanity* (Wuhan: Central China Normal University Press, 2005).

Hughes, Freida, *Forty-Five* (New York: HarperCollins, 2008).

Kazzer, Claas, 'Difficulties of a Bridegroom', *Q/W/E/R/T/Y* 9 (1999): 187–201.

Kendall, Tim, *Modern English War Poetry* (Oxford: Oxford University Press, 2006).

Larrissy, Edward, *Reading Twentieth Century Poetry* (Oxford: Blackwell, 1990).

Lucas, John, *Modern English Poetry from Hardy to Hughes* (London: Batsford, 1986).

Malcolm, Janet, *The Silent Woman: Sylvia Plath and Ted Hughes* (London: Macmillan, 1994).

Maslen, Elizabeth, 'Counterpoint: Collaborations between Ted Hughes and Three Visual Artists', *Word and Image* 2(1) (Jan.–March 1986): 33–44.

Middlebrook, Diane, 'The Poetry of Sylvia Plath and Ted Hughes: Call and Response', in Jo Gill (ed.), *The Cambridge Companion to Sylvia Plath* (Cambridge: Cambridge University Press, 2006).

Moat, John, *The Founding of Arvon* (London: Frances Lincoln, 2005).

Moody, David, 'Telling It Like It's Not', *Yearbook of English Studies*, 17 (1987): 166–78.

Moulin, Joanny, *Ted Hughes: New Selected Poems* (Paris: Didier Érudition, 1999).

Muldoon, Paul, *The End of the Poem* (London: Faber & Faber, 2006).

O'Brien, Sean, *The Deregulated Muse* (Newcastle-upon-Tyne: Bloodaxe, 1998).

Owen, Jane, *The Poetry of Ted Hughes: Author Study Activities for Key Stage 2/3* (London: David Fulton, 2003).

Paulin, Tom, *Minotaur: Poetry and the Nation State* (London: Faber & Faber, 1992).

Roberts, Neil, 'Ted Hughes and the Laureateship', *Critical Quarterly* 27(2) (1985): 3–5.

Roberts, Neil, *Narrative and Voice in Postwar Poetry* (Harlow: Longman, 1999).

Roberts, Neil, 'The Common Text of Sylvia Plath and Ted Hughes', *Symbiosis* 7(1) (2003): 157–73.

Roberts, Neil, *Ted Hughes: New Selected Poems* (Penrith: Humanities-Ebooks. co.uk, 2007).

Sagar, Keith, *Ted Hughes* (Harlow: Longman for the British Council, 1972).

Sagar, Keith, *Literature and the Crime Against Nature* (London: Chaucer Press, 2004).

Sagar, Keith, 'Ted Hughes', *Dictionary of National Biography*, Vol. 28 (Oxford: Oxford University Press, 2004).

Schmidt, Michael and Grevel Lindop (eds), *British Poetry Since 1960* (Chatham: W. & J. Mackay, 1972).

Smith, A.C.H., *Orghast at Persepolis* (London: Methuen, 1972).

Thurley, Geoffrey, *The Ironic Harvest* (London: Arnold, 1974).

Uroff, Margaret Dickie, *Sylvia Plath and Ted Hughes* (Chicago: University of Illinois Press, 1979).

Usha VT, 'Remembering Ted Hughes', *Journal of Literature and Aesthetics*, 7(2) (1999): 81–4.

Wagner, Erica, *Ariel's Gift: Ted Hughes, Sylvia Plath and the Story of* Birthday Letters (London: Faber & Faber, 2000).

Winterson, Jeanette, 'Foreword', in *Great Poets of the 20th Century: Ted Hughes* (London: *Guardian*, 2008).

Wright, Carolyn, 'What Happens in the Heart', *Poetry Review*, 89(3) (1999): 3–9.

General Index

Index of Works by Ted Hughes